. . .

TRANSLATING WORLDS,
DEFENDING LAND

. . .

TRANSLATING WORLDS, DEFENDING LAND

Collaborations for Indigenous Rights and Environmental Politics in Amazonia

CASEY HIGH

STANFORD UNIVERSITY PRESS
Stanford, California

Stanford University Press
Stanford, California

Printed in the United States of America on acid-free, archival-quality paper

Library of Congress Cataloging-in-Publication Data
Names: High, Casey, 1977- author.
Title: Translating worlds, defending land : collaborations for indigenous rights and
    environmental politics in Amazonia / Casey High.
Description: Stanford, California : Stanford University Press, 2025. | Includes
    bibliographical references and index.
Identifiers: LCCN 2024027215 (print) | LCCN 2024027216 (ebook) |
    ISBN 9781503640481 (cloth) | ISBN 9781503641464 (paperback) |
    ISBN 9781503641471 (ebook)
Subjects: LCSH: Huao Indians—Ecuador—Oriente—Politics and government.
    | Huao Indians—Civil rights—Ecuador—Oriente. | Environmentalism—
    Ecuador—Oriente. | Petroleum industry and trade—Environmental aspects—
    Ecuador—Oriente.
Classification: LCC F3722.1.H83 H54 2025 (print) | LCC F3722.1.H83 (ebook) |
    DDC 304.208998/909866—dc23/eng/20240808
LC record available at https://lccn.loc.gov/2024027215
LC ebook record available at https://lccn.loc.gov/2024027216

Cover design: Daniel Benneworth-Gray
Cover photo: Courtesy of the author

This book is dedicated to the memory of Ñai Gaba and Wareka Gaba.

CONTENTS

LIST OF MAPS AND ILLUSTRATIONS

ACKNOWLEDGMENTS

I owe thanks to many people who have helped make this book possible. It is primarily a result of the generosity, care, and contributions of Waorani people who have shared their lives with me over the past twenty-five years. Countless people have welcomed me into their homes, gardens, forest treks, parties, community meetings, and conversations—all of which have contributed to my very partial understanding of the world I describe in this book. It would be difficult to include a complete list of those who have made my fieldwork possible, and enjoyable, over the years, but I am especially grateful to the families in Toñampari and other villages in Pastaza province where I have spent my longest periods of fieldwork in Ecuador.

First and foremost, I thank Amowa Gaba and Ñai Gaba—and their ten children—for being my host family over the years and for supporting my research and well-being in so many ways. Their care, laughter, and seemingly endless tolerance have made my time with them especially memorable. The first Waorani household to welcome me in the late 1990s was that of Awanka and Yato, Ñai's elderly parents. After staying with Amowa and Ñai's family for the better part of two years during my doctoral fieldwork in the early 2000s, their children—many now adults with families of their own—have become my primary hosts in Ecuador. My fieldwork has followed this third generation—and their marriages—to distant villages, some located in more isolated areas of Pastaza and others along oil roads in the province of Orellana. I thank Uboye Gaba and Marci Enqueri, as well as Ana Gaba and Moipa Nihua, for extending their care and generosity to me in their homes. Several other friends have helped me in various ways in fieldwork, such as Toca Caiga,

Rosa Gaba, Camilo Huaomani, Timoteo Huaomoni, Manuela Ima, and Antonio Quemperi. Some elders who taught me much about Waorani life are no longer with us: Awa, Awanka, Dayuma, Koba, Ñai, and Paa. Although the purpose of this book is not to record their knowledge and stories, I hope my reflections at least honor what their words and lives mean to younger Waorani generations today.

I also want to give special thanks to the people who participated in the Waorani Language Documentation Project that began in 2009. Along with the many speakers who were recorded, I want to acknowledge the work of those Waorani who became language researchers: Uboye Gaba, Marci Enqueri, Mery Nenquihui, Nemonte Nenquimo and Opi Nenquimo. Their work—and reflections on it—are a key part of the story I tell in this book. But the recordings and texts they contributed are also more important than a book like this one—particularly for their own communities. Special thanks to Uboye Gaba who, as a host-brother, researcher, and activist, figures prominently in this book and in my thinking about Waorani environmental politics. I also want to recognize linguist Connie Dickinson's dedication in supporting Indigenous communities in Ecuador to document their own languages. Her commitment to training Waorani researchers and managing most aspects of the language project reflects an ongoing ethical commitment to collaboration that I greatly admire.

Thanks to the official Waorani organization (NAWE) for supporting my fieldwork in the Waorani territory, whether finding me an extra seat on a plane or pickup truck or providing me with communications in the communities. My research has also benefited from conversations with representatives of the Association of Waorani Women (AMWAE) and the Waorani Organization of Pastaza (OWAP). In Quito, my fieldwork was made possible in part by the sponsorship of Editorial Abya-Yala. The research for this book was funded by grants from the Wenner-Gren Foundation, the Fulbright Commission, the UK Economic and Social Research Council (ESRC), the French Centre National de la Recherche Scientifique (CNRS), the Endangered Languages Documentation Programme (ELDP), the Munro Fund (University of Edinburgh), and the UK Global Challenges Research Fund. I also thank Goldsmiths, University of London, and the School of Social and Political Science at the University of Edinburgh for supporting shorter research trips and for managing the ELDP grant.

Many colleagues helped me think through the ideas in this book. I have benefited from conversations with several scholars who have done ethnographic research with Waorani communities, including Andrea Bravo Díaz, Ciara Wirth, Laura Rival, and Margherita Scazza. Working with Elliott Oakley helped me rethink my approach to Amazonian environmental politics, and conversations with Mike Cepek, Luiz Costa, Mary-Elizabeth Reeve, Michael Uzendoski, Pirjo Virtanen, Harry Walker, and Norman Whitten have all contributed to my thinking on a range of topics in Amazonia. In Edinburgh, I am grateful to Maya Mayblin for her feedback on several draft chapters of the book. I also thank Magnus Course and Agustin Diz for their support, as well as Sophie Haines, Laurie Denyer-Willis, and Alex Edmonds for commenting on the introduction and helping me to revive this project after the COVID pandemic. Thanks to Josh Reno for his support and valuable comments on the book proposal and to colleagues who provided critical feedback at anthropology research seminars at Cambridge University, Manchester University, the École des Hautes Études en Sciences Sociales (EHESS) in Paris, and the Center for Research and Collaboration in the Indigenous Americas (CRACIA) at the University of Maryland. I do not assume that any of these people, whether Waorani researchers or seasoned academics, will agree with what I say in this book, but I thank them all for their support.

Special thanks are also due to my editor, Dylan Kyung-Lim White, for taking an interest in this project and for his feedback and encouragement from start to finish, and to the anonymous reviewers whose comments and suggestions have much improved the book.

Finally, I want to thank my parents, Fred and Sue, my brothers, Shawn and Seth, my wife Elizabeth, and my boys, Toby and Russell, for their love and support through the many phases of my life in this book.

Some of the material in chapter 2 appeared in the 2018 article "Bodies That Speak: Languages of Differentiation and Becoming in Amazonia," *Language and Communication* 63: 65–75.

Some of the material in chapter 3 appeared in the 2020 article "'Our Land Is Not For Sale!' Contesting Oil and Translating Environmental Politics in Amazonian Ecuador," *Journal of Latin American and Caribbean Anthropology* 25, no. 2: 301–23.

A NOTE ON ORTHOGRAPHY

In this book I use italics to distinguish words in the Waorani language, Wao-terero. While some authors use the Spanish spelling "Huaorani," I use the "Waorani" currently adopted by most Waorani people, their official political organizations, as well as most Ecuadorian institutions, news media and academic scholarship. Spelling conventions in Wao-terero vary greatly among its speakers and in texts written about them. There are also differences in pronunciation between Waorani communities in distant areas of their territory. Here I use an orthography adopted fairly consistently in the Waorani Language Documentation Project that I describe in this book, which emphasized ease of use for Waorani speakers accustomed to using the Spanish language alphabet. This spelling follows the sounds of Spanish vowels a, e, i, and o, and most Spanish consonants, including ñ (which sounds like "ny" to English speakers). However, I use diacritics to distinguish nasalized vowel sounds common in Wao-terero, such as the -ö- in the word öko ("house"), which has a sound similar to "ongko." I also use italics for Spanish and Kichwa words but make explicit in the text when I am referring to words in these other languages.

INTRODUCTION

. . .

SHARING UNCOMMON GROUND

SEVERAL YEARS AGO, I made a brief trip to Toñampari, a Waorani village in the Ecuadorian Amazon where I began fieldwork in the late 1990s. One evening during my stay I listened to Amowa, one of the people I know best there, speak about his family and their sporadic contact with outsiders in the 1950s. Amowa, his wife Ñai, and their ten children, many now adults with families of their own, have been my host family during much of my fieldwork. Since Amowa and Ñai, as elders, are well known for telling stories of the adventures, comedic follies, and tragic fates of ancestors and mythic characters, I was already familiar with some of the stories I heard that night. But this time was different. On this occasion, Amowa's adult son Uboye carefully orchestrated the scene around his father, setting the stage to make a video recording. This involved using candles to improve the lighting for the camera, which was attached to a tripod standing on the dirt floor of the house, and setting up microphones in the appropriate positions as Amowa sat patiently in his hammock.

Once the story began, interactions around the house followed a familiar pattern. The many children and grandchildren sat silently, focusing their attention on Amowa as he voiced and gestured the sounds, movements, and actions of ancestors who came across oil workers, missionaries, and other outsiders at a time when relations between Waorani and other Ecuadorians were fraught with mistrust, fear, and violence. Those in the audience only occasionally broke their silence with laughter, making the sound *ooo!* to affirm events in the story, or to ask questions like *emonano* (who was it?) or *eyemono* (where?) about the people and places Amowa described. Whether it was due to the camera, his son's interest in making the recording, or simply his pleasure in telling stories, Amowa spoke for more than three hours, pausing only to respond briefly to these interjections and for Uboye to change the tape in the camera.

Uboye's recording of an everyday context with his family, and his thinking about it, reflects what I think is an increasingly familiar scene of ethnographic fieldwork. Whether in remote corners of Amazonia or in no less exotic scientific research labs, we must recognize and engage with the imaginative horizons our interlocutors find in new technical expertise and knowledge. In some cases, like that which I describe in this book, such expertise is not entirely separable from ethnographic description and analysis—much less politics. As people like Uboye become ethnographers in their own right, we must reconsider not only who is representing what, but also what is at stake in these encounters beyond writing texts or methods of participant observation. They engage creatively not only with the ideas of "culture" around them, but also the differences, shared interests, and potential solidarity they find in collaborations with people and projects that extend well beyond their home communities.

Uboye's recording was part of one such collaboration: research to document his native language, Wao-terero. For me, this project—involving a linguist, an anthropologist (me) and speakers like Uboye and his parents—was an opportunity to engage in research in which Waorani people would have a stake in the results. But this work does not simply reveal shared interests or meanings—the common ground often implicit in the very idea of collaboration. As our interlocutors find new languages, practices, and technologies for reflecting on their lives in this work, their purposes are often different from conventional anthropologists. Their epistemological and political commitments require thinking about the value of collaboration beyond addressing preconceived problems or writing ethnography. Rather than erasing these differences—much less overcoming the inequalities in which academic research in Amazonia is embedded—Waorani researchers find in this work new ways of engaging conflicts with outsiders and within their own communities.

As our interlocutors become researchers, they bring distinct purposes and understandings to these projects, often leading to unanticipated consequences. While Uboye's interest in recording his father suited the goal of documenting an "endangered language," he also came to see in the words of his elders a particular power, a "truth" he contrasts to the speech of younger Waorani political leaders. For him, video became not just a tool for documenting language and culture, but to hold politicians to account for what they said. I was both fascinated and horrified when, two years after making the recording of his father, Uboye received threats from his neighbors while recording a meeting in which the Waorani political leadership was hotly contested. As he and other Waorani researchers had their own purposes in this work, it revealed a distinct ethics and politics that, at times, exposed them to real risks.

These engagements, and especially the skills and technologies they involve, do not exist in a vacuum. They take unanticipated directions, becoming part of ever-more translocal relationships and political projects. In 2019, I met with Uboye in Puyo, a frontier city in Amazonian Ecuador, where he recorded what became the most successful protest against the Ecuadorian government's selling of contracts to exploit oil on Waorani lands. By then he had acquired his own professional camera, which rested on his shoulder as he filmed other Waorani people marching alongside international environmentalists and Indigenous rights activists. Now married and with small children of his own, Uboye walked alongside his wife, Marci—also a Waorani language researcher—who carried their infant daughter in her arms. After the march snaked through the city streets, he joined a crowd of journalists in recording the speech of Nemonte Nenquimo, a Waorani language researcher who was now becoming an internationally renowned environmental leader. Uboye too was becoming an anti-oil activist, working with an international network that led to him becoming delegate at the 2021 UN Climate Change Conference in Glasgow (COP26).

In this book I explore how Waorani people engage in a changing sociopolitical world, whether as researchers and videographers or through campaigns to defend their lands and combat climate change. Their collaborations, both with academic researchers and international environmental activists, bring about new problems and possibilities for those involved. The book is at once an ethnography of these engagements and a critical reflection on how collaboration is conceptualized in anthropology and beyond. Rather than accepting this term as a generic buzzword or a coherent sociopolitical imperative, I describe the possibilities and limits of anthropological collaboration and what our interlocutors find when they become enmeshed in it. In this way, I approach collaboration as both an open-ended method and a complex ethnographic object through which we can better understand novel conceptual horizons emerging in Amazonia and elsewhere.

MAP 0.1: Map of Ecuador. Source: High 2015a, 4.

Translation is an integral part of the collaborations I describe in this Amazonian contemporary. Whether facilitating relationships across social worlds or highlighting their differences, translations have consequences for Amazonian people—and their allies—well beyond questions of anthropological theory. In a context premised as much on solidarity between Indigenous people and environmentalists as ideas of difference, translating Indigenous concepts into the language of nature, culture, and conservation allows some young Waorani leaders to engage a social and political scale beyond their home villages, Ecuador, or South America. The process of translating across worlds, whether in language documentation or environment politics, highlights the possibilities for collaboration in Amazonia today. It at once challenges the tendency to imagine Amazonia as a place of natural isolation or essential difference and defies conventional ideas of tradition and modernity

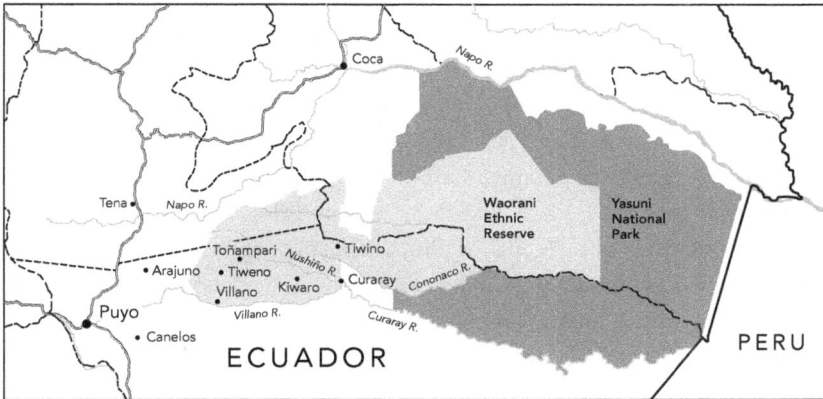

MAP 0.2: The Waorani Ethnic Reserve and Yasuní National Park in Amazonian Ecuador. Source: High 2015a, 5.

that accompany such imagination. Waorani collaborations in this contemporary also offer specific ways of rethinking the methods, purposes, and possibilities of academic research.

Conceptualizing Collaboration Anthropologically

While questions of collaboration have long been central to anthropology, conventional methodological and ethical commitments fall well short of recent calls for more deliberately collaborative practices.[1] As we embrace diverse sites, methods, and social dynamics in fieldwork today, most anthropologists still depend on long-term relationships with the people they write about—and sometimes with. As a result our work relies, more than in other fields, on collaborations that go beyond the age-old trope of participating in and observing the lives of others. Today anthropologists grapple with difficult questions about collaboration in research and writing: What does it entail and what is the point? How can anthropology be more collaborative, and with whom? Who stands to benefit and who does it belong to? What does it mean to people with different understandings and priorities? What are its limits?

These are some of the questions that come with Waorani involvement in academic research and other collaborations. For people like Uboye, what is the point, if any, of documenting an "endangered language"? What knowledge and skills do they derive from recording and transcribing language videos, and how might these technologies figure in other contexts? In what ways do they present new ways of reflecting on what it means to be Waorani and speak their language? How are their priorities and ethical commitments different from academics? What novelty, opportunity, and risk do they find in these collaborations? These are some of the questions I consider as I try to make sense of what language documentation and environmental politics mean to Waorani researchers, leaders, and their communities. In asking these questions, my interest is not in collaboration as a form of applied anthropology or even the material outcomes of such projects, but as a context for understanding a contemporary Waorani world as it unfolds.

My exploration of this process points to how, whether in Amazonia or Europe, "at home" or abroad, anthropologists today encounter new expectations, accountabilities, and possibilities in fieldwork and writing. Questions of collaboration will have different implications everywhere. But I want to highlight their particular salience to an academic community that, broadly speaking, is as engaged with ideas of difference as it is committed to various forms of solidarity. Whether in critiques of claims to scientific authority in ethnographic writing (Clifford and Marcus 1986), including critical feminist approaches (di Leonardo 1991), calls for decolonizing anthropology (Harrison 1997), or the emphasis on coauthorship (Lassiter 2005), the purposes, methods, and ethical commitments of an engaged anthropology increasingly depend on what kind of engagement in the world we understand anthropology to be (Beck and Maida 2013; Low and Merry 2010).

While efforts to place anthropologists and their interlocutors on more equal footing is an important part of the current "collaborative moment" (Sillitoe 2015), in this book I also engage critically with collaboration as a concept and practice. In a world where this idea often implies an ethic of mutual benefit, social innovation, and self-realization (Riles 2015; Strathern 2012),[2] I explore the creative possibilities and limits of collaborative anthropology (Konrad 2012). In moving beyond critiques of the detached academic observer of generations past, anthropologists are well positioned to appreciate the knowledge this work engenders. Though often envisioned as a more inclusive and democratic method for documenting preexisting forms, or serving goals negotiated with interlocutors, collaboration also involves much more than the common ground many of us seek. It is the tensions, conflicts, and unpredictable nature of this work that I suggest both reveals differences and evokes new imaginative possibilities for anthropologists and their "others." The fact that such possibilities may end up challenging, distorting, or rejecting our initial epistemological and political commitments is part of what makes them important.

I draw on insights from collaborative ethnography, interdisciplinarity, decolonization, feminist anthropology, Indigenous methodologies, and other approaches that make clear the need to consider the meanings, uses, and predicaments of collaboration beyond assuming shared purposes or harmonious engagements with the communities that anthropologists study. As Faye Harrison cautions, collaboration often implies a claim to ethnographic authority (2012, 92). How, then, might we envision anthropological collaborations that do not presume a common ground between "our" and "their" conceptual, political, and practical engagements?

In some cases this requires thinking about the purposes of collaboration beyond outcomes, such as coauthored texts, that tend to be valued more in academic settings than elsewhere (Kirsch 2018). In language documentation, it quickly became clear that Waorani researchers were more interested in the videos they recorded than linguistic texts derived from them, much less ethnographic writing like this book. In communities where reading is often limited to official contexts of necessity, the videos are more accessible and have greater entertainment and political value. But this interest also reflects epistemological differences that problematize the authority of ethnographic representation. For some Waorani researchers, the words of their elders, which they associate with the "truth" of "direct" experience, stand in stark contrast to speculative claims about the thoughts and intentions of others.

What, then, might make a particular collaboration anthropological? Tim Ingold (2018) envisions anthropology as a practice of correspondence, "an imaginative stretch of attention" in which anthropologists and their hosts "reach an accord that goes beyond existing understandings" (65). Rather than juxtaposing different "worlds" outside one another or applying anthropology to solve preconceived problems, such practices of "commoning" or "togethering" ultimately lead to things that neither anthropologists nor their interlocutors initially imagined (61).[3] And yet, tension, discord, and divergent interests are as central to anthropology as rapport, agreement, or "togethering." Marisol de la Cadena (2015) contrasts collaboration toward a mutual goal from "co-laboring" in which anthropologists and their interlocutors know and make distinct—yet partially connected—worlds. Similarly, alliances between Indigenous peoples and environmentalists can involve a process of "uncommoning" where divergent notions of nature become the basis of solidarity (de la Cadena 2019). The tensions in these projects are often embedded in long-standing inequalities that anthropologists and their hosts can hardly ignore. Positioning oneself as an engaged or activist anthropologist does not simply eclipse such realities, regardless of our political convictions.

The fact that I am a white man from the United States who normally lives in Scotland is part of what constitutes my relationships with Waorani people. But questions of relative power are only part of what often makes collaboration fraught with disagreement and misunderstanding, especially when the people written about share stakes in research and come to hold specific expectations of it. Part of the challenge is in recognizing how our "epistemic partners" (Holmes and Marcus 2008) come to value and demand things that academic researchers may not anticipate. The potential of collaboration is as much a result of conflict as it is agreement,[4] and this should move us to take differences seriously without taking for granted the exact nature of our collaborations, or even the content or meaning of what is transacted in them.

Rather than taking ideas of essential difference as our object—whether in the guise of culture or ontology—or assuming that all relationships are shaped by political and economic inequalities, collaborative anthropology can bring about new ways of positioning self and other in knowledge production (Heffernan et al. 2020, 7; Konrad 2012, 20). This is as much the case with interdisciplinary projects as it is work that situates anthropology's "natives" as ethnographers and anthropologists in their own right.[5] For example, Waorani language videos present a wealth of linguistic, ethnographic, and historical data. But Waorani involvement in their making and commentary about their value also reflects an epistemology that departs from the conventional purposes of documentation. Just as what they call "Waorani land" (*wao öme*) challenges ideas of nature, environment, and conservation in environmental politics, their analysis of these projects evokes distinct understandings of the nature of language and what constitutes "truth."

In this way collaboration is itself a complex ethnographic object that, while already a central concern in fieldwork and writing, merits further attention as a provocative anthropological concept. As Annelise Riles (2015) suggests, it is "our problematic term" in the sense that it can "allow us to closely observe the process of persons *becoming interested*" (180). My central focus is precisely this process of certain Waorani people becoming interested in new things and in new ways, and what promise this holds for them.[6] The practices, relationships, and imagination that constitute emergent forms of collaboration are an important part of what I call a Waorani contemporary. They highlight not just novelty, but equally, enduring ideas about the nature of knowledge, language, the body, and what it means to be a Waorani person.

Waorani Collaborations

This book draws on my fieldwork with Waorani communities in the Ecuadorian Amazon with whom I have been involved for the past twenty-five years. These communities have experienced extraordinary changes in recent decades since coming into regular contact with nonindigenous people in the late 1950s. In the wake of Christian missionization, the settlement of highly mobile groups into more permanent villages, and the devastating effects of oil drilling on their lands, Waorani people have come to understand their place as Amazonian "Indians" and "warriors" under dramatic conditions. Anthropologists and other researchers, like the missionaries who preceded them, have become part of a *kowori* (non-Waorani) world that defines them as one Indigenous culture or nationality among others. The conditions under which these sociopolitical identities have taken shape point to striking and sometimes painful generational differences.

It is a generation of young adults, mostly in their late twenties and thirties, who are the focus of this book. It is less about "Waorani people"—if such a generalization is useful at all—than people like Uboye, a man who became involved in our collaborative work more than a decade after I first came to live with his family. Starting in 2009, he and I were part of a three-and-a-half-year multidisciplinary project funded by the Endangered Languages Documentation Programme (ELDP), then based in the University of London, to document the Waorani language (Wao-terero). The project emerged from years of discussion with parents, schoolteachers, and political leaders about the possibility of incorporating Waorani language materials into their local schools. Until recently, village schools were conducted almost exclusively in Spanish, with *kowori* teachers adopting a national curriculum that devalued and undermined local social and economic life (High 2015b; Rival 2002).

The project also came about through my previous discussions with linguists interested in documenting endangered languages. Wao-terero is a clear example of such a language, spoken by only around 4,000 people in a context where Spanish, the national language, dominates most official contexts. The central premise of the project was that of documentation. It involved video-

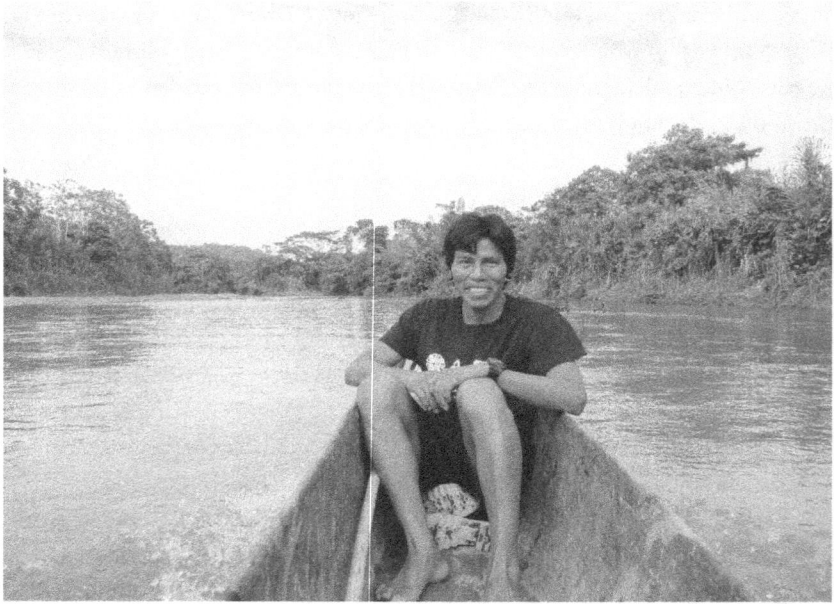

FIGURE 0.1: Waorani researcher Uboye Gaba travels by canoe to his home village on the Curaray River. Photo by author.

recording Waorani speakers and subsequently transcribing and translating the videos, resulting in a growing body of linguistic texts to be made available in an archive. I was initially uneasy with the idea of documenting an "endangered language" as a form of Indigenous knowledge, as it smacked of anthropology's long-abandoned tradition of salvage ethnography (Clifford 1989). However, the project was also premised on extensive collaboration with a linguist and Waorani language consultants who, in addition to being recorded as speakers and receiving training in linguistic research methods, became key protagonists in deciding what to record.

Up to this point, my work as an anthropologist was of little if any consequence to the Waorani families who had generously welcomed me into their lives for years. This is why the idea of their priorities being central to language research, along with the new skills they would acquire through it, was of particular interest to me. The elders I approached were happy to have their stories recorded and were supportive of the project. But it was younger, bilingual Waorani adults who became the primary researchers. Having studied at village schools, they were open to living in the city for extended periods and working long hours in front of computer screens. Some embraced language research as a rare opportunity to secure income and free room and board in the city. For some it was an alternative to working for oil companies—a key source of employment for men. Young Waorani women, who until recently had less presence in urban areas, also participated, sometimes bringing their small children with them to live temporarily in the city.

Language documentation research is often tedious and boring, especially for those not accustomed to the routines of wage labor or repetitive work on computers. It involved hours of listening carefully—and repeatedly—to recordings of people speaking, and using a keyboard to transcribe them into an alphabet established at the start of the project, eventually to be translated into Spanish. Perhaps not surprisingly, Waorani researchers were often more interested in traveling to remote locations to make language videos. They

FIGURE O.2: *Durani öko*: A traditional Waorani house. Photo by author.

sometimes visited specific villages for the first time for this purpose, or sought to record relatives living in distant places. After receiving training in video and sound recording, they made their own choices about who—and what themes—to record. These decisions led to videos of diverse contexts, both in Waorani villages and outside their territory.

The language research laid bare different understandings of collaboration, ethics, and what constitutes knowledge. Importantly, it offered young Waorani adults something more than its material outcomes. Without diminishing the value of language videos and texts as a form of documented knowledge, the processes by which they became researchers and experts in their own right became an unanticipated focus of my ethnography. Perhaps by necessity, I came to see my previous "informants"—including my host family—in a new light. This is not the first or only context in which people like Uboye and his family have worked closely with *kowori* people like me. Not entirely unlike their work with the early missionaries, or hosting schoolteachers and anthropologists, language research situates them in new ways and reflects changes in their lived world. It is precisely these changes—particularly the new possibilities and problems that come with them—that are the focus of this book.

I consider how Waorani people engage in and translate a changing sociopolitical world as speakers, researchers, and political actors. As I set out to study these engagements, new and more visible forms of collaboration were coming into view. By 2019, three Waorani language researchers had become key figures in environmental politics, working closely with international organizations to stop further oil drilling on their lands. It was apparent that these collaborations, whether with academics or foreign environmental activists, were bringing about new concerns and aspirations. Some Waorani researchers came to see the words of the elders they recorded as a resource for defending their land and engaging with outsiders. Others found alliances with environmentalists to be a platform to challenge oil and other threats to their livelihoods.

It is the goals, challenges, conflicts, and contradictions emerging from these processes that reveal both ontological differences and Waorani people working and speaking across them. These collaborations and the translations they entail are central to understanding Amazonia as a distinct contemporary context. As an increasingly visible part of social and political life in much of Amazonia today, anthropologists can ill afford to ignore the new imaginative horizons they present. By focusing on Amazonian people as epistemic partners, and the ways in which they translate and engage across different "worlds" (Hanks and Severi 2014), I describe the unanticipated consequences of such projects. Waorani engagements in them requires thinking about their changing relations with each other and outsiders in new ways.

In Amazonian Ecuador, going to school, migrating temporarily to frontier cities, and engaging in Indigenous politics are all part of how young Waorani adults experience the demands of their cultural specificity and citizenship. None of this exists outside of a wider politics of recognition that, in settler colonial contexts, often defines Indigenous people through essentialist measures of authenticity based on imagined spatial and cultural continuities.[7] Language research is not independent from these processes, nor does participation in it somehow liberate Waorani people from the inequalities in which their lives are embedded. But it does render language a cultural object in ways that challenge reductive understandings of indigeneity within a dominant multiculturalist framework. As videographers and linguists, they produce a form of Indigenous media that reaches beyond the remit of documenting an "endangered language" or "culture." Video has become a powerful technology by which they reflect on their lives, language, and communities.[8]

For some Waorani, documenting language has become a technology for learning new things, whether about ancestors, key places in their territory, or techniques for making things. It has led some to think about specific features of their language itself as something that distinguishes them from other people. For others, the words of elders in the videos are a source of power, political inspiration, or even prophecy. And still for others, making recordings involves risky political engagements across Waorani communities, particularly in efforts to hold their own leaders to account. Recently, Waorani language researchers have turned their cameras toward challenging the government's selling of oil concessions on their lands. Here they employ video as a tool for documenting their protests, demanding the state's accountability, and forging alliances with lawyers, environmentalists, and Indigenous rights activists. Beyond recording protests in Ecuador, this engagement has placed some Waorani adults on a global stage of international meetings and media coverage.

In this way deliberately collaborative work can challenge age-old stereotypes about culture with which anthropologists have often been complicit. Rather than just generate new knowledge for academic debate, the Waorani people who engage in it mobilize alternative forms of knowledge, experience,

FIGURE 0.3: Witnessing: Uboye films a Waorani protest against oil in 2019. Photo by author.

and critique as researchers and activists. This work does not simply serve to document, preserve, or revive preexisting forms of Indigenous knowledge; it makes something new. Such creative potential can make these collaborations risky or undesirable to some people in contexts of social transformation and political conflict.

Rather than present a wholesale solution to the methodological and ethical problems of contemporary anthropology, the collaborations I describe in this book complicate things. They reconfigure relationships and audiences in ways that are difficult to foresee. When the language documentation project began, I had no idea that Waorani researchers would later become prominent environmental leaders, with one leader featured in *Time* magazine and receiving a prestigious international prize for her activism, and another speaking in front of world leaders at COP26. Nor did I anticipate the challenges they would face, such as criticism from other Waorani suspicious of their close links to outsiders, or *kowori* people questioning their authenticity as Amazonian people simply for using a state-of-the-art video camera.

This illustrates how, in ceding control of certain aspects of research, and in so doing appreciating alternative purposes in it, the uncontained nature of collaboration reveals unanticipated risks for everyone involved. Our interlocutors often risk much more than we do in this work. But it still may be well worth it to them. Becoming researchers and environmental activists offers some Waorani new ways of thinking about social transformation beyond essentialist measures of cultural authenticity. In this way conceptualizing collaboration anthropologically complements debates about ethnographic authority, coauthorship, fieldwork ethics, and the possibilities of an engaged anthropology. It also presents a key method for understanding what constitutes a distinctly Waorani contemporary.

Translating beyond Language

As anthropologists often observe, acts of translation take us well beyond questions of language alone. Much more than their elders, young Waorani adults are ever more involved in the work of translating across differences in language, cosmology, and power. For some, this has involved years of engaging in Spanish at school or dealing with shopkeepers, jungle pilots, and provincial authorities during visits to the city. For others, translation is part of Indigenous politics, including negotiations with oil companies, the state, and international organizations. And for those young adults who have worked as language researchers, the process of recording, transcribing, and translating Wao-terero has become a professional skill at the same time as it positions them to reflect in new ways on what it means to speak their language.

While the primary goals of documenting an endangered language are aligned with linguistics (Haig et al. 2011), my conceptual and methodological focus is not language, or linguistic anthropology's rich tradition of studying socially situated discourse as culture (Sherzer and Urban 1986; Urban 1991). I explore what Waorani collaborations in language documentation and environmental politics reveal about the power of speaking Wao-terero.[9] While my interlocutors envision speaking their language as an ability that is seemingly inseparable from the body, language research renders speech visible and translatable in new ways. In presenting Wao-terero as a particular kind of acoustic and visual object, the videos offer them new opportunities to consider what makes their language—and specific ways of speaking it—distinct.

This is especially the case with videos of elders and the gestures they often use in tandem with expressions that are difficult to translate. And yet, an increasing number of young adults are becoming skilled translators. Whether in language research, environmental politics, or elsewhere, their translations create new understandings and potential alliances (Gal 2015; Tsing 2005), sometimes bringing things into being (Di Giminiani and Haines 2020). But these contexts, which often involve working closely with outsiders, also show how Amazonian people are not confined to a single language ideology (Ahearn 2012) or ontological commitment (Hage 2015). I suggest that the ability to operate across what academics often see as incommensurable differences is a key feature of Indigenous life in contemporary Amazonia. It involves living with what de la Cadena (2015) describes as "partially translated connections" where the languages and practices of multiple worlds "constantly overlap and exceed each other" (4–5).

The ways in which Amazonian people translate between their native languages and the national languages of the countries where they live are but one example of this. Most Indigenous Amazonian people are, to at least some extent, bilingual. As Indigenous citizens, learning national languages in school presents both a burden and an opportunity to engage wider publics. Whether in political speeches, at school, or in everyday interactions with outsiders, speaking Spanish involves constant acts of translation.[10] But Waorani efforts at translating their own words, concepts, and struggles into Spanish and the language of environmental politics both highlight and at times elide differences between *kowori* and Waorani ideas in significant ways.[11]

Documenting Wao-terero has involved many hours focused on specific technical aspects of the language and their translation. In this book, however, I step outside the texts to explore how my interlocutors communicate across different ideas about their land and way of life. As de la Cadena observes, "translating implies a movement from one world to a different one" that separates certain things or beings from their representation (2015, 30). But it is in part through translations that a new generation of Waorani leaders communicates across different linguistic and ideological frameworks. This process sometimes appears relatively unreflexive or even automatic; in others, translations are precise, strategic, or identified by Waorani speakers as problematic. In this way translation, more than simply "rendering in one language that which is expressed in another" (Hanks 2014, 18), is an epistemological space that enables "passage from one context of communication to another" (Hanks and Severi 2014, 8). This process of translating worlds is an increasingly important facet of Waorani collaborations.

Translations are thus a concern not just for linguists and philosophers, but also for anthropology. They serve different purposes and are inevitably tied to relations of power, authority, and legitimacy that extend beyond questions of language (Asad 1986; Blaser 2010; Maranhão and Streck 2003). These purposes are diverse and overlapping: translators may seek as technically accurate or literal a translation as possible, or to render it more accessible to speakers of another language. Others, not unlike ethnographers, focus on fidelity to the source language and its cultural context, sometimes emphasizing the impossibility of accurately translating across languages, cultures, or worlds. All of these purposes figure in the myriad contexts in which my Waorani interlocutors engage and communicate across differences.

The idea of allowing one's own language to be affected by others (Benjamin 1923), or a "foreignizing translation," is an apt description of what anthropologists often seek (Rubel and Rosman 2003, 7; Venuti 2000). Eduardo Viveiros de Castro (2004) describes how in Amazonia the "multinaturalism" of Amerindian thought implies a method of translation (as differentiation) that is distinct from the Western tendency to draw equivalences in translation. Leaving aside the problem of generalized regional models, these approaches illustrate how translation can evoke—or conflate—different worlds (Blaser 2010; de la Cadena 2015; A. Escobar 2018).

Anthropologists and their interlocutors engage in translating not just language and meaning but "worlds" in the sense of "orientated contexts for the apprehension of reality" (Hanks and Severi 2014, 8). It is this process that interests me, whether in Waorani language research or environmental activism against the oil industry. These collaborations, like the "co-laboring" practices through which de la Cadena seeks to destabilize conventional ethnographic expertise, require "inhabiting the partial connection between both worlds" (2015, 14). In contexts like these, Waorani people translate not just words or concepts, but sometimes very different ideas about what constitutes Waorani and *kowori* worlds. This is why we must think beyond the Spanish terms— such as *naturaleza* (nature), *cultura* (culture) and *buen vivir* (good living)— that often frame environmental politics in Ecuador and beyond.

From Language Documentation to Environmental Politics

The Waorani researchers who have become environmental activists illustrate the growing stakes of translating worlds. Their collaborations highlight not only Amazonian environmental knowledge but also an ability to speak and work across different understandings of their land and life. The global visibility of their work shows the consequences of translation beyond a specific Waorani theory of language. If transcribing and translating hours of video evokes for them the agency of speaking Wao-terero, environmental politics involves talking about their ancestral lands as "nature" or a bounded "Indigenous territory" in need of conservation. They describe the land on which they live, *wao öme* ("Waorani land"),[12] not as a passive background "environment" of natural resources for human economic activity, but a dynamic socionatural world in which Waorani and numerous nonhuman beings interact and communicate. The animals, plants, forests, and waterways of *wao öme* are as social as they are natural, even as relations between humans and other beings can be dangerous and confrontational. Engaging successfully in these relations, whether in shamanism, gardening, hunting, or interpreting the language of specific birds, is closely connected to what Waorani people describe as "living well" (Bravo Díaz 2023; High 2020).

The differences between *wao öme* and Western ideas of "nature" will not surprise readers familiar with Amazonian ethnography, which is best known for challenging ideas about nature, culture, and relationships with nonhuman beings.[13] Such differences are important for understanding what *wao öme* and "living well" mean to Waorani people. However, beyond engaging in translation as a form of anthropological analysis, I am interested specifically in how Waorani activists communicate and effectively work across what they call, in Spanish, different *mundos* ("worlds"). Environmental politics is a key context for this, but it is one where translation can distort or erase differences, especially when adopting the dominant language is an urgent political necessity.

In these contexts, the practice of drawing equivalences between different concepts is an important skill. It is part of a wider sociopolitical context that situates Amazonians—and Indigenous peoples elsewhere—as "environmental citizens" whose territorial sovereignty is closely connected to conservation.[14] As Paige West (2006) observes, conservation does not simply protect the environment; it can undermine local practices and threaten to dispossess communities of their territorial sovereignty. In Ecuador, a global regime of environmentality has taken many forms, including international funding for conservation partnerships and projects to demarcate and map Indigenous territories. But becoming environmental citizens does not simply remake the identities, values, and beliefs of Indigenous people who work across different

FIGURE 0.4: *Wao öme*: Waorani territory extends across three provinces in Amazonian Ecuador. Photo by author.

understandings of conservation and the governance of their territories (Cepek 2011, 502; West 2006; Zanotti 2016). In some cases, they challenge the political and economic forces that threaten their lands and dominant notions of conservation.

Much of the second half of this book focuses on how Waorani environmental leaders talk about their struggle to defend land in terms of nature, culture, and conservation. This does not reflect a younger generation simply dismissing the knowledge of their elders, much less embracing Western environmentalism. Rather, adopting this language allows them to engage with a range of outsiders who have very different ideas about their land and way of life. In this way translation is fundamental to both the translocal alliances and misunderstandings that constitute contemporary Amazonian environmental politics. Here translating worlds not only points to how translation exceeds language but also how such practices involve thinking and operating in different contexts (Hanks and Severi 2014, 10).

While many scholars challenge the idea that people inhabit distinct or incommensurable realities,[15] I follow what my interlocutors describe as distinctly Waorani and *kowori* worlds and how they work across different languages and concepts in contexts they have come to share with *kowori* outsiders. Rather than envisioning people confined to different worlds, whether Western or Amazonian, I am interested in how they engage across differences. This is especially important in postcolonial contexts like the Americas, where for centuries Indigenous people have experienced racism, violence, and dispossession from their lands. In most contexts, they have had little choice but to live between different modes of existence.[16]

The multilingualism of places like Amazonia makes these processes all the more open to creative possibilities. The ability to speak confidently in Spanish to outsiders about the need to protect *wao öme* as "nature," or Waorani elders as emblematic of "culture," indicates more than simply a hegemonic understanding. In environmental activism it has proven to be a valuable tool for resisting oil extraction on Waorani lands. Some young Waorani adults today express pride in their ability to speak and work successfully with such differences, sometimes in contrast to their local peers. When I asked one young man where he was currently living, he responded that he lives in "many places" and in "two worlds," referring to his regular travel between Waorani villages for language research and to Ecuadorian cities to attend meetings with environmental organizations.

In multilingual contexts, the ways in which translation can at least partially bring "incommensurable cultural worlds" into alignment (Hanks 2014, 30–31; Gal 2015) has important bearing on contemporary Waorani politics. While translation is a feature of everyday life, especially for bilingual speakers, it becomes explicit in environmental activism, where even seemingly failed translations do not always get in the way of communication and political alliance. In this process Waorani leaders insist on the difference in living as Waorani people on their ancestral lands and also align their struggle with global discourses of indigeneity, conservation, and even climate change. Their skill is in communicating urgent concerns to powerful outsiders in a common language of environmentalism and Indigenous rights.

Relationships between Amazonian people and a diverse community of environmental allies are less distant and more tangible than ever before. In contrast to the 1980s, when Indigenous people became a symbol of conservation for Western activists hoping to save the Amazon rainforest from the onslaught of economic development (Conklin and Graham 1995), some

Amazonian leaders today have themselves become experienced activists on a global stage. This involves close working relationships with NGOs, academics, and state institutions concerned with territorial rights and conservation. They also encounter other Indigenous groups with similar experiences of extractive industries and hostile state policies. Even as anthropologists highlight differences between "Western" and "Amerindian" cosmologies, some Indigenous people are becoming adept at working across such differences (Bodenhorn 2012; Cepek 2012; Oakdale 2022). The global connections reflected in these collaborations in no way guarantees their success in defending lands and livelihoods. But the new possibilities (and risks) Amazonian people are finding in them—and the work of translation they entail—are part of contemporary political life.

Beyond Common Ground

If Amazonian environmental politics involves working and speaking across different worlds, anthropologists too must rethink the nature and purpose of our collaborations with Indigenous communities. Recognizing the inequalities embedded in traditional fieldwork and representations of difference,[17] many anthropologists today foreground empathy, solidarity, and common experience in ethnographic fieldwork and writing.[18] However, calls to decolonize research make clear that we can no longer reasonably assume that anthropology's "others" share interests in research—even if premised on solidarity or applied to social problems.[19]

Efforts to make anthropology more equitable and empathetically attuned to the lives of others have led to new forms of ethnographic writing framed as "dialogic" (Bauman and Briggs 1990; Tedlock 1991) "reciprocal" (Lawless 1993), or "collaborative" (Field 1999; Lassiter 2005).[20] In different ways, these approaches envision ethnography as a shared process where our interlocutors have a more visible and influential voice in terms of what happens in fieldwork, what is written down, and for whom.[21] While collaborative ethnographies can be more accountable and relevant to the people anthropologists work with, the common ground they seek tends to focus on the texts they produce. But writing ethnography is not a value shared by everyone, especially where differences in literacy and experiences of race, class, and gender make it an unlikely bridge to mutual interest. Research participants may expect more from anthropologists than just texts (Kirsch 2018), which may be of little use to them.

In questioning this common ground, we should recognize the skills and technologies by which our interlocutors themselves reflect on their lives, even when they do not fit conventional ideas of ethnography. What, then, of collaborations beyond text? Is there any use for collaboration as a method of anthropological engagement not orientated toward writing or applied to preconceived problems? I think there is, but projects like those I describe in this book are often no less challenging than coauthored texts.

In language documentation, Waorani researchers are often more interested in video recordings than the texts derived from them. Abstract questions about "Waorani culture" take backseat to the value they see in the words of speakers they choose to record. Some have become interested in the statements of elders who describe an apocalyptic future where the Waorani ideal of "living well" breaks down and *wao öme* is ultimately destroyed by *kowori* exploits. As Waorani collaborations bring priorities and questions that are distinct from those of environmentalists and academics, the possibilities and limits they find in this work should push us to rethink the form and purpose of the collaborations we seek.

In many aspects of life, collaboration has come to be valued as more creative, empowering, and beneficial than the work of individuals or institutions (Riles 2015). If rendering differences more comfortable in working toward a common goal is now an ethical imperative,[22] the risk of erasing differences, whether in political power or cosmology, presents problems for any anthropological collaboration. Rather than only seek shared goals from the outset, we should embrace and learn from divergent purposes in collaboration. As this work is as much about building relationships as producing descriptions, it involves experimenting with how meaningful communication and political action is possible across differences (169).

Such practices are an important part of the contemporary context I describe in this book. Despite the differences Waorani researchers and leaders see between their own and *kowori* worlds, documenting an "endangered language" and "protecting nature" involves communicating across seemingly irreconcilable ideas about language, land, and conservation. Whether translating into Spanish sounds they identify as unique to their own language or contrasting Waorani and capitalist ways of valuing land through the language of environmental politics, they find this work increasingly meaningful—and sometimes effective.

Questioning the common ground often assumed in collaboration is especially important in settler colonial contexts, where research can itself be a site of political struggle between Western and other ways of knowing (Simpson 2014; Smith 1999).[23] Even where these tensions are less apparent, we must anticipate future consequences. Despite the close relationships that often come with fieldwork, ethnographic research is often of little if any use to the people we study (Smith 1999). Even writing against injustices is not always of direct consequence to the people we write about—especially when confined to academic publications.

Simply envisioning research as more collaborative is unlikely to resolve these issues—especially when embedded in long-standing inequalities.[24] Why should we expect any such work to involve entirely shared interests? Is a common ground always desirable or even possible?[25] Rather than erasing differences between self and other through dialogue, mutual understanding, and solidarity, certain collaborations can highlight the tensions in such differences as a positive site of productive work.[26] The ways in which some Waorani researchers contrast the "truth" embodied in the speech of their elders to the "lies" they see in claims to represent others—whether in politics or ethnographic writing—are but one example of this.

A key priority for collaborative anthropology is thus to shift the purpose of ethnography from primarily one of description and analysis to one that defers to our interlocutors' modes of knowledge (Holmes and Marcus 2008, 82). For me this has in part meant recognizing the choices and purposes of Waorani researchers in making particular recordings. The conventional focus on accurate translation, building a linguistic corpus, or documenting Indigenous knowledge is secondary to their own epistemological values and political goals. For some Waorani researchers, video is a tool for witnessing political events, or to record the "direct" or "true" experiences reflected in the words of their elders—sometimes in contrast to what outsiders say about "Waorani culture." While divergent expectations in this work make its outcomes risky and uncertain, the critical conversations that emerge from it can make research more relevant to the people we write about and with (Holmes and Marcus 2008, 84).

A collaborative anthropology that questions the erasure of difference in the name of common ground can contribute to new solidarities across long-standing inequalities. However, in the messiness of fieldwork, we should not expect to always end up sharing the political commitments of our "others," much less assume they are part of a clearly bounded community with shared goals. This is as important for thinking about the limits of collaboration as it is for recognizing the constraints and risks young Waorani adults face in their current political action. They sometimes work not only across Waorani and *kowori* worlds but in a contentious political terrain within their own communities.

This raises a broader conceptual problem that I address with Waorani language research and environmental politics: what we can reasonably assume the people we engage with in collaboration share among themselves? As a small Indigenous Amazonian group who speak an isolated language, Waorani are exactly the kind of people often imagined as a "community." Whether described as a "culture," "society," or "tribe," there is an implicit assumption that they live in a natural state of collective solidarity, with shared understandings and commitments to specific traditions (High 2013).[27] The success of Indigenous politics often depends on such images of unity—most often identified as "culture"—not least because negotiations with the state and other outsiders depend on it.

However, the collaborations I describe in this book can open spaces for conceptualizing and expressing differences beyond conventional identity politics. In language research, some young Waorani adults have found a technology for thinking about culture and indigeneity in ways that undermine essentialist stereotypes. Their work sometimes lays bare dissenting views and conflicting agendas—the differences often ignored in romanticized representations of culture and resistance (Abu-Lughod 1990b; Ortner 1995). The contingent and unpredictable nature of these collaborations push us to think about Waorani and other Indigenous peoples more in terms of innovation than essences.

If language research and environmental politics suggest the potential of collaboration beyond common ground, working with differences is anything but easy for Waorani researchers and leaders. Rather than a clear path to harmony or social justice, their work often becomes entangled in unpredictable conflicts (Davis 2016). It can also place anthropologists like me on uncertain ground. This may not be a bad thing for a profession whose strength is more in questioning certainties than proving them. In this way the "crisis of participation" some see in the current collaborative moment is a logical next step from anthropology's well-worn crisis of representation (Kirsch 2018, 2). This collaboration, located in the clashes and misunderstandings in fieldwork and politics, indicates the experimental character of research that challenges the positioning of the anthropologist as sole "ethnographer" and all others as "informants." The fraught nature of these projects is part of what makes them important, even when they do not achieve the horizontal relations we desire.

Toward an Amazonian Contemporary

Language research and environmental politics illustrate how young Waorani adults engage with new opportunities and challenges in their lives. The technologies, relationships, and knowledge they entail indicate not a transition from "tradition" to "modernity," but collaborations in a contemporary world they share with outsiders. The anthropology of the contemporary (Rabinow 2007), often focused on global connectivity, expertise, and innovation, is fundamentally premised on such practices (Faubion 2016, 373).[28] In locating researchers, their subjects and their collaborations in the same, mutually constituted temporal frame (Guyer 2016, 373), this approach moves beyond enduring notions of tradition and modernity by which social transformation is often imagined in places like Amazonia.

Anthropologists tend to apprehend this moving, experimental domain of the contemporary through studies of science labs, the work of artists, museum collaborations, and international bankers (Holmes and Marcus 2008). These contexts of technical expertise and innovation are interesting sites to explore novel problems and risks. But we should also look to less obvious spaces of the contemporary—even those not conventionally associated with scientific innovation or global connectivity (Sanchez Criado and Estalello 2018, 5). Today we find these spaces in new and unexpected locations, and among people whose rights, livelihoods, and political clout may depend in large part on their status as antithetical to modernity.

Outsiders often measure Waorani cultural authenticity, like that of many Indigenous peoples, in terms of continuities. But even if Waorani language researchers are less connected to global flows of capital than bankers or lab scientists, and their language videos are unlikely to garner attention from an international arts scene, their transcriptions and experimentations in videography produce something new. As technologies of "para-ethnographic" imagination (Holmes and Marcus 2008), their expertise leads not only to new knowledge but also reflexive understandings of themselves, their communities, and their place in them. This is why their work can, in unexpected ways, unfold in conjunction with more visible and politically engaged forms of collaboration, such as environmental activism.

I doubt that the young Waorani adults who became language researchers more than a decade ago would have then imagined becoming prominent environmental activists. I do not suggest that Uboye's participation at COP26 or Nemonte Nenquimo's emergence as a global environmental celebrity are a direct result of their work in language documentation. These are of course very different projects, with different purposes. But I approach both as collaborations in an Amazonian contemporary that extends beyond their home communities: a contemporary made as much of new knowledge and expertise as entrenched understandings of what it means to be Waorani, to live, as they say, "like the ancient ones," and to speak Wao-terero.

The contemporary is of little analytical use if restricted to allegedly modern contexts of knowledge production. In language documentation the experts are not just linguists and anthropologists with PhDs, but Waorani people who learn new skills and imagine new possibilities through their work. Though not qualified according to conventional measures of scientific expertise, some develop the technical skills of professional linguists at the same time as they display the curiosity and critical reflexivity of ethnographers. My initial surprise at how quickly they learned specialist computer programs for text transcription revealed my own prejudice about people with few educational qualifications. Whether we call them informants, language consultants, interlocutors, or epistemic partners, they make clear that thinking and working as a researcher does not require the education accessible only to the privileged few recognized as scholars.

It should not be controversial to include Waorani researchers and environmental activists in the domain of the contemporary—even if they do not write ethnography. This has important implications for questions of collaboration. Dialogue and collaboration with Indigenous scholars are crucial to making anthropological descriptions more meaningful to Indigenous communities (Sillitoe 2015). Indigenous scholarship, written by and for Indigenous people rather than about them, is an important part of decolonizing anthropology and the knowledge it creates (Todd 2016). But writing is not the only way of recognizing and valuing Indigenous perspectives. For clear historical reasons, Indigenous people have more access to academic credentials in some places than others. In Waorani communities, where few adults access higher education, ethnographic texts are—at least now—an unlikely tool for expressing views on issues that matter most to them.

However, they still have much to say as critical observers. Young adult activists openly challenge not only a multi-billion-dollar oil industry and a government that sells oil concessions on their lands to the highest international bidder, but also Waorani politicians they see failing to protect *wao öme* or bring significant benefits to their communities. These critiques are also voiced—often more subtly—in language research, where they contrast the skilled oratory of "the ancient ones" to the ineffective speech of politicians and lack of knowledge among younger peers. Such insights emerge from the very processes of research and activism. Waorani language researchers are not Indigenous scholars in any conventional sense. But their work is ethnographic, even as it challenges the idea that research should simply serve to document enduring, preexisting knowledge.

For the non-Waorani linguist involved in the project, a major purpose of language documentation was to record—and thus preserve—Indigenous knowledge. In no way do I diminish the knowledge of speakers recorded for this project, nor can I absolve myself from the interest in documenting it. But that knowledge is not my focus in this book. It is instead Waorani engagement with this process as a form of social imagination and reflection on what it means to be Waorani in the midst of social transformation: an Amazonian contemporary.

These engagements offer a perspective distinct from both conventional anthropology and Indigenous scholarship. In recording videos of family, friends, distant elders met for the first time, church sermons, and the speeches of aspiring politicians, Waorani language researchers engage critically with their world at the same time as they document it. Rather than becoming "culture-bearer-scholars" (Sillitoe 2015, 20) who complement or correct my outsider perspective on their culture, Waorani have their own purposes in making recordings. For some it is a way of earning cash income. For others it is an opportunity to learn about and reflect on social differences and what is going on around them—something not entirely distinct from anthropology. For others still, it is a tool for holding oil companies and political leaders to account. What emerges in this work is not a consensus about Waorani culture and how (or to whom) it should be represented, but the conflicts and contradictions in their social and political lives—of which oil companies, state institutions, and outsiders like me have long been part.

The novelty and lack of consensus revealed in collaborations of this kind are what make them such a complex ethnographic context. Releasing our hold on the idea of Indigenous knowledge as something long finished and awaiting discovery, the anthropology of (and in) collaboration that I am arguing for requires sensitivity to new ideas, practices, and relations that emerge from these engagements. It approaches Amazonian people not simply as bearers of an "Indigenous culture" but as fully human beings whose contemporary both includes others and has a distinct shape and texture. Waorani language documentation and environmental activism are thus part of how we might understand a distinct contemporary taking shape in Amazonia.

In sum, the collaboration I describe in this book is as transformative as it is documentary—both in the knowledge and the relations it creates. Its unpredictable character highlights limitations for everyone involved. For me, it has required becoming part of other people's lives in more challenging ways, with new risks and responsibilities, whether in archiving language videos in distant locations or managing the work and salaries of people with little previous experience of wage labor. In such processes, the relationships we have maintained for many years can easily fall apart and turn to resentments about failed expectations. We may be revealed as liars, thieves, or ungenerous kin. Some Waorani people risk much more in collaboration. For them the consequences can be close to home, and unlike foreign academics who return to our home countries, these consequences may follow them closely throughout their lives. Even as some gain new skills and opportunities, they can face difficult challenges and bitter humiliations at the hands of local peers and international audiences. We should not romanticize collaboration any more than the assumed coherence or unity of Indigenous communities who engage in it.

All of this indicates how the methodological challenges of collaboration also bring ethical questions. What does "informed consent" or "ensuring no harm to research participants" mean in research premised on Waorani people making their own choices about what they record and participate in? When they turn their cameras to the issues that matter most to them—sometimes risking their own safety—to what extent can academics claim (or deny) responsibility in such work? Here ethics cannot be addressed by received wisdom from previous generations of anthropologists who understood collaboration primarily in terms of participant observation in the service of collecting data. When my interlocutors contrast the "true" speech of their elders to the "lies" of many *kowori*—including politicians and anthropologists—they bring their own ethics to this work. Departing from the conventional epistemology, ethics, and politics of anthropology, they evoke a distinct understanding of the relationships between knowledge, language, and being in the world. I hope to show why, for Waorani researchers and environmental activists, as well as anthropology, collaboration might still be worthwhile despite such differences.

Summary of Chapters

In the first two chapters I describe what documenting an endangered language entailed for the academics and Waorani researchers who became involved in it. Chapter 1 focuses on the collaborations this involved, placing Waorani language documentation in the historical context of communities that have experienced profound transformations since coming into regular contact with *kowori* people and state institutions in the 1960s. I explore how, alongside different disciplinary visions of collaborative methods and ethics, Waorani researchers have engaged in this work beyond the technical requirements of language documentation. While the videos they recorded are a form of Indigenous media that renders language a cultural object in new ways, they became more interested in the words of elders as a resource for addressing current problems than as an index of cultural authenticity.

Chapter 2 explores the power Waorani people see in speaking Wao-terero and how it figured in their work to document it. The agency attributed to speech in shamanism, funerary practices, and language videos all situate language as a force inseparable from the bodies of speakers. Here Waorani researchers highlight divergent ideas about the nature of language and demonstrate how people operate across these differences. In this way, they draw on elders' speech as a critique of their own political leaders and as a model for environmental activism. In this context, the methods of language documentation and ethnographic research become intimately connected to the distinct logic of Waorani environmental politics.

Chapters 3 and 4 move the discussion of collaboration to environmental activism, where questions of translation are as central as they are to language documentation. Chapter 3 describes Waorani environmental leaders who work closely with international activists, translating across differences to defend their lands against the oil industry. Central to this collaboration is the ability to translate between *wao öme* ("Waorani land") and a *kowori* logic of conservation premised on "nature," "culture," and "environment." While adopting these discourses, they conceive of conservation in terms of the rights and needs of specific nonhuman beings and their relationships to Waorani people that constitute *wao öme*. As "living well" increasingly depends on an ability to operate across different conceptions of Indigenous lands and life, translations reveal not just differences between "Western" and "Amerindian" ontologies but the need to locate contemporary Amazonia in relation to wider sociopolitical processes. This is evident in chapter 4, where I describe Uboye's experiences at the COP26 climate change conference. While environmental politics evokes new possibilities, it also illustrates the limits of contemporary collaborations that are as much about structural inequalities as Waorani ideas of autonomy, responsibility, and the limits of political authority.

The point of departure for chapter 5 is a casual comment I heard from a Waorani friend that "anthropologists lie." I draw on this statement to unpack a theory of knowledge that evokes the possibilities and limits of the collaborations I describe in this book. I describe a Waorani epistemology in which "truth" is associated with direct, embodied experiences, in contrast to abstract forms of representation or claims about others. While bodies, persons, and households are mutually constituted in everyday social life, speculative claims about the thoughts or experiences of others are understood to be a form of deception or "lying." The understanding of autonomy—and its link to the body—in this theory of knowledge underscores Waorani moral evaluations of environmental politics, their own leaders, and ethnographic writing. I suggest that such a contention, rather than making a collaborative anthropology futile in this Amazonian contemporary, points to the distinct form and purpose of anthropology for Waorani researchers.

The concluding chapter asks: what do these collaborations mean for anthropological methods and engaged anthropology more broadly? Despite embracing concrete goals, such projects remain unfinished and open-ended—both for Waorani people involved in them and for outsiders. Unlike ethnographic texts, the practices, relations, and technologies they bring remain embedded in Waorani social and political life. Their unpredictable consequences indicate not a transition to a version of "modernity" imagined by outsiders, nor simply the extension of an enduring tradition, but the new possibilities of an Amazonian contemporary. This points to what is at stake for a generation of Waorani researchers and leaders engaged in collaborative projects that extend well beyond their home communities.

ONE

. . .

COLLABORATIONS IN AN
AMAZONIAN CONTEMPORARY

IN MARCH 2019, I sat in front of a laptop computer with Uboye, listening carefully to a video recording of his mother, Ñai, sitting in her hammock telling a story called "the son of the boa." Having just returned from visiting Ñai at a village feast, Uboye and I were now many miles away at the home of linguist Connie Dickinson, on the outskirts of the Amazonian city of Tena. Our task was to complete the final transcription and translation of the video—which was soon to be archived in London. For a number of reasons, we had chosen Ñai's telling of "the son of the boa" and a second story about the mythic character Pagueñemo as recordings to make available for public access through the online archive. Ñai was well known among her kin and community for her extensive knowledge of Waorani oral tradition and her ability to captivate audiences with her stories. More often than not, her audience consisted of her husband, one or more of her ten adult children, and an ever-growing number of grandchildren who visited her. Small in stature, usually soft-spoken, but also known for her generosity and sharp humor, Ñai made the stories come alive powerfully through sound and gesture. It is clear in the video how humor—a seemingly constant aspect of Waorani social life—is a key feature in her story, as small contextual details and onomatopoeic expressions add comedy to otherwise well-known stories.

Ñai's oratory skill made the recording a good candidate for public access in the archive. It's content—stories about characters from a mythic past—also made it more viable to share than other videos. One of the myths recounts how a woman is impregnated by a boa, and the drama that follows when a grandmother cuts what appears to her as the boa-child's hair—but is actually his heart—unwittingly killing him. The second story describes how Pagueñemo, master of butterfly-people, helps the lost survivor of a burning lightning bolt find his way back home to his family. Both of these myths evoke beings, whether plants, animals, or insects, that take human form in certain situations, and the consequences of misreading their true bodies.

Stories like these, whether about palm trees appearing as people and entering a house or butterflies searching for a manioc beer drinking party, exemplify key features of Waorani language and cosmology. Recordings of heated political meetings and intimate accounts of revenge killings between rival families, though equally important for the purposes of language documentation, can require more complex ethical consideration for public access. Alongside their content, the contexts surrounding recordings in part define their importance to Waorani people and determine what can and cannot be done with them. In this case, the fact that Ñai is Uboye's mother, a person whose stories I had listened to on many occasions while living in her home, were part of what framed our work on this particular translation.

As we sat in front of the computer, Uboye and I shared an unspoken awareness that Ñai was in her final days of battling terminal cancer. For me, this made the video as much a tribute to an extraordinary person as it was an evocative example of verbal artistry in Wao-terero. Ñai, between telling her stories, planting extensive gardens of manioc and plantains, and offering commentary on people and events in the village, always found the time to welcome me into her home with her characteristic care and humor. If my presence was a burden to her and others, which I am sure it was at times, this did not stop her also welcoming my *kowori* wife with a familiar ease, generosity—and determination to teach her a key skill of Waorani women: chewing cooked manioc tubers to prepare manioc beer.

Our work that day on the recordings of Ñai was in some ways also the culmination of nearly a decade of collaboration in language documentation—a project in which Uboye has taken a leading role. It took us the better part of three days to go over the text, correcting countless mistakes in the original transcription and translating it into Spanish. As we went, the work oscillated between arduous periods of listening and reinterpreting Ñai's words, Uboye's nuanced explanations of the context, speculation about linguistic details, and above all, laughter. Uboye's now expansive knowledge of sound symbolism in his language made the story and its translation more understandable and enjoyable.

FIGURE 1.1: The late Ñai Gaba Caiga in front of her house in 2017. Photo by author.

As we worked, with Uboye patiently accommodating my struggles to understand and translate unfamiliar Waorani phrasings, he described to me how the particularity of his language made our translation uniquely challenging. Over the years he has become an expert at identifying, differentiating, and explaining ideophones—a remarkably prevalent feature of Wao-terero. Stories like "the son of the boa" are replete with these expressions, in which speakers vividly simulate—often through accompanying gestures—sensations and perceptions from everyday life. For example, in this recording the sound of forest fruits landing on the forest floor after being cut high up in a tree is *tei! tei!*, and the sound of a person stamping on the ground is *teik!* After much discussion of the differences between his mother's use of the ideophones *bage bage* and *doge doge* in the story, Uboye managed to explain to me, with his characteristic laughter, that the first refers to the flopping up-and-down movement of a man's penis when running naked, while the second refers to a penis becoming erect.

But this work is not just fun and games for Waorani language researchers like Uboye; it is a demanding and often boring job that requires being away from their communities for weeks or months at a time. They participate in it at least in part to meet specific financial needs, whether to pay for the repair of a broken chainsaw, new clothes, or medicines for family members. As we translated "the son of the boa," I knew from our previous conversations that Uboye had several things on his mind beyond ideophones: he had a sick newborn baby, needed money to travel back to his home community to vote in the national elections, and was anxiously waiting for his elected position in the Waorani organization to be officially recognized. His situation was indicative of the scarcity of cash and employment opportunities that are part of the context of collaborative work with Waorani people.

*

Every anthropological project involving fieldwork presents its own collaborative opportunities and challenges, even if simply in the ambition to participate in other peoples' lives. The ethical considerations of this work are always embedded in specific sociopolitical histories of which ethnographers become part. The Waorani people I have come to know in the Ecuadorian Amazon are particularly interesting in this respect. Their historical positioning in Ecuador as well as ongoing changes in their communities have had a major impact on the nature of our collaborative work. In this chapter I locate the Waorani Language Documentation Project in the context of recent transformations and generational differences that have emerged since many Waorani came to live at a missionary settlement starting in the late 1950s. These changes help make sense of how young adults engage in and talk about language documentation and their relationships with *kowori* (outsiders).

The specific interests Waorani language researchers have in collaboration are often distinct from those of academics. As videographers, linguists, and speakers, they produce a form of Indigenous media that renders their language a cultural object and also challenges the essentialist notions of "culture" often associated with Amazonia. Their work evokes new ways of imagining what it means to be Waorani in the contemporary world. Rather than suggesting a reified notion of tradition or indigeneity, the contemporary that Waorani researchers construct through language documentation includes *kowori* people and technologies. It is in part this social and technological interface, which includes anthropologists and linguists, among others, that makes Waorani collaborations a particular kind of political engagement.

Recognizing Waorani language consultants as researchers may sound like an obvious or even necessary move for anthropology today. And yet, rather than overcoming familiar ethical and epistemological problems in fieldwork, efforts to place collaboration at the forefront of anthropology, especially in settler colonial contexts, is likely to complicate or intensify these problems. The different understandings and engagements this involves raise age-old questions about representation, relative power, adequate compensation, and positionality not only for academics but also for their epistemic partners involved in claiming Indigenous rights. Some of the products and politics of such projects are difficult to anticipate—or to reconcile with our own priorities—because they are not entirely our own.

It is not just the differences between Waorani and academics that complicate and enrich collaboration. In this chapter I also highlight how anthropologists and linguists bring different visions of collaboration into language documentation research. These differences evoke new and sometimes challenging conceptual horizons for all those involved. The point is not to conflate disciplines and "cultures" as analogous fields of difference, but to highlight that such engagement mobilizes alternative forms of knowledge and experience (Barry and Born 2013, 20). It is precisely the emergent possibilities and commitments in collaboration that make it a key setting for ethnographic reflection. Here I explore such novelty in Waorani participation in language documentation, but also in other ways of asserting autonomy in a wider scene that includes oil companies, schools, and Indigenous politics.

Waorani Life on an Amazonian Frontier

Most Waorani people live on a vast rainforest reserve of more than one million acres between the Curaray and Napo Rivers in the Ecuadorian Amazon. Their population of around 3,500 lives across more than forty villages, some in remote areas reached by small aircraft or several days travel by foot, or less by canoe. Others are located along oil roads that traverse the northern boundary of the reserve, especially to the east. Their reserve, initially established as a Protectorate in 1983 including only the western part of their ancestral lands, was expanded and legally recognized as the official Waorani territory in 1990.

Today it stretches across the provinces of Pastaza to the west, Napo to the north, and Orellana to the east. In all of these areas, some Waorani live in close proximity to other Indigenous peoples, colonists, and other Ecuadorians. Recently, upwards of fifty Waorani families have relocated to the frontier town of Shell or the nearby regional capital, Puyo.[1] The eastern part of the reserve is surrounded by the Yasuní National Park, one of the world's richest areas of biodiversity and home to Waorani and related groups living in voluntary isolation.[2] Waorani people have deep historical links to the Yasuní, a controversial site of oil extraction, and claim it is part of their ancestral territory.

Much of my fieldwork has been in the western part of the reserve associated with Waorani who came to live at the evangelical mission settlement of Tiweno in the late 1950s and 1960s. Most of the young adults who became language researchers are from this area. However, since many of their parents and grandparents are from areas to the east, some were interested in recording language videos with relatives in other parts of the reserve. As they visited distant locations, in some cases for the first time, their recordings included a much more geographically diverse group of Waorani voices than in typical ethnographic fieldwork conducted by a single researcher. Waorani researchers often commented on this diversity, whether about regional linguistic differences, the biographies of people they met, or mythic characters that appear in their recordings. For me, this diversity laid bare the circumscribed nature of my previous fieldwork, which typically involved long stays with specific families in villages I have come to know well. Working with multiple Waorani language researchers—each with their own curiosity and family background— significantly broadened the scope and complexity of the research.

In most areas Waorani livelihoods depend primarily on hunting, gardening, fishing, and gathering forest fruits on the lands surrounding their villages. This economy has diversified in recent decades in large part due to the oil industry and increasing access to frontier cities. In areas where oil drilling is most extensive, the wages men earn from employment with oil companies are an important source of income. In some areas, polluted soils and rivers make gardening and fishing less viable. Elsewhere, fishing and gardening are of greater importance. Almost everywhere, with the exception of isolated groups within the reserve, Waorani communities have important links to the wider cash economy. In some villages this includes ecotourism projects and temporary work with environmental NGOs and state agencies. Even in areas not close to oil installations, young men travel long distances to work on temporary contracts with oil companies.

The vast majority of Waorani people speak their distinctive native language, Wao-terero, as a first and primary language. The focus of the language documentation project, Wao-terero is understood to be an isolated language insofar as linguists have not established any substantial links to other Indigenous languages (Peeke 1979; Klein and Stark 1985). Most Waorani, with the exception of some elders, speak at least some Spanish. This is in part a result of intensifying relations with *kowori* people in recent decades, including the introduction of state schools in some villages, oil work, migration to frontier cities, and interethnic marriages.

Since the 1970s an increasing number of Waorani have married Kichwa-speaking Runa people, the demographically and politically dominant Indigenous group in Amazonian Ecuador. As a result, some Waorani adults and children speak Kichwa, and despite Runa spouses most often relocating to live in Waorani villages, some Waorani today live in towns outside the reserve. Some of the children of these interethnic marriages do not learn the Waorani language, and there is a degree of speculation about whether these children are Waorani or *kowori*. Such claims and attributions of identity are contextually dependent and highly variable (High 2006, 2015), making the exact size of the Waorani population open to different interpretations. This situation also raises questions about who should be allowed to represent Waorani people as political leaders in their official Indigenous organization.

Even as interethnic marriages and residential movement to areas outside the Waorani reserve to some extent blur the boundaries of what it means to be a Waorani person, participation in a national and global scene of Indigenous politics has simultaneously shaped a more concrete sense of Waorani ethnic identity. This identification as a specific Indigenous ethnicity—or more typically in Ecuador as a distinct *nacionalidad* ("nationality")—is part of Waorani involvement in a broader political arena that recognizes Indigenous identities in specific ways in Latin America (Hale 1997; Postero 2007; Warren and Jackson 2002). Waorani ethnopolitics has emerged in relation to a burgeoning oil economy and in the wake of an intense period of violence and distrust between Waorani groups. In comparison to other Amazonian peoples in Ecuador, such as Runa and Shuar, Waorani are relative newcomers to a strong national Indigenous movement.[3] And yet they live in one of the most contested frontier areas of Ecuador in terms of oil, illegal logging, conservation, and conflicts with "uncontacted" groups.

Many pages have been written about Waorani isolation and resistance to contact with outsiders prior to mission settlement.[4] Often described as the last

Indigenous group in Ecuador to accept peaceful contact with missionaries, neighboring Indigenous peoples, and the state, they have long been associated with violence. While often assumed to be an essential feature of Waorani life, spear-killings between rival families and against *kowori* outsiders should be understood in relation to an expanding frontier epitomized by slave-raiding rubber barons in the early 1900s and subsequent extractive economies (Wasserstrom 2016).

For much of the twentieth century, in Ecuador and beyond Waorani people were emblematic of the "wild" Amazonian Indians of colonial imagination (High 2015a). Until recently they were most often referred to as *aucas*, a Kichwa term that means "wild" or "enemy" forest-dwelling people and in Ecuadorian Spanish has connotations of savagery associated with Amazonia (Taussig 1987). Accounts of violent resistance to outsiders who entered Waorani lands, recorded in twentieth-century chronicles (Cabodevilla 1999; Labaka 2003), were hardly challenged by early missionary and anthropological writings that described a society so enmeshed in internal blood vendettas that it might soon disappear altogether without missionary intervention (Yost 1981).

Seen as a "savage" people in need of receiving the word of God, Waorani people became a prized target of Christian missionization in the 1950s. They rose to prominence in evangelical imagination in 1956 when five US missionaries were speared and killed in a failed effort to establish peaceful contact with Waorani along the Curaray River.[5] The killings, which were widely reported in US news media and later missionary writing as an act of Christian martyrdom (Life 1956; Wallace 1960, 1973), became a key event in the unfolding relationship between Waorani people and missionaries in the second half of the twentieth century (High 2009a). In particular, Elisabeth Elliot, the wife of one of the deceased missionaries, and Rachel Saint, the sister of another, later established a Waorani mission settlement. They did this with the help of Dayuma, a young Waorani woman who had sought refuge at a plantation after fleeing revenge killings involving her family. She taught Saint Wao-terero and later accompanied the missionaries to establish a mission settlement, Tiweno, in 1958. Dayuma, celebrated as the first Waorani convert to Christianity, became a key figure in brokering marriages between former enemy groups— including those between upriver and downriver Waorani and with Runas.

Though the missionaries initially struggled to bring mutually mistrustful families to live together, in the coming years they attracted the majority of

Waorani to live at Tiweno. The mission became a site of tentative alliances and social change, with many Waorani converting to Christianity by the 1970s and marrying Runa spouses. Despite suffering newly introduced diseases at the mission, punctuated by a deadly polio outbreak in 1969, the violence between Waorani groups and against outsiders steadily lessened. At the same time, an oil industry that had begun exploratory work on Waorani lands in the 1940s found new allies in the missionaries, as the relocation of distant groups to the mission laid the groundwork for oil extraction to begin in earnest on Waorani lands in subsequent decades (Kimerling 1993; Stoll 1982). By the mid-1970s overpopulation, food shortages, and strained relations at the mission led many Waorani to disperse and establish new villages. Even after the missionary organization, the Summer Institute of Linguistics (SIL), was banned from Ecuador in 1981, Rachel Saint remained with Dayuma to continue mission work until her death in 1994.

By that time oil drilling by Texaco on Waorani lands to the north had brought deforestation, industrial pollution, and colonization along the main oil road known as the "Via Auca."[6] Even as the Waorani reserve gained an expanded legal title in the 1990s, the government sold concessions to extract oil in several areas of it. Most notably, the contentious Block 16 concession—sold to the Maxus Corporation in the early 1990s—included parts of the reserve to the east and the Yasuní National Park. It was later developed by the Repsol-YPF consortium, which brought expansive oil installations and roads to an area inhabited by Waorani who had refused mission settlement in previous decades. Oil production in the park and adjacent areas of the Waorani reserve is a hotly contested issue in Waorani communities, as are proposals to develop Block 22 in the province of Pastaza to the west. As oil and other extractive economies have harmful effects on isolated groups in these areas, and Waorani relations with them, the social and ecological consequences of oil have become part of a national debate that includes mestizo activists.[7]

The combination of mission settlement, the impacts of oil, and the introduction of state schools has transformed Waorani life in many ways. While some elders today recall a time before missionization when they feared *kowori* were cannibals, many of their children have learned Spanish, worked for oil companies, and in some cases married nonindigenous (mestizo) people. Some of their grandchildren have become teachers, Indigenous politicians, or activists involved in international campaigns to defend Waorani lands. These generational changes, which have been an ongoing focus of my conversations with Waorani people for years, are part of the broader context of language documentation. Particularly for the young Waorani adults who have become language researchers, this context today includes a rapidly deteriorating security situation in Ecuador, where the influence of criminal gangs linked to drug cartels has made public life increasingly uncertain and dangerous—even in the Amazonian provinces.[8]

Most *kowori* like me who come to live and work in Waorani communities find them to be very welcoming. Without ignoring enduring interfamily conflicts and growing resentment of oil companies and colonists in some areas, Waorani routinely incorporate outsiders into their villages and homes in large part through generosity, care, and seemingly constant humor. By now there is ample evidence to dispel misleading representations of them living in a state of constant violence and isolation.[9] The revenge killings that were intense in the middle of the twentieth century have not been constant, nor have Waorani always rejected peaceful relations with other Indigenous groups (Cabodevilla 1999; Cipolletti 2002; Reeve and High 2012).

As relations with outsiders have become more viable, engagements with the national Indigenous movement and international activists are today an important part of Waorani political life. Since the 1990s Waorani leaders have negotiated with the Ecuadorian government, oil companies, and other external interests through their own Indigenous organizations. Their overarching political office, the Waorani Nationality of Amazonian Ecuador (NAWE), consists of elected Waorani representatives assigned to areas such as health, territory, education, and tourism.[10] Located in the frontier city of Puyo, NAWE operates alongside the Association of Waorani Women (AMWAE), which has a key role in producing and marketing sustainable crafts and agricultural products. In addition to providing training workshops for women, AMWAE also challenges oil companies, illegal logging, and other threats to Waorani territory. This changing political landscape also includes regional Indigenous organizations, such as the Waorani Organization of Pastaza (OWAP),[11] which has been instrumental in protesting oil drilling and works closely with Ecuadorian and international Indigenous rights advocacy groups.

Whether welcoming outsiders, learning Spanish, or creating new designs for an international craft market, relationships with *kowori* can be productive and desirable. In contrast to certain stereotypes, I rarely hear Waorani people talk about this process in terms of their "culture" being threatened by a "modern" world around them. While their ideas and practices challenge conventional understandings of culture and social change, relatively new ideas, such as "nature" and "culture," are becoming prominent in Amazonian social and political life. As we shall see in the following chapters, Waorani—like many other Indigenous peoples around the world—have little choice but to engage with the global discourses of multiculturalism and environmentalism around them. Their territorial rights—and their alliances with outsiders—may depend on the ability to engage and translate these ideas. This does not mean that new encounters entail a complete break with the past—at least many Waorani and other Amazonian people do not tend to describe them in this way.

Language documentation is part of this changing sociopolitical landscape. Even if the stakes are smaller than in oil extraction and environmental politics, it is also a process through which my interlocutors reflect, often critically, on what being Waorani and engaging with *kowori* means to them. For some, it brings the stories of elders and their legacy of violence to bear on questions of what life ought to be like. It is part of a larger intergenerational process of imagining how things might be different in the future. So language documentation is political (England 2003), even if Waorani researchers find in it a form of engagement quite different from that of their official organizations. In the following sections, I describe what this has involved and how language videos, as a form of Indigenous media, situate language and culture beyond conventional measures of authenticity.

The Waorani Language Documentation Project

This book began with a description of a young man named Uboye recording his father's stories about the time prior to the arrival of missionaries. It was part of a language documentation project involving a field linguist (Connie Dickinson), an anthropologist (myself), Waorani language researchers like Uboye, and speakers like his parents. A few years before, inspired by Dickinson's work to document Indigenous languages elsewhere in Ecuador, I began recording videos of Waorani people speaking. My interest in language documentation stemmed from my previous work on how memories of spear-killings and missionization figure in ongoing Waorani transformations. Discussions with linguists also made me reflect on how, despite Wao-terero being the primary language spoken in most households, migration to frontier cities and the use of Spanish in village schools place this minority language under threat in a national context. Although spoken by nearly all of the Waorani population, it has received little attention since the first missionary linguists arrived in the 1960s (Peeke 1973, 1979; Pike and Saint 1988).[12] For linguists involved in language documentation and revitalization work, Wao-terero is a classic example of an endangered language (Austin and Sallabank 2011; Evans 2009; Thomason 2015).

When I began making recordings, I was not surprised that several young adults like Uboye quickly became interested in the videos. During my previous fieldwork, young people were excited to see their still images on my digital camera and later receiving paper copies. Access to video increased in the early 2000s, with some families bringing generators from the city to watch popular Hollywood films in their homes. Although I did not record video until several years after my initial fieldwork, it became clear when I made my first recordings in the mid-2000s that I would have little difficulty recruiting Waorani people to work with video. Several elders, especially those renowned for their storytelling and extensive knowledge of *wao öme* (Waorani land), were happy to participate as speakers. The knowledge and "beautiful" speech in their stories about past times is integral to what Waorani call *waponi kiwimonipa*, which loosely translates as "living well." For elders and young adults alike, these stories are a valued way of sharing knowledge across generations.

I was more surprised to find that some young adults, after initial training by the linguist, also became interested in the laborious process of transcribing the videos through a computer program designed for language documentation. On the basis of this initial work and the initiative the linguist took in expanding it, we began a three-and-a-half-year project to carry out more extensive research with a grant from the Endangered Languages Documentation Programme (ELDP).[13] The idea was to collect more than one hundred hours of video to be transcribed, translated, and analyzed, creating an electronic database with thousands of examples from which to produce a dictionary, grammar, and other language resources. The recordings and corresponding texts would then been deposited at the Endangered Languages Archive (ELAR), to be accessed where permission is granted by the speakers and researchers involved in the recordings.

One of my main interests in this project, beyond making an ever-expanding source of linguistic and cultural data accessible to future generations of Waorani people, was Dickinson's (2011) approach to collaborative documentation. Having already worked on a successful project to document the Tsafiki language on Ecuador's Pacific coast, she was committed to the idea that this work should involve a high degree of collaboration with Indigenous language consultants and be orientated toward meeting the needs of native speakers. In a context where Wao-terero is the first language of most Waorani people, this in part meant identifying what they thought should be recorded with whom and adopting an orthography that could be easily used on a Spanish keyboard. Though focused specifically on documentation, the linguistic data resulting from the project would make it possible to create educational materials in the native language.

The rationale was to train Waorani people to do as much of the documentation work as possible, from recording video to transcribing and translating texts, to eventually parsing and glossing individual words, just as a professional linguist would. To this end Dickinson, in addition to managing most of the project, trained several Waorani in the technical aspects of documentation. Some worked on a full-time basis for extended periods, while others only occasionally transcribed specific videos. This required temporary relocation from villages or Amazonian frontier towns to Dickinson's house in the city, where they had access to computers and other equipment for documentation. In addition to receiving room and board at the house for themselves and their families, they were normally paid on the basis of how many hours of video they transcribed, which was designed to be the rough equivalent of a low professional salary in Ecuador.[14] Some Waorani researchers who became skilled videographers were eventually able to make trips independently to communities and public events to record video.[15]

As is common in language documentation, there is an emphasis on oral histories in the videos Waorani researchers record. To some extent this reflects their interest in learning new knowledge from elders about past events, people, and places. However, even outside the specific context of recording language videos, storytelling is a speech genre that often emerges when elders speak in the home. The recordings also include everyday conversations, political speeches, and descriptions of hunting and other activities. I recently accompanied a Waorani researcher who recorded a protest against oil in the regional capital, which included elders singing and a young Waorani woman speaking to reporters against the Ecuadorian government's decision to grant further concessions on Waorani lands. The diversity in these videos reflects Waorani political and intellectual engagements as much as it does the practical requirements of language documentation.

My own technical role in this project has been relatively small. Having introduced the proposal to some Waorani elders and the young adults who worked as language researchers, I had planned to spend a year working alongside them and the linguist. However, I was only able to make several shorter trips to Ecuador, where I learned the basics of language documentation alongside Waorani researchers, assisting in the transcription of videos and revising and translating texts. More recently, I interviewed Waorani language researchers about their experiences in language documentation, and the work of preparing the videos for the archive continues at present. In 2019, I met with several Waorani researchers to talk about the potential uses they see in language videos and to reflect on their current work beyond language documentation. At present three of them are in leadership positions in Waorani organizations. In November 2021, the fieldwork came to Scotland, when Uboye attended the COP26 climate change conference in Glasgow and then stayed with my family in Edinburgh for a week. My most recent fieldwork trip to Ecuador, which I describe in the final chapter, was in July 2023.

Part of the idea from the start of the project was to enable Waorani people to conduct their own language documentation in the future, independently from linguists or other academics. Of course, the needs and wishes of Waorani speakers and their communities are likely to change over time, as will the ethical dimensions of accessing the videos. This means that, in addition to the linguist's commitment to training speakers in the use of video and processing texts, this work involves anticipating future possibilities. The unpredictable and relatively uncontrolled ethical implications of collaborative work are closely connected to the novel potential of projects that expand the scope of who participates as researchers. As we shall see, for good reasons, Waorani language researchers, as ethnographers, have their own agendas in recording videos that can complicate conventional academic approaches. They are also subject to ethical scrutiny within their communities.

The project was borne out of a shared interest in collaboration that recognizes Waorani people as researchers in their own right. Dickinson's goal was to generate data about an endangered language in an ethical way that is accessible to speakers. Though critical of outsiders claiming to be involved in "saving" Indigenous cultures, she subscribed to the dominant perspective in endangered languages research: that key aspects of culture are lost when Indigenous language use ceases (Hill 2002). I was interested in how closer attention to language would allow me to learn more about Waorani ideas and practices, but was wary of the idea of collecting or "salvaging" knowledge assumed to be vanishing.[16] Moreover, having never previously met Waorani people who did not speak Wao-terero, the immediacy of language endangerment was less apparent to me than other threats to their way of life.

This would soon change, as I have since met Waorani parents living with *kowori* spouses in urban areas whose children speak little or no Wao-terero. To a lesser extent, this language shift is also part of life in Waorani villages. During a visit to Ñai and her husband's home a few years ago, I noticed Ñai struggling to communicate with two of her visiting grandchildren. The children, who were probably four or five years old at the time, belonged to Ñai's oldest son and his Kichwa-speaking wife. They had lived for years in a frontier city, where they spoke Spanish in school and primarily Kichwa in a home shared with the mother's parents. Despite speaking little of either language, Ñai constantly engaged with the children during the visit, using gestures to communicate and teach them as much as she could in Wao-terero. She approached what I assumed to be a major social and linguistic barrier with her characteristic calm and humor—reminding me that multilingualism is not a foreign or unusual feature of life in much of Amazonia.

If my interest in language documentation was in some ways different from my colleagues in linguistics, I saw in this work a possibility for more meaningful collaboration with Waorani people. As several young adults became interested in making recordings, I found an opportunity to involve them in research in which they themselves would have stakes in the results. Even if this work has not led them to study linguistics or anthropology, it offered a rare opportunity for them to acquire professional skills outside the school curriculum in Ecuador. Some have since worked with documentary film crews and other projects. While language research is only temporary, at the very least it presents an alternative to oil work—a primary source of employment for Waorani men. Several young women also contributed significantly to the project both as speakers and researchers who transcribed and translated videos. They have also been involved in discussions of the challenges and values of collaborative language documentation for Waorani people. In chapter 4 I describe how one of these women, Nemonte Nenquimo, became a key figure in international environmental activism against oil.

Converging Visions of Collaboration

The complexity of collaborations I describe comes not only from Waorani people becoming researchers with their own agendas, but also from how linguists and anthropologists tend to approach language documentation in different ways. Anthropologists today offer diverse proposals to situate their "others" on more equal footing. Whether envisioned as coauthorship, cotheorization, or joint political action, this work reveals not just differences, but how our interlocutors inhabit and negotiate these differences. By insisting on an epistemological equality between "us" and "them," deliberately collaborative work posits a common ground from which we might better appreciate differences that exceed ideas of "culture." In this way, anthropological studies in and of collaboration can evoke new possibilities that emerge where different worlds meet. It is often the conflicting views and priorities in these encounters—whether between different disciplines or between academics and Waorani researchers—that lay bare the creative potential of collaboration for anthropologists and their interlocutors.

While most anthropologists, including linguistic anthropologists who share a similar ethnographic approach, tend to make questions of power, positionality, and subjectivity in fieldwork central to their writing, linguistic fieldwork specifically for the purposes of language documentation often focuses more on scientific accuracy and the range of data to be collected (Ahlers and Wertheim 2009). Envisioning language preservation as a singular ethical outcome and developing methods to answer preexisting questions (Ahlers 2009), this approach has affinities with applied anthropology (Shulist 2013, 10). However, the heightened ethical implications of sharing information and managing digital archives beyond the academy can make linguistic fieldworkers more sensitive to issues of copyright and ownership of data (Seifart et al. 2008; O'Meara and Good 2010).

Anthropologists often envision research questions as more open-ended, ideally derived from the fieldwork encounter itself. Since Indigenous people participate in language documentation for reasons that are distinct from academics, part of the complexity of collaboration derives from the divergent agendas they bring to it, particularly when it becomes part of Indigenous political practice (Field 1999). In Amazonia, this work inevitably becomes entangled with experiences of social transformation, whether in urbanization, state education, wage labor, or Indigenous politics (Shulist 2013, 2018; Wroblewski 2021). Since it is difficult in these contexts to assume a preexisting "community" to whom the products of collaboration can be addressed or given, we should recognize competing local objectives in language documentation beyond discourses of cultural diversity and pan-indigeneity often emphasized in linguistic policy (Shulist 2013, 18–19).

But the differences between approaches to collaboration in anthropology and language documentation should not be overdrawn. It quickly became clear in Waorani language research that, to the linguist involved, the videos and transcribed texts were valuable scientific data, whereas my ethnographic writing was—for her—a purely theoretical endeavor. But she was sensitive to complex ethical questions well beyond conventional approaches to documentation. Training and working alongside Waorani people to document their language required confronting these issues in much more sophisticated ways than most ethnographers would. She often voiced frustration with the ethical shortcomings of academic researchers who fail to recognize the intellectual contributions of Indigenous peoples or compensate them accordingly. In 2016 she brought together members of diverse Indigenous groups in Ecuador to the Amazonian Regional University (IKIAM) to draft a new ethical framework for research with Indigenous communities. Dickinson was also integral to establishing an Indigenous council at IKIAM—the first of its kind at an Ecuadorian university.

So, if the linguist embraced a systematic approach and envisioned language preservation as an ethical goal, she was no stranger to the messiness of collaboration. Whether in determining how to compensate Waorani speakers fairly, who should have access to the finished videos, or what parts of the texts can be published online, her work involved closer attention to ethics and questions of collaboration than most anthropologists or Waorani people are accustomed to. She also supported Waorani priorities that emerged through the project, such as opportunities for professional training in filmmaking, visits to remote villages to record elders with particular knowledge, and Waorani researchers making trips to international conferences to present their work. But collaboration in these contexts also revealed conflicts regarding not only the purpose of language documentation but also what roles and responsibilities different people should have in it.

Language documentation lends itself well to mutual interests in work that goes beyond purely academic debates. There are also ethnographic insights to be gained from the consequences of collaboration across disciplines and with different communities. Although these projects may seem anachronistic to everyday life in Amazonia, they can tell us something about how people navigate new and challenging relationships. Such collaborations—whether in language documentation or environmental politics—generate situations that demand novel responses, and thus new possibilities for effecting change. The chapters that follow describe how Waorani people find novelty not only in filming each other speaking Wao-terero but also in more explicitly political forms of collaboration that take them well beyond their home communities to defend Waorani lands.

Language beyond Cultural Authenticity

Waorani language documentation is an example of how the use of audiovisual media contributes to new kinds of social, historical, and political consciousness among Indigenous communities that have long been the object of colonial imagination and oppression. Indigenous people bring their own diverse ideas about video's capacity to create, sustain, or revive social relations at multiple levels, and this "embedded aesthetics" expresses values and principles that outsiders often fail to understand (Ginsburg 1994, 368; Pace 2018). Waorani videography in language documentation involves such an aesthetics, even as it becomes entangled with wider processes of objectifying Indigenous culture in Amazonia.[17]

Waorani people are aware of their symbolic position as "wild Indians" in the national imagination when they appear at protests and folklore festivals with long spears and painted bodies (High 2009b). As with this bodily imagery, the ability to speak an Indigenous language is also a key marker of cultural authenticity in much of Amazonia (Graham 2002). These external expectations are part of the wider context in which Waorani language researchers and videographers navigate between foreign measures of authenticity and the expectations of their own people.

In the 1990s and early 2000s, when most Waorani language researchers attended school, mestizo teachers routinely complained to me about the challenge of educating and "civilizing" Waorani students. Required to wear school uniforms, adopt Spanish names, and speak in Spanish as they learned reading, writing, and math skills orientated explicitly toward life outside their communities, students also participated in events designed to celebrate Waorani "culture" as a distinct Indigenous "nationality."[18] The ways in which schooling disconnected young people from the lives of their parents and elders,[19] while also emphasizing their cultural particularity, is part of what frames Waorani interests in language documentation.

Elders, despite generally valuing school education, often comment that it has contributed to generational differences, whether regarding young people adopting *kowori* ways or their bodies becoming relatively weak (High 2010).

But I rarely hear Waorani people—young or old—describe themselves as victims of this process. Parents direct criticisms less at the discrimination their children face in school than at teachers who fail in their expected duties—such as those who abandon their classes for extended periods or appear drunk in the community (High 2015b). For many young Waorani people, schooling is part of becoming Ecuadorian—an identity many have embraced in recent decades. And yet, the resulting generational differences also inform the value some Waorani language researchers see in making video recordings.

They often draw on discourses of "culture" to describe the stories, knowledge, and ways of speaking associated with elders that they learn about. In their own language, young Waorani adults describe the painted bodies, colorful feathers, and other decorations they wear at protests and other public events as being *durani bai* ("like the ancient ones")—a term they most often translate to Spanish as *la cultura* ("culture") (High 2015a, 61). These terms also refer to practices, abilities, and values associated with elders, such as sharing, generosity, physical endurance, personal autonomy, or being able to speak and sing "beautifully." Whether referring to elders, ancestors, or young people performing images and values associated with them, Waorani discourses of *durani bai* and culture imply a sense of historical continuity.

While the purposes, methods, and products of language documentation are different to Indigenous filmmaking, both involve Amazonian people in new forms of objectification that engage and exceed culturalist discourses. Indigenous people have their own purposes in public performances of Amazonian "culture," which are not always clear to nonindigenous audiences (Graham 2005, 625; Oakdale 2004; 2005). Even as making language videos is projected less toward external audiences, it values language in ways that were not initially obvious to Waorani researchers. It frames language as an object that, like other things cultural, can be lost. The linguist involved made clear her view of language preservation as integral to recognizing and defending Waorani culture in the face of external pressures. In this view, the prospect of the Spanish language replacing Wao-terero is part and parcel to the threat of impending cultural loss (Errington 2003).

Prior to the language project I had not heard Waorani people talk about their language as a cultural object in this way. Their organizations have at times supported the development of basic educational materials in Wao-terero for use in village schools—sometimes approaching me for assistance in this area. Locally, however, families tend to value school education primarily as a way to learn skills and language orientated toward the *kowori* world (Rival 2002), rather than a space for Waorani language or "culture." However, becoming bilingual Ecuadorians does not appear to erode their sense of being Waorani. Advocates of language preservation might argue that this lack of concern for language displacement is part of why many minority languages around the world are disappearing.

I am sympathetic to this concern on the part of linguists who commit much of their professional and personal lives to these projects despite little prospect of recognition in the academy (Hill 2002, 120). Yet the connections drawn between language and culture in revitalization projects often involve an "ideological shift" for Indigenous people (Shulist 2013, 23). These shifts can affect local politics in unanticipated ways, since their reasons for participating in this work may diverge from those of linguists and anthropologists.[20] For some young Waorani adults involved in language documentation this has meant imagining their relations with outsiders and each other in new ways.

Waorani researchers have their own purposes in choosing what to record in language videos. Some are keenly interested in documenting everyday life

FIGURE 1.2: Waorani researchers make a recording for the language documentation project in 2011. Photo by Connie Dickinson. Used with permission.

or learning something new, whether technical skills or the details of a particular story. Their recordings can reveal more nuanced ideas than outsiders appreciate and sometimes come into conflict with the sensibilities of other Waorani people. The day after Uboye filmed his father's stories described in the opening of this book, he decided to record hours of teenagers sitting around talking in the village. When I asked why, he said, "I want to record young and old people who speak differently . . . and people who speak different dialects of Wao-terero . . . from distant communities." Having by then worked for months alongside a linguist, his response reflected a priority of language documentation: to include as much diversity in speakers and speech genres as possible. But Uboye also has his own agendas in making language videos. His ideas about their purpose and value have changed over the years through his experiences of becoming a researcher, a parent, and an activist. One of these is the growing emphasis some Waorani researchers place on making recordings to hold political leaders to account—including their own.

Participation in language documentation is part of a much wider process of redefining what it means to be Waorani. Many of my interlocutors are critical of conventional Indigenous politics—a skepticism borne in part out of the positioning of their leaders between Waorani and *kowori* worlds. When a Waorani political organization was established in the 1990s, some of the first Waorani high school graduates became Indigenous leaders tasked with negotiating with the state, NGOs, and oil companies operating on Waorani lands (Zeigler-Otero 2004). These primarily male leaders struggled to mediate between a multi-billion-dollar oil industry backed by the Ecuadorian state and the expectations of Waorani villages where there is little tolerance for political and material inequalities (High 2007).

In this context a Waorani ethnic identity has taken shape that draws in part on popular imagery of Amazonian people, whether as custodians of nature or the "wild Indians" of colonial imagination. Many school-educated adults are not involved in the Waorani political organization and, like their elders, are quick to point out when they see urban Waorani leaders departing from specific egalitarian values. Some Waorani language researchers contrast ethnopoliticians to what they describe as "Waorani culture" and engage in alternative forms of leadership in alliance with international activists. But what does "Waorani culture" mean in this criticism? Language recordings, more than just documentary evidence of authentic culture or history, are a way of asserting what it means to be Waorani in new and changing contexts.

Rather than recording people displaying the body decorations and spears expected at festivals and political meetings, Waorani researchers tend to be more interested in knowledge of plants and animals, techniques for making objects, oral histories and everyday conversation. Uboye's attention to differences between how older and younger people speak is part of his curiosity about changes since what Waorani people call "the time of civilization" at the mission (High 2016). He prioritizes recording elders because, as he says, they "speak differently" than younger people, and to learn "what Waorani leaders were like in the past." This work is part of a wider Waorani conversation about the perceived lack of accountability and incessant political in-fighting among Indigenous leaders, a situation they lament playing into the hands of oil companies and preventing economic benefits reaching villages. These criticisms indicate how some Waorani use language research as a technology to evaluate contemporary problems in their communities.

Some young adults look to the words of elders for knowledge and ways of speaking they fear are being lost. They describe living elders and their knowledge of "the ancient ones" as emblematic of the past strength and unity of Waorani people. Emphasizing a relentless autonomy and determination to defend Waorani land, they draw comparisons between elders, ancestors, and the remaining groups living in voluntary isolation within the Waorani territorial reserve. As a form of social memory linking past and present to future aspirations, this narrative contrasts with how many Waorani elders remember the deep divisions between Waorani groups during the intense warfare prior to mission settlement (High 2015a).

Thinking beyond questions of historical accuracy, some Waorani people see language documentation as an opportunity to draw on the words of elders as a powerful political tool. Uboye, for example, describes some of his recordings as a source for learning ways of speaking that made past generations effective leaders. For him, the words of elders embody a Waorani "world"—distinct from the *kowori*—that enabled them to effect change in the past. Waorani people should thus be able to defend their lands from oil companies—or achieve substantially greater compensation—if they learn to speak "strongly" as their ancestors did. His call to embrace the verbal skills of elders attributes a specific power to speaking Wao-terero.[21] It also offers a way of thinking about difference beyond conventional images of Indigenous culture in Amazonia and elsewhere.

Uboye and others look to the words of elders not for authoritative commands about how to live or how to deal with the pressures of oil, but for ways of speaking that convey the collective power of being Waorani to younger generations and outsiders. Their words are also a source of prophecy, as some Waorani adults explain to me that they warn others of what will happen in the future. Rather than predicting events regarding specific people, elders increasingly express concerns about the fate of all Waorani people—whether in reference to internal problems or the prospect of succumbing to a hostile and ever-expanding *kowori* world.

Waorani language researchers have interests in video that are distinct from other people in their communities. While I was making a recording in a village along the Curaray River several years ago, a family I know well organized the children to perform, as they described it, "like the ancient ones," by singing and dancing together. A young mother, who had painted her children's faces red with achiote dye and tied palm fronds around their heads, told me: "record this and take it back to your country for your family to see." Such spectacles, like those at urban festivals, are what many Waorani expect video to capture. The interests of Waorani researchers are quite different in this respect. In some contexts, they value stereotypical imagery of "Indianness" as entertainment or as an integral part of their relations with *kowori*. But their choices in filming Waorani language are in many ways ethnographic in their own right. Video has become a technology through which they not only project a sense of who they are but also engage with outsiders and each other in new ways.

Whereas imagery that mediates relations between Amazonian people and outsiders is often visible and material—unaccompanied by verbal expression—in language videos Waorani researchers explore the visual and audible aspects of their social world. Several have explained to me how they seek recordings to learn about things they did not previously know, such as details about deceased relatives in oral histories or techniques for building houses, weaving baskets, and making hunting poison. As they record videos for their own purposes, questions of one practice or image being a more or less authentic expression of Waorani "culture" appear to be less important than learning how elders speak and what they see the future to hold.

*

In this chapter I have described how the questions Waorani researchers ask in language documentation—and the meanings they find in it—take new directions working alongside linguists and anthropologists. After many months transcribing videos, I discovered that some of them not only described the knowledge of elders they learned about in the recordings but also how the particularities of their language are part of what makes Waorani people distinct. The point is not that their interests are more genuine than the images that tend to mediate relations with outsiders, but that they express new ways of thinking about themselves and others through their collaborations as researchers. This novelty is the product of both cooperation and conflict in ongoing practices that cannot simply be reduced to ideas of tradition and modernity that tend to frame questions of cultural authenticity.

The purposes Waorani people have in language documentation, including what they choose to record and how they value it, are central to the collaborative context I describe in this book. But understanding these engagements—and how they become expressions of Indigenous autonomy—also requires attention to a Waorani theory of language observable in social life. In the following chapter I explore the power of speaking Wao-terero and how it figures in language documentation and other situations that situate language as integral to Waorani "culture."

TWO

. . .

SPEAKING DIFFERENTLY

IN JULY 2017 I traveled to Toñampari, a Waorani village where I carried out much of my fieldwork from 2002 to 2004 and have since visited every year or two. Members of my host family there were closely involved with language documentation, so I had come to ask them what they thought about the project and possible future uses of the language videos. As we sat in hammocks in the shade of their longhouse one hot afternoon, I listened to my hosts talk hopefully about the game meat that Amowa, the father of the family who had gone hunting early that morning, might soon bring back to the house. Given my long absence from the community and the profound changes it has seen since I first began fieldwork in the late 1990s, I admit feeling a certain satisfaction with such a familiar household scene. On countless occasions I have been at home with this family, patiently anticipating Amowa's arrival with fish and various game animals for the afternoon meal. His wife, Ñai, along with two of their young adult daughters, had already collected manioc from gardens across the river to cook with the meat.

On this occasion the family was hopeful, speculating that Amowa might return with a collared peccary, a large forest bird, or perhaps a deer. When I asked why they were so confident, Amowa and Ñai's daughter-in-law explained that they had heard a birdcall "*tititi*" outside, thus foretelling a successful hunt. She and her husband explained that the calls of certain birds, in this case the *geñëta*, not only indicate a successful or unsuccessful hunt, but also can warn that animals or people are nearby. So while the *geñëta* bird's call "*tïka*" indicates that a hunter will not find game, "*tititi*" communicates the presence of animals to Waorani hunters and gardeners. Another bird, the *kaäta*, also warns that rain is coming. Such prophetic communication, they explained, is not limited to birds.[1] Frogs, for example, also anticipate rain with their calls "*wewewe*," and the nocturnal monkey's (*amöka*) call, "*urururu*," warns that enemies are coming to attack.

Ñai, listening to these explanations by her young adult children and probably noting my superficial understanding of how birds speak to humans, interjected with the following story about two birds:

> One of the birds, *geñëta*, was thin and unattractive, like a Kichwa person. The other, *koyomene*, was very beautiful and strong. Two girls wanted to marry the attractive bird. He told both of the girls to come to his [mother's] house to be with him, where he would be waiting. There were two paths in the forest, one leading to his house, the other leading to the ugly bird's (*geñëta's*) house. So the beautiful bird told the girls that he would leave a feathered crown on the correct path to his house, so they would know which way to go. But *geñëta* overheard *koyomene* saying this, so he secretly switched the crown to the other path, to trick the girls into going to his [mother's] house. Then, to trick the girls into staying at his house, the ugly bird would spend the whole day out hunting, not revealing his true identity to them. He would only come home at night, when it was too dark for the girls to see who he really was. This went on for a long time. But the girls eventually became suspicious and asked his mother why the bird never came home during the day. Finally, one night they grabbed him and held him down until they could see him in the morning light. When they discovered who he really was, they left and went to the beautiful bird's house. When they arrived *koyomene* asked why they had never come. The girls explained the trick *geñëta* played on them, but *koyomene* sent them away.

Ñai's story illustrates an expert ability to draw on historical and mythical accounts to enrich and contextualize knowledge and its exchange in everyday dialogue.[2] I certainly benefited from her ability to do this throughout my fieldwork, even if I have not always been able to follow her connections between mythic characters and household conversations. This aspect of verbal artistry—exemplified by Waorani elders—is difficult to adequately capture in language documentation videos. Though unable to record her account in the natural flow of conversation, I wrote it down in my notebook that evening in as much detail as I could.

After hearing her story, I asked Ñai why the calls of the *geñëta* bird, and not *koyomene*, foretell a successful hunt. She explained that, while *koyomene* is able to hunt game himself, *geñëta* makes calls to others since he cannot hunt well. Observing that some Waorani words for birds, such as *yawe* (toucan), are the same as the sounds associated with their calls, I asked what birdcalls might have in common with the Waorani language (Wao-terero). Ñai and others who were present explained that the calls of birds and other animals are not exactly Waorani language, but sounds that require interpretation and translation. They offered the example of the *geñëta* bird, whose call "*tïka*"—communicating an unsuccessful hunt—is like the word *onöke* in Wao-terero, meaning to lie or mislead. They translated its "*titititi*" call—affirming a successful hunt—as *nawäga*, meaning serious or true. However, my interlocutors emphasized that these birdcalls, rather than just translations or prophetic announcements, also interject in response to when a person says something true (*titititi/nawäga*) or untrue (*tïka/onöke*). On this occasion, the words of my hosts—and the call of the *geñëta* bird—proved to be accurate, as Amowa soon returned home with a deer carcass draped over his shoulder.

In this chapter I describe Waorani understandings of language in terms of what it means to speak Wao-terero, engage with nonhuman beings, and

FIGURE 2.1: Ñai roasts deer meat in her home in 2017. Photo by author.

document their language through video recordings. While language documentation involves imagining language in new ways, the work of Waorani researchers also builds from an Indigenous theory of language that challenges the multiculturalist frameworks in which documentary linguistics, anthropology, and Indigenous politics are embedded. I consider the metaphysical underpinnings of this theory by comparing Waorani ideas about the power of speaking in shamanism and funerary practices to their collaborative work in language documentation. Central to this understanding is a conception of language as a force that is seemingly inseparable from the bodies of speakers—whether animal or human. The distinct features of Wao-terero that Waorani researchers identify in their video recordings highlight how collaboration in linguistic research evokes divergent ideas about the nature of language at the same time as it demonstrates how people operate across distinct concepts of difference.

The Power of Language

Among Indigenous peoples of the Americas, language is often seen less as a system of representation than a practice that brings things into being or effects changes.[3] In some contexts, being spoken to or spoken of, even at a distance, can have material consequences for people. In Amazonia the relational power of speaking implies distinct ways of imagining the very nature of language.[4] In contexts where social relations routinely transcend conventional distinctions between "nature" and "culture," nonhuman beings also have important stakes in linguistic practices. Amazonian understandings of the force of language emerge in shamanism, ritual, and various forms of singing that transform or create something in the world.[5] Waorani language, or more specifically the embodied act of speaking it, has a status distinct to that with which many *kowori* are familiar. But what is language exactly that allows it to have such a force in these contexts? How much is this power understood to be specific to their own language, and how much of it do they see as a general feature of speech in any language?

Waorani people appear to understand the act of speaking Wao-terero to have a particular kind of power. Although I rarely hear my interlocutors reflect on the nature of language in abstract terms, they describe how certain kinds of speech contribute to making or unmaking relationships, whether between humans or with nonhuman beings. While the spoken words of a shaman can themselves do harm, in funerary practices speaking unintelligibly is part of how Waorani differentiate and separate themselves from deceased kin and the dangers associated with them. These contexts present certain contrasts to the idea of language as "culture" in the social dynamics of collaborative work to document their language through video recordings, transcriptions, and translations. Whether in shamanism or the foregrounding of perspective in specific ways of speaking, the affective properties of language point to the inseparability of body and voice in Waorani understandings of becoming.

While I want to highlight differences between Waorani and conventional Western ideas about language, the purpose of this chapter is not to contrast them as polar opposites. Even if "Western" and "Amerindian" language ideologies may appear logically incommensurable, in practice Amazonian peoples engage in diverse social contexts that cannot be reduced to a single, coherent understanding of language. Alongside situations where Waorani people describe the power of speech to make or unmake social relations in distinct ways, emergent ideas of language as emblematic of "culture"—whether in bilingual education or language documentation—also involve thinking through differences in new ways. I suggest that collaborative projects premised on shared ideas of language and culture are precisely the sites where we can better understand these differences as part of what shapes contemporary social dynamics in Amazonia.

Body and Voice

The specific power of language can be seen in Waorani shamanism, and particularly sorcery.[6] Shamans, who have a special adoptive relationship with jaguars, are at times inhabited by jaguar-spirits who speak through a shaman's body in dreams. While jaguar speech is said to bring about successful hunting (Rival 2002), for many Waorani people it is also associated with a dangerous predatory perspective (High 2012a). One of the risks in shamanism is that the jaguar/shaman's speech can harm other human beings. Though my Waorani interlocutors generally claim to know little about the technical process of assault sorcery, on several occasions it was explained to me that shamans can cause harm by merely speaking the names of specific people. Part of the danger in a jaguar-spirit inhabiting the body/voice of a shaman is that other people present may (even inadvertently) bring misfortune on people by talking about them—even jokingly—during jaguar speech. This is why elders remind young people to take great care in what they say in the presence of a jaguar shaman.

I would be wary of reading a generalized theory of language into a specific context like jaguar shamanism. Animals do not normally speak—at least not in ways that are intelligible to Waorani people in the way human language is. In fact, in everyday life they generally find troubling the idea of nonhuman beings speaking to them in human language. This is evident in concerns about sorcery and encounters with nonhuman beings in the forest who appear and speak deceptively as humans.[7] I remember watching a *Star Wars* movie (dubbed in Spanish) in a Waorani village about twenty years ago, when, after a scene where Yoda talks with Luke Skywalker, a teenager asked me: "Do animals really talk to people in your country?" At that time, in Waorani villages there was relatively little access to movies, which my hosts associated with a *kowori* world. As elsewhere in Amazonia (Descola 1994), they routinely point out parallels between the social lives of certain animals and humans. A typical example is peccaries, whose muddy forest trails are often compared to the paths Waorani groups leave behind when traveling together to feasts. Peccaries are also said to invade manioc gardens much like human thieves, and hunting them with spears has associations with warfare (Rival 1996). Birds too are often said to share common aspects of sociability with human beings (Bravo Díaz 2023, 111; Rival 2002).

What I think baffled the teenager who asked me about Yoda, however, was the idea of a clearly nonhuman body speaking in human form. For him and other Waorani, speaking, rather than being a uniquely human capacity, under normal circumstances implies relations with beings who share the same bodily form. So although it did not make sense for Yoda, a clearly nonhuman being, to talk with Luke, a jaguar can speak to human beings—in human language— insofar as it inhabits the body/voice of a shaman. What this appears to suggest is that "body" and "voice" are intrinsically connected insofar as they define the specific character of a relationship.[8] Birdcalls, like those of the prophetic *geñëta* bird, require translation because they are not human language, but that of nonhuman bodies.

This connection between language and the body evokes Viveiros de Castro's (1998) proposal that Amerindian perspectivism situates the body—rather than "culture"—as the principal site of differentiation. While illustrating how Amazonian concepts of difference exceed the idea of cultures as representations of a single natural world,[9] the apparent inversion of multiculturalism he sees in multinaturalism risks ignoring the ways in which many Indigenous cosmologies collapse Cartesian dualisms altogether.[10] Leaving aside familiar mind/body and nature/culture distinctions allows us to better understand the inseparability of body and voice in a Waorani metaphysics of language. Rather than a symbolic system, separate from human action, language is in this context a bodily practice that has a distinct capacity to affect relationships and bring about changes in the world.[11]

Such an understanding sheds light on how Waorani people approach a wide range of relationships, whether between coresident kin, their own Indigenous leaders, or various *kowori* "others." If sorcery highlights the potentially dangerous consequences language can bring about, in everyday life speaking with, to, and about people is understood to have creative properties, even if in less formalized ways than in shamanism.[12] Much as acts of eating, drinking, and living together entail shared bodily transformations, speaking together is an essential part of how people and households are made (High 2018; A.C. Taylor 2007; Vilaça 2016), even, it seems, in situations where speaking to others is anything but straightforward.

Speaking and Eating with Others

For many of my interlocutors, speaking Wao-terero is an important part of what constitutes being a Waorani person. Elders describe how, before the missionaries arrived, they debated whether outsiders were indeed people. Still today they refer to non-Waorani people generally as *kowori*, a term that until recently denoted aggression and a semihuman state of cannibalism. Many Waorani feared that *kowori*—whether other Indigenous groups, missionaries, or mestizos—were intent on eating them. Rather than real people, whose bodies are the product of eating food fit for human consumption, *kowori* were a kind of predatory being, not entirely unlike the dead. The word *kowori* is closely related to the word for the "deceased" (*wori*). In this sense *kowori* were not understood to share the same kind of human body (or food) that constitutes Waorani people. Since speaking Wao-terero corresponds to a particular kind of relation between human bodies, which are made from the household consumption of human food (and not human flesh), it would have made little sense to try to relate to or speak with cannibals. And this was in fact the case: many Waorani went to great lengths to distance themselves from *kowori*—some still do.

This changed in the late 1950s and 1960s with the arrival of missionaries. Visiting and living with missionaries and the Kichwa-speaking Runa people who accompanied them appears to have changed the predatory status of *kowori*, who proved not to be cannibals. In living with and eating real food with them, Waorani came to understand *kowori* as people with human bodies—even if somewhat odd ones. They even started speaking to them as people. One of the first missionaries observed how this happened in the early days of contact in 1957, when two Waorani women arrived at a Runa village. The US missionary there, Elisabeth Elliot, was surprised to see that as the two women began cooking and eating with their Kichwa-speaking hosts, they spoke to her and the Runa in Wao-terero as if they could understand (Elliot 1961). The missionary, who understood almost nothing of Wao-terero at the time, was baffled by their incessant speech directed at her and their apparent insistence that she could understand them.[13] Elliot wrote that the Runas present, who understood the Waorani to be "wild" forest-dwelling Indians, were surprised to see that the Waorani women had the capacity for language at all.

It appears that if *kowori* were indeed people with human bodies, rather than cannibals or the deceased, they should be able to speak or at least understand Wao-terero. This is to say that speaking, like eating together, was part of how Waorani envisioned themselves creating a human relationship with *kowori*. In this way living together appears to have been simultaneously about coming to share corresponding bodies and voices. The power of language to make relations with "others" is part of a more general Amazonian emphasis on "becoming" that Viveiros de Castro (1992, 2011) contrasts to relatively fixed ideas of kinship, identity, and humanity familiar to Western contexts. Just as Waorani babies become people and kin through sharing food and drink and learning to speak with people in their household (*nanicabo*), shared consumption, language, and the body appear inseparable in this process of becoming.

While I can only speculate about this process historically, a close connection between the capacity to speak Wao-terero and becoming part of proper human relationships was evident in my own fieldwork decades later. By then many Waorani households had incorporated Kichwa-speaking spouses who, despite their continuing status as *kowori*, invariably learned to speak Wao-terero and came to share a consubstantial body with people in their household. Other *kowori*, such as missionaries and anthropologists, have also come to share the body/voice that constitutes Waorani household life. I often found it odd how, despite my struggles to learn Wao-terero, my hosts openly commented to other Waorani people and outsiders that I speak their language. Just as they would comment on my body becoming more like theirs as a result of living and eating with them—and thus requiring that I observe specific

dietary taboos when a household member fell ill, their insistence on my capacity to speak and hear their language was inseparable from my identity as a
coresident.[14] This meant that I ended up, to some extent, in a similar position
to that of the missionary Elliot in the late 1950s.

Differentiating the Dead and the Living

This understanding of speech as an embodied form, rather than a distinct
mental capacity distinguishable from the body, is perhaps most clear in Waorani attempts to unmake relations. The death of a kinsperson requires just
the opposite of the intended effects of language in making people and relations. Several Waorani have described to me how the deceased are dangerous
because, not knowing or accepting themselves as dead, they may resist letting
go of their relationships with living people. Affective relations with the dead
can only be harmful to the living, who risk falling ill or dying if they fail to differentiate themselves from them. Waorani describe being alone—particularly
at night—as making people especially vulnerable in this respect. This emphasis on the dangers of the dead and the need to separate them from the living is
widespread in Amazonia and elsewhere in South America.[15]

For Waorani people unmaking relations with the dead kin involves temporarily forgetting their deceased kin. In some contexts, this can mean speaking and acting as if the deceased did not exist. On one occasion, when relatives gathered in the home of the bereaved after a burial, I observed two men
clowning around the house laughing and appearing to speak in tongues. One
of them later explained to me that they were speaking in French "as gringos"
(white people) do,[16] hoping that their comedic performance would lessen the
grief of the bereaved and make those present unidentifiable to the deceased.[17]
The coming together of living kin speaking in Wao-terero or the emotional
cries of a bereaved mother might otherwise attract unwanted attention from
them. Speaking in tongues and making jokes was part of an effort to exclude
the deceased from relationships in which they can no longer safely participate.
As one of the jokers explained, a person who grieves alone or too openly risks
succumbing to the deceased relative's desire for ongoing interaction with the
living, ultimately causing them to adopt the perspective of the dead. Attempts
to forget the dead are temporary, as stories about how ancestors were killed in
the past are prominent in Waorani oral histories, but only once they are safely
separated from the social world of the living.

The practice of speaking unintelligibly to deflect attention from the dead underscores the power of language to bring people together. It begins to address the question of whether, in Waorani understanding, such a capacity is specific to their own speech or is a more general feature of language. Whether in their insistence on my ability to speak their language, or speaking "French" to unmake relations, Wao-terero appears to have a certain force that other languages do not—at least when it comes to Waorani relations and Waorani bodies. This is subtly evident in their attention to specific features of Wao-terero. Although I have not heard Waorani explicitly state that "gringo languages" are less conducive to the social practices they value, there is a sense that different languages correspond to different bodily forms—both human and animal. As the practice of speaking "like gringos" at funerals illustrates, Wao-terero and *kowori* languages appear to evoke distinct bodily forms and corresponding social properties.

The central issue here, then, is not just one of different languages having distinct kinds of agency, but how they correspond to different bodies. What was troubling about Yoda in the *Star Wars* movie, for example, was not that he could speak, or even that he spoke to Luke, but that he spoke to Luke in a human language that did not correspond to his own evidently animal body. In contrast, Waorani routinely observe that members of a variety of animal species speak—both with each other and, at times, to human beings. As we have seen, birds in particular are known for their prophetic calls, often foretelling a successful or unsuccessful hunt, dramatic changes in weather, or even the imminent arrival of an attacking group.[18] As in much of Amazonia (Berlin 1994; Berlin and O'Neill 1981), most bird names in Wao-terero correspond (as ideophones) to the sounds associated with them. In some cases, like in Ñai's story about *geñëta*, their calls are interpreted as messages with reference to mythic narratives.[19] Although Waorani are able to learn the meanings of these calls, they draw a clear distinction between bird messages and human speech. There is nothing troubling or unusual about the intelligibility of birdcalls since, in contrast to Yoda conversing with Luke or a jaguar speaking through the body of a shaman, their language corresponds to their distinct bodily form.[20]

For Waorani people, linguistic differences—whether those between human groups or between human and nonhuman beings—correspond in certain ways to bodily differences. Of course, today they are not only aware of *kowori* languages; many of them are bilingual in Spanish or Kichwa as a result of schooling, interethnic marriages, or experiences outside their home villages.[21] Other Ecuadorians and foreigners are still *kowori*, even if this category no longer has connotations of cannibalism. *Kowori* do have human bodies (and thus human language), but our bodies (like our languages) are different. Waorani elders say that the bodies of young people have changed substantially at the same time as they have come to speak a foreign language. At school, where they learn Spanish, children eat food that elders see as making their bodies weaker and less able to hunt or endure long treks in the forest (High 2010). So even if it is clear that many people who perceive themselves as humans do not share the same language, there remains an association between bodily differences and speaking or learning different languages. This may help explain why, in language documentation, some Waorani researchers have become interested in specific features of Wao-terero that correspond to bodily gestures.

Documenting Language, Translating Difference

Engagements with diverse *kowori* in Ecuador and beyond involve new ways of thinking about language and difference. If I have described a universalist Waorani understanding of language as something intrinsic to relations between human bodies, bilingual education, cultural politics, and language documentation research all insist on language as something that differentiates them "culturally." Like the long spears and distinct body decorations Waorani have become known for in Ecuador, their language acquires the status of an object to be defined, presented, and even preserved as part of the very integrity of "Indigenous culture." In these emerging contexts, languages are distinguished not in terms of bodily experiences and capacities but as distinct representations of a single world that are at once disembodied from speakers and objectified as an essential characteristic of indigeneity[22].

The link between language and culture is often essentialized in Western language ideologies that assume monolingualism to be the norm (Graham 2002, 183). As a result, Amazonian leaders risk being seen as "inauthentic" or "corrupted" when they make public speeches in European languages, even in contexts where speaking in a native language may compromise their ability to effectively communicate with outsiders (189). In this way language has become part of the unrealistic expectations and fundamental misunderstandings Indigenous people often encounter—even among Indigenous rights activists and other allies (Conklin and Graham 1995; Kelly 2011). Like anthropological fieldwork in Amazonia generally, Waorani collaborations with foreign linguists and anthropologists in language documentation research funded by international institutions should be understood within this context.

Language research is not the only or even the primary way in which Wa-orani people engage in new ideas about language and "culture" in contemporary Amazonia. But it does envision Wao-terero in ways that depart from what I have described in shamanism, funerary practices, and previous encounters with *kowori* people. Rather than an embodied form of human sociality with a seemingly universal force of its own, in language documentation research Waorani researchers must to some extent also come to understand their language as a symbolic system of representation.[23] Without ignoring what they see as unique to their language, they understand that much of the very premise of documentation is to record, transcribe, and translate Wao-terero into textual representations that have meaning and value beyond the recorded speech acts.

Making language videos is a technology of objectification through which Waorani language researchers reflect on what it means to be Indigenous Amazonian people and speakers of Wao-terero. This is part of what makes videography interesting and politically important to many Indigenous people. In language documentation, Wao-terero is something that can be interpreted, written, and translated as representations of a world ostensibly shared between Waorani and *kowori* people. While this process values Wao-terero "culturally"—as a distinct object that differentiates Waorani people from others—it simultaneously devalues the power of language as a force in the world. Subjected to the language ideology of documentation, it becomes an endangered cultural resource to be collected, analyzed, and archived for future generations, rather than an immediate, embodied force in social life.

These contrasting theories of language are not mutually exclusive, nor does being a Waorani language researcher involve simply trading one for another. Waorani people involved in language documentation continue to recognize the power of words to effect relationships, whether in shamanism, funerary practices, or everyday life. At the same time, some come to understand their language as a different kind of force in the world as they struggle to translate words and concepts on a computer keyboard. More than constituting relations between beings who share the same bodily form, Wao-terero has acquired a new, seemingly disembodied power as a cultural object that is highly valued by outsiders—whether by linguistic researchers or mestizo Ecuadorian audiences who listen to their speeches at urban folklore festivals.

Some young Waorani adults are more invested than others in this new understanding of language. Some speculate about why *kowori* people would want to record and document their language, wondering if their language videos might have a special economic value in foreign countries. On certain occasions I have been asked questions like: "how much money do gringos pay for recordings of Waorani people speaking?" Others see the videos themselves as expressions of their "culture" that should be valued both by outsiders and younger generations of Waorani people who stand to learn from them. In the following sections I explore how the school-educated bilingual adults who participated as researchers in Waorani language documentation have come to see certain features of their language, such as the extensive use of ideophones, and video recordings of speakers, as cultural objects. At the same time, however, their engagements evoke differences that exceed the conventional politics of recognition in Ecuador and beyond.

The Limits of Translation

Even as language documentation to some extent introduces a separation between body and voice, one of the strengths of using video in this work is that it integrates images of speakers with sound in the process of transcription. This is particularly important for working with Wao-terero, a language so replete with expressions that simulate the sounds speakers sense in the world around them that it is sometimes difficult to follow without seeing the corresponding gestures. And yet, documentation ultimately disembodies language from its speakers, especially as the videos become "texts" to be translated on computers and archived in distant institutions. The process of translating from Wao-terero to Spanish is exactly what Waorani language researchers find most difficult in language documentation. Even the most skilled among them can become exasperated in their attempts to translate Waorani language, often using lengthy contextual descriptions to describe to me why a speaker used a particular word or grammatical form. This is in part because they are attempting to translate not just words, but "worlds" (Hanks and Severi 2014).

For example, when asked to translate a term like *woro-woro*, an ideophonic expression that simulates the sound of a person or animal moving through forest foliage, they often describe contextual details of an encounter, such as the point of view of a hunter and certain behavioral characteristics of the animal. In some cases they conclude that it simply "does not translate" to Spanish. Despite the difficulties in separating speech in Wao-terero from its speakers or translating it in a straightforward way, these contexts are part of what interests Waorani language researchers most. Ideophones are interesting in this respect because they do not lend themselves well to being translated as an abstract representational form. Through corresponding physical gestures, they simulate sensations, perceptions, and shifts in perspective rather than just refer to them (Nuckolls 2010). Described as "a vivid representation of an idea in sound" (Doke 1935, 118), "sensory words" (Dingemanse and Akita 2016), or "vocal gestures" (Voeltz and Kilian-Hatz 2001, 3), ideophones are characterized by expressivity and "communicate by imitating a variety of subjective impressions" (Nuckolls 2010, 29). While onomatopoeia familiar to European languages tend to be restricted to words that imitate sounds, ideophones refer to a wider variety of sound symbolism, such as visual effects, texture, aspect, and other sensory domains.

While a linguistic analysis of ideophones is beyond the scope of this book,[24] their use in Wao-terero appears to share much in common with neighboring Kichwa-speaking Runa people in Amazonian Ecuador. As Janis Nuckolls observes:

> Quichua speakers . . . reconfigure what are conventionally understood as background components into the foreground. Ideophonic performances . . . baldly call attention to a change in perspective. The speaking self of the speech event communicates by imitating and thereby becoming the force that creates a movement, sound, or rhythm. (Nuckolls 2010, 31)

This "becoming" in momentary shifts in perspective involves not just an alignment between human participants, but also a form of "ecological dialogism" with nonhuman beings (Nuckolls 2010, 49).[25] Though there are significant differences between Kichwa and Wao-terero, one of the striking features of many Waorani language videos is a similar foregrounding of other perspectives in ideophones and corresponding gestures. Despite the difficulties in translating them, these expressions often capture the imagination of Waorani researchers. Whether marking the point of view of other human beings or animals, they illustrate again how body and voice are not easily separated in Waorani understandings of language. It is this inseparability that gives sound symbolism its relational force and makes it difficult for Waorani people to translate into Spanish. As they come to associate language with "culture," it is perhaps no surprise that ideophones are central to what the most experienced Waorani researchers see as particular to their language.

These expressions have a heightened presence in language videos in part as a result of what Waorani language researchers choose to record. They are aware that, for the purposes of documentation, the videos should include as much diversity as possible in terms of the age and gender of speakers, the themes addressed, and the social contexts of the recordings. Still, most of the videos are recorded in comfortable settings—often with close kin or people with whom the Waorani researchers are at least familiar. As a result, many of them include myths, autobiographical narratives, or stories about the past experiences of the narrator's family. What these stories tend to share in common, particularly for the people who tell and record them, is an aesthetic of storytelling characteristic of household life. This is precisely the kind of intimate setting where ideophones appear to be most common (Nuckolls 2010, 44). Their extensive use in these contexts points to the emotive and relational force of linguistic forms that express experiential knowledge.

Ideophonic expressions are part of what makes these stories so enjoyable to Waorani listeners. A typical example is hunting stories, which men tell in the evening while others are gathered around the cooking hearth. These are entertaining accounts because they tend to focus on the dramatic movements, sounds, and perceptions of hunters and the game animals attempting to evade them. Whether describing the distant calls of toucans (*yawe*), the sound of a spear hitting its target (*tek!*), a poison dart blasted from a blowpipe penetrating the body of a monkey overhead (*pereik!*), or the sound of a white-lipped peccary stomping on forest leaves (*ua! ua!*) as it attempts to escape a hunter, ideophones mark a shift in perspective whereby the hunter temporarily "becomes" the hunted. They are prevalent in the speech of women and men, whether in comedic accounts of individual folly, well-known myths, or tragic accounts of spear-killings from the distant past. I find that young people also use such expressions extensively, though not as skillfully or to the same extent as elders.

As part of a Waorani sensory ecology linked to health and vitality (Bravo Díaz 2023), ideophones also express perceptions of new and challenging situations. Andrea Bravo Díaz describes how Waorani people who live along an oil road use the ideophone "*toc toc toc*" to describe the sound of oil drilling and "*buuu*" for trucks passing along the dusty road—both of which they see as offensive "noise" in contrast to the forest (122). Whether reporting a recent experience in a manioc garden, or telling a detailed story about the adventures of ancestors or a first encounter with an oil company helicopter, there appears to be a correlation between the prevalence of ideophones in speech and the depth of knowledge and oratory skill recognized in the speaker. This ability is precisely what many Waorani—and especially language researchers—recognize and admire in the speech of elders.

What is most striking to me as a listener is how Waorani speakers powerfully convey the experience of an encounter through a simultaneous expression of sound and bodily movement.[26] This keen attention to sensory perception points to why they are so highly valued by Waorani audiences. In this way, what is often in the background in conventional Western thinking about language becomes central to what is being expressed—whether from the point of view of a human or an animal. Waorani researchers routinely point out, after working long hours to translate texts, the difficulty of translat-

FIGURE 2.2: Amowa Gaba carving an axe handle in his home in 2017. Photo by author.

ing or explaining in Spanish the meanings of ideophones in Wao-terero. And yet, the work of language documentation involves translating ideophones, however clumsily, into textual representations of language. Sounds that are, for Waorani, sensory experiences inseparable from the bodies that express them, must come to stand for something. In the absence of an approximate equivalence, Waorani translations involve moving between radically different "worlds" or "contexts for the apprehension of reality" (Hanks and Severi 2014, 8). This is one way in which the work of Waorani language researchers has certain parallels with anthropology.

Political Speech and the Truth of Becoming

As a marker of cultural difference, Wao-terero is becoming a source of power and interest beyond relationships between Waorani people. But Waorani language researchers and many of their peers see key differences between speaking Wao-terero in everyday life and the words that often characterize Waorani relations with outsiders. In contrast to the ways of speaking that make and unmake relations in the home, or the vivid sense of "becoming" expressed in ideophones, their leaders appear to have a different power in addressing *kowori* audiences in Spanish.[27] Whether directed at oil companies, the state, or foreign environmentalists, many Waorani understand political speech to have less credibility and efficacy than other forms of speaking—especially that of elders.

I suspect that many Waorani people give relatively little weight to the words of their leaders in part because of the limited extent of dialogue in political speech. While most see Indigenous politics as necessary for dealing with outsiders, the distinct values they attribute to the words of leaders and everyday language reflects an egalitarian ethic that limits the authority of individuals (High 2007). After being elected at large assembly meetings within their reserve, Waorani representatives of their formal Indigenous organization often face intense criticism from their peers, whether for their perceived access to external wealth, dealings with oil companies, or the general idea that their words should not be trusted (Baihua and Kimerling 2018). These observations are typically couched in a broader criticism that leaders spend too little time in Waorani communities. Rather than eating, drinking, and speaking together with their kin and neighbors, their lives are often understood to be closely connected to a *kowori* world in the city. In a context where hierarchy and representational democracy have little traction, Waorani leaders are to some extent understood to speak for themselves.

In contrast, the speech of elders—who have little presence in formal Indigenous politics—is often received with considerable weight in Waorani communities. Like young adult leaders, older men and women have little hierarchical authority over others—even their own children (High 2015b). But what they say, particularly in household contexts of storytelling, attracts focused attention in part because it is pleasurable to hear and because it is perceived as credible. Waorani language researchers, when reviewing recordings, often reflect on how elders speak "beautifully," "truthfully," or "seriously." These qualities are also associated with their ability to speak as ancestors did in the past, or "like the ancient ones." In these discussions, again, the knowledge and oratory skill Waorani language researchers identify in recordings is also what makes the work of transcribing and translating them so difficult. Some describe to me how many young Waorani people don't "know/hear" (*iñinamai*) the words of elders, an observation that at once points to generational differences between themselves and elders and frames part of the value they see in their work.

Even as elders often talk about things that happened long ago or in distant places, they express a depth of experiential knowledge of people and events. Their words and gestures are often compelling, whether provoking raucous laughter about a particular person's eccentric behavior or quiet contemplation of the deep suffering of another. Elders express the kind of veracity of experience that is often lacking in political speech as they mimic and "become" the sounds they express. Their words, it seems, are understood to have precisely the truth value and social force that politicians lack. Their stories exemplify the qualities that, for language researchers like Uboye, make the speech of certain elders powerful and even prophetic.

Elders' stories often contain implicit moral imperatives that subtly connect past events or characters from myths to present issues and future possibilities (High 2015a). Even Ñai's account of the prophetic *geñëta* bird at the start of this chapter was, to my ear, more a warning about the art of deception and a guide to help me translate birdcalls than it was an event to be remembered with exact accuracy. While the lessons to be taken from these stories are rarely dogmatic—or even made explicit—in recent years many Waorani people have described to me how elders foretell future events. Waorani language researchers in particular have become interested in their accounts of an apocalyptic future in which Waorani people and their territory no longer exist. These prophecies describe violence between rival Waorani families, ecological damage from oil companies, fights over money, and the prospect of a *kowori* world ultimately destroying their own. Even as these accounts foretell a future beyond the direct experiential knowledge associated with elders, as with mythical narratives and other forms of speaking, what elders say is taken very seriously.

On one occasion, after listening to an elder speak publicly at a contentious meeting to discuss the possibility of a new road being built through Waorani territory, a young Waorani man explained to me the "power" of such speech:

> When elders speak, they have power . . . it makes you feel like you are the same as the person speaking. It can protect you from attacks, like when someone shoots at you but the bullet misses. . . . Many young people don't understand the way elders speak.

While the idea of elders' words protecting people from attack was unusual to me, this comment indicates the power many Waorani young adults attribute to their speech. The speech of elders is powerful not because it conveys orders to be followed, but because it embodies a certain truth of experience associated with them. Even as many Waorani people describe and value their knowledge as "truth"—whether as a record of the past or prophecy for the future—this truth should not be mistaken for something independent from diverse experiences and perspectives. The objectivity of their speech and knowledge instead stems from skillfully embodying sounds and temporarily "becoming" the people and other beings they describe. This is part of what gives the stories and prophetic accounts told by elders their weight, credibility, and entertainment value. While some Waorani language researchers record videos of political speech in part to hold leaders to account, it is the beauty and experiential qualities of elders' words that appears to make them so pleasurable to Waorani audiences.

It is elders—more than young people—who engage in what Waorani people refer to as "strong speech" (*nägi tereka*). As Bravo Díaz (2021, 2023) observes, this is a loud and grave form of political speech in which a person shouts complaints and publicly scolds others—including *kowori*—for moral transgressions. Understood to emerge spontaneously in contentious meetings, "strong speech" is a skill that requires the strength or vitality embodied in specific ritual practices (2023, 74).[28] While this is an example of how the power of speaking is closely linked to the body, "strong speech" is also to some extent gendered. Bravo Díaz notes that while older people are more polished in it than younger people, older women are particularly adept at speaking "strongly" in public contexts (2023, 138). This form of speech has an increasingly important role in encounters and meetings with state authorities and oil companies who fail to meet Waorani demands.

In contrast to the power of "strong speech" and the diverse perspectives exchanged in everyday conversation, the political speech of official Waorani leaders often draws on a more generic expression of dialogue with *kowori* people. While this often involves adopting discourses of "culture" to express and translate differences, for the younger generations of Waorani adults who become political leaders, language researchers, and teachers, the idea of "culture" is still up for grabs. I was struck by the contrast some Waorani language researchers drew between their documentation work and that of their official political organization, which one described as not being "real Waorani culture." Emerging political discourses of culture and indigeneity often imply questions of authenticity that are antithetical to anthropology (Hale 2006). But it is worth thinking about how and why Amazonian people evaluate these discourses and translate them in diverse contexts. While some forms of political speech necessarily engage the language of culture, for some Waorani researchers it is antithetical to the distinct qualities they see in speaking Wao-terero.

*

Indigenous understandings of the nature and power of speaking can shed new light on the ways Amazonian people experience a changing world. Rather than abstracting a generalized Amerindian ontology from the content of myths, shamanic cosmologies, or hunting practices, in this chapter I have described how speaking can itself be a bodily practice of becoming in everyday life. Whether in making others into kin, differentiating the living from the dead by speaking in a foreign language, or in the ecological dialogism of ideophones, speaking can involve shifting perspectives in everyday life. As we have seen, these shifts may be from one human perspective to another or between humans and other beings. All of these contexts point to an intrinsic connection between language and the body that at once resonates with theorizations of multinaturalism but dissolves familiar body/mind, nature/culture dualisms.

In conveying other perspectives and the affective properties of an encounter through sound and gesture, Waorani speech points to how the power of words derives from the inseparability of body and voice. Since the beauty and relational power of speech is seemingly inseparable from sensory experience, speaking Wao-terero foregrounds what is often in the background in thinking about language as a system of symbolic representation. This should cause us to take a step back from the dualisms often used to describe Indigenous Amazonian people. One of the immediate problems in talking about ontological differences with regard to language is the tendency to imagine seemingly absolute logical contradictions between, for example, Western "naturalism" or "multiculturalism" and Amerindian "multinaturalism." My main interest here is the interconnections between Waorani understandings of what language is and the culturalist thinking that frames the politics of recognition in much of South America. Although these interactions suggest different ideas about what speaking can do, they also illustrate how Indigenous people operate simultaneously across contrasting ideas of what makes people and the languages they speak different.

Waorani collaborations in language documentation—as speakers, linguists, videographers, and ethnographers—illustrate the complexity of this process. I do not think that their work as researchers involves simply trading one idea of what language is for another. While I have highlighted the differences between official political speech and the kinds of language that constitute everyday life, the positioning of Waorani language researchers, like other young adults in Amazonia today, requires that they speak simultaneously to local and external audiences (Ball 2018; Graham 2002).[29] These dialogues, often conducted today in the language of culture, involve not only different and contradictory expectations but also highly unequal power relations.

Waorani researchers work, live, and develop new ideas about their language in this dynamic space, which they sometimes share directly with *kowori* people. More than simply reflecting a dominant Western language ideology, this space, of which language documentation research is part, highlights different ideas of what language is and what speaking can do. It also involves efforts to translate across languages and concepts, the consequences of which are becoming ever more apparent in Amazonia (High 2020). Through their work Waorani researchers to some extent come to understand their language as one symbolic representation of the world among others, a cultural object that differentiates them from other people. And yet, they still find it difficult to translate Wao-terero to Spanish, which requires separating language from the vivid sensory experiences and gestures of Waorani speakers. In this way their understanding of ideophones at once reflects a distinct Waorani theory of language as a force in the world and Western understandings of language as "culture."

More than simply objects of intellectual curiosity, the distinct worlds anthropologists describe in Amazonia and elsewhere should help us reflect on how state development agendas, educational programs, and research projects accommodate, suppress, or come into conflict with differences. Whether in bilingual education, collaborative projects to document endangered languages, or efforts to revitalize their use, this work requires thinking beyond a conventional Western metaphysics of language. The Waorani theory of language I have described points not just to the difficulties of translation but more importantly to how the power of language is in some ways inseparable from the everyday contexts in which it is spoken.[30] The ways in which my interlocutors understand the power of Wao-terero to diminish when dislocated from the bodies of speakers illustrates the challenges of political and educational projects that decontextualize language use.

Collaborative research in language documentation is not an easy solution to this challenge. At the very least, it tends to complicate things. It not only has serious limitations, but may be impossible or undesirable in some communities. But this kind of work, where possible, can lay bare differences in how people understand the power of language. Recognition of such differences, whether by anthropologists, linguists, or Waorani language researchers, may offer tentative bridges between seemingly irreconcilable understandings. These collaborations—and the translations they entail—are important in part because of their novelty and unintended consequences. Rather than a straightforward technical solution to the problem of endangered languages, they highlight Indigenous engagements with language that both adopt and exceed essentialist notions of culture that surround contemporary Waorani sociopolitical life. As we shall see in the next chapter, these engagements are unpredictable as they become part of imaginative horizons well beyond the practice of documenting an endangered language.

THREE

. . .

TRANSLATING
ENVIRONMENTAL POLITICS

LANGUAGE DOCUMENTATION RESEARCH IS of course not the only—or the most important—kind of collaboration between Indigenous people and outsiders in Amazonia. Waorani people today engage in close working relationships with diverse nonindigenous people and institutions, whether in wage labor, research, or politics. In this chapter I highlight the opportunities some young Waorani adults are finding in environmental activism, an arena that brings unprecedented recognition of the challenges they face. Their collaboration with an international community of activists is creating new possibilities to challenge powerful oil interests, even as this involves divergent understandings of environment and the role of Indigenous people in conservation. As with language research, Waorani environmental leaders must learn to work across significant conceptual and linguistic differences. In translating between what they call *wao öme* ("Waorani land") and a *kowori* logics of conservation, their efforts to protect their lands and ways of life involve voicing differences between concepts—and at times drawing equivalences between them.

As they become "environmental citizens" (Agrawal 2005; K. Escobar 2015), some Waorani are challenging oil through development agendas that claim post-neoliberal models of well-being and conservation. And yet, their defense of *wao öme* also challenges the premise of nature as something independent from human action or resources to be extracted, managed, or conserved. Conservation projects often envision Indigenous people in harmonious relationships with their environments in ways that render them less visible ecopolitical agents. In this chapter I describe how, in adopting discourses of "nature" and "culture," Waorani activists also conceive of conservation in terms of the needs of specific animals and their relationships to Waorani people. In environmental politics, what they call "living well" (*waponi kiwimonipa*) depends on working between different conceptions of Indigenous lands. These translations reveal not just differences between "Western" and "Amerindian" worlds but also the need to approach Amazonian social transformations in relation to wider sociopolitical processes in Ecuador and Latin America.

"Our Land Is Not For Sale!"

In February 2019, I traveled with Uboye, his wife Marci, and their two small children to the city of Puyo, the capital city of Pastaza province in Amazonian Ecuador. We had come to join a protest against the government's selling of concessions to drill oil wells on Waorani lands. As a seasoned language researcher and emerging environmental activist, Uboye planned to make a video recording of the event. Upon arriving we were soon surrounded by acquaintances from several distant villages I have come to know during fieldwork, many wearing colorful feathered crowns and palm fiber strings tied around their chests. Some women had painted vivid red dye around their eyes and wore stretched tree bark skirts, while several men carried long spears over their shoulders. Many others appeared in ordinary street clothes. As more protestors arrived, the joking and laughter that typically accompanies Waorani public encounters set the stage for what would soon become one of the largest ever political mobilizations of Waorani people.

The protest concerned Block 22, one of several areas designated by the government for oil development in the Ecuadorian Amazon—often overlapping with Indigenous reserves and areas of rich biodiversity. It was the latest of many oil contracts granted on Waorani lands in recent decades, often without adequate consultation with local communities. I felt the weight of this particular concession personally, as Block 22 includes the communities where I have lived during my longest periods of fieldwork since the late 1990s. The prospect of oil drilling threatens the forests and rivers many of my closest friends and interlocutors depend on for their livelihoods in an area already under threat from logging, mining, and colonization. During my most recent visit, several people described to me their concerns about these threats and the prospect of a road being extended into the area where they live. As one elder warned, "With the road . . . the colonists will come, and the animals will be gone."

The protest involved delivering a lawsuit against the Ecuadorian government. The case, brought by the Coordinating Council of the Waorani Nationality of Ecuador-Pastaza (CONCONAWEP)[1] and circulated on social media under the banner of "Waorani Resistance Pastaza," highlighted the lack of community consultation required by Ecuadorian law prior to selling oil concessions. As the number of Waorani protestors gathered at the central plaza grew, many Waorani took photographs and recorded video with their phones. A press officer from the regional Indigenous organization began yelling out slogans against oil from a megaphone. Protestors blocked traffic in the busy city center, carrying giant cloth signs denouncing the oil industry and insisting on their right to decide the fate of their lands. One in Spanish read *"la selva es nuestra vida, no más petróleo"* ("the jungle is our life, no more oil"). Another, written in the Wao-terero, read *"monito ome goronte enamai,"* with a Spanish translation: *"nuestra selva no se vende"* ("our jungle is not for sale"). Adding to the spectacle were at least a dozen international activists who

FIGURE 3.1: "Our Land Is Not For Sale!" On February 27, 2019, Waorani and other Indigenous people marched in the Amazonian city of Puyo to protest the government's decision to sell oil concessions on Waorani lands in the province of Pastaza without free, prior, and informed consent. Photo by author.

darted skillfully between lines of Waorani protestors, photographing beautifully adorned elders and recording anti-oil slogans.

The previous evening Waorani people had arrived by bus from villages
throughout their territory to a meeting point a few miles outside of town,
where preparations were made for the protest. As a Waorani language researcher recorded video of Waorani people of all ages and international activists making colorful banners, I was introduced to two veteran political
activists from other areas of Amazonian Ecuador—one Cofan and another
Siona—who came to support the Waorani cause after successfully challenging
a similar oil concession on Indigenous lands to the north. The solidarity, both
from other Indigenous peoples and international activists, distinguished this
Waorani protest from others I have attended over the years. Equally striking
was the scale of Waorani participation in the march the following day. The
largest gathering of this kind I have seen, it was the culmination of a Waorani Resistance Pastaza movement that had been growing in momentum for
months.

I was also struck by the reactions of local Puyo residents we passed on
the streets during the march. Many observed with curiosity from shops and
restaurants or from the upstairs windows of their homes overlooking the
street, voicing or gesturing their support. Some casually photographed the
protest with their phones. This support from a majority mestizo urban population, and the absence of overt hostility toward the Waorani cause, was remarkable given the history of discrimination against Indigenous people in
Ecuador. Block 22 was part of the government's Ronda Suroriente auction of
new oil concessions that met considerable resistance in Ecuador. Protestors
from several other Indigenous nationalities whose lands are located within
these areas marched alongside Waorani people in Puyo. Some mestizo Ecuadorians also joined, including an elderly woman who drew attention with
her loud screams "*Carajo! Petróleo afuera!*" ("Damn it! Out with Oil!"). Only
a few meters away, Waorani elders calmly walked barefoot, arm in arm, down
the streets. Their body adornments, unified steps, and collective singing in
Wao-terero drew attention from photographers and onlookers.

At the protest I met several activists from the United States involved with
NGOs supporting the Waorani Resistance campaign, such as Amazon Frontlines and Digital Democracy. In recent years these organizations have promoted Waorani struggles for territorial autonomy—both online and in various projects in Ecuador. I joined the march somewhat awkwardly, unsure

FIGURE 3.2: Waorani women marching arm in arm to deliver a lawsuit against the government at Puyo's Judiciary office. Photo by author.

what my role should be in an event premised both on Indigenous autonomy and an unprecedented degree of international collaboration. As I walked along the sidewalk, to the side of the main protest, my awkwardness lessened when the wife of a Waorani language researcher handed me her baby to carry. As the march progressed beyond the city center and toward the judiciary office on the outskirts of town, Waorani acquaintances from my previous fieldwork seemed to appear almost out of nowhere. Having grown up in the rural villages where I first met them, some are now permanent residents of Shell—the town adjacent to Puyo where the regional airport is located.

Alongside foreign activists and their cameras, some Waorani protestors were also keenly interested in documenting the event. Uboye brought his video camera, at one point jumping onto the back of a pickup truck driven by a leading North American Indigenous rights activist at the front of the march to film the protest. His participation laid bare how language documentation and other forms of witnessing and political engagement are increasingly intertwined with *kowori* people, their technologies, and emerging forms of collaboration evident in the march. He and other Waorani wanted to record the international character of this scene, including the participation of foreign activists. Uboye explained how recording the protest would show the "truth" about Waorani resistance to oil—challenging claims that they agreed to the Block 22 concession. In contrast, the international activists were cleverly cropped out of the many photographs that appeared in subsequent media coverage of the protest around the world.

Finally, when we arrived at the gate of the Pastaza judiciary office, the *demanda*—the lawsuit against the government—was delivered in a wheelbarrow of folders. Filed against Ecuador's Ministry of Energy and Non-Renewable Natural Resources, the Ministry of Environment, and the Secretary of Hydrocarbons, it sued the government for selling oil concessions without the free, prior, and informed consent of Waorani communities. It claimed that the Block 22 concession was illegal because consultations carried out in 2012 failed to comply with requirements protected in the Ecuadorian constitution and international law.[2] The scale of the paperwork delivered by the protes-

FIGURE 3.3: Waorani and international activists recording the 2019 protest. Photo by author.

tors was emblematic of the power of official documents to dictate the fate of Indigenous lands in Amazonia. As we waited, two leading activists in the Waorani resistance movement—both key researchers in Waorani language documentation—gave interviews to TV reporters as a helicopter hovered in the sky overhead. One of them, Nemonte Nenquimo, a woman in her mid-thirties and then president of CONCONAWEP, made a public statement in Spanish:

> Our land is full of life. Inside the jungle there are sacred animals, our rivers, our community, and that is what we want to protect. Our land is our life, without our land we cannot live. We are here, all of us community members together, to speak. Many other communities came to support us. They are going to demand our rights, and we hope they [the government] will listen to us and respect us, respect our lives. Our land is not for sale.

Soon a lawyer supporting the Waorani legal case took center stage in delivering the *demanda* and negotiating the entrance of Waorani people into the grounds of the judiciary. After a prolonged discussion at the gate, lined with dozens of police in a nervous standoff, a few dozen protestors were allowed into the large courtyard garden in front of the main building. Not long after this, the gates were opened to the remaining crowd, and the grounds of the judiciary became a jovial gathering of Waorani protestors and their allies while the leaders of Waorani Resistance Pastaza and their lawyer entered the office to formally deliver the *demanda*.

In the weeks following the protest there was much uncertainty about the fate of the lawsuit. After Waorani elders at one point drowned out a court hearing by singing collectively in their native language, the presiding judge rejected proposals to hold the hearing in their territory. However, on April 26, two months after the march in Puyo, the Pastaza Provincial Court decided in favor of the lawsuit, ruling that the 2012 consultation process was invalid and suspending indefinitely the selling of oil concessions on Waorani lands in Pastaza.[3] Waorani struggles against oil are far from over, not least because oil drilling continues apace in other parts of their territory. But this was a historic victory. In addition to substantially frustrating the Ecuadorian state's plans to further develop oil on Waorani lands, the lawsuit also has implications for other Indigenous communities living in adjacent areas with oil resources.[4]

The court ruling soon received media attention around the world as a vic-

FIGURE 3.4: Waorani environmental leader Nemonte Nenquimo speaks to reporters at the protest. Photo by author.

tory for Indigenous rights and conservation in the global south. The success of the Waorani resistance movement, even if tentative, marks an important achievement in terms of Waorani solidarity and international collaboration. As a new chapter in Amazonian ecopolitical alliances, it also illustrates how language documentation research does not exist in isolation but is linked to a wider political scene that entails other kinds of collaboration—both between Waorani people and with outsiders. As the 2019 protest illustrates, some of the same young adults who worked as researchers have since become key environmental leaders who engage in increasingly international contexts. Whether transcribing texts in front of a computer screen or demanding their rights on the streets of capital cities, these young adults are engaging with questions of Waorani land and autonomy in new ways.

Translating *Wao Öme*

Waorani people talk about their ancestral territory—what they call *wao öme* ("Waorani land") or *monito öme* ("our land")—as a place where bountiful game animals, forest products, and gardens allow them to "live well." They describe *wao öme* not as a domain separate from themselves, or a natural resource to be managed, but in terms of interconnected relations between human and nonhuman beings. The 2019 protest indicates how many Waorani today see oil posing a major threat to this socionatural world. Their recent success in defending *wao öme* is in part the result of decades of dealing with oil companies, missionaries, state institutions, and international environmentalists. While these relationships have often been premised on misleading stereotypes, Waorani leaders are forging close working relationships with diverse *kowori* allies committed to the struggle against extractive industries. Alongside growing concerns about scarcity, pollution, and territorial boundaries, face-to-face relationships with environmentalists involve engaging across different understandings of their territory and its conservation.

Acts of translation are central to the politics of oil and conservation, in which outsiders often envision Waorani people as an Amazonian "culture" and their land as "nature." Ecopolitical alliances involve multiple ways of translating between Waorani concepts and *kowori* discourses of conservation. Viveiros de Castro (2004) notes that, when met with radical differences, the tendency in Western thinking is to transform them into similarities, as versions of a single reality we all share. So, the world Waorani call *wao öme* becomes "nature" or "environment," and their notion of "living well" becomes "culture." This method of translation—what Viveiros de Castro calls uncontrolled equivocation—envisions differences as representations of a single world, rather than distinct worlds in and of themselves (18).[5] In this model Amazonian people, in contrast, prioritize differences in their translations. In positing "difference rather than identity as the principle of relationality," their controlled equivocations "connect the two discourses to the precise extent to which they are *not* saying the same thing" (18–20).

If the distinction between "controlled" and "uncontrolled" equivocations sheds light on how differences are translated in Amazonian environmental politics, the statements of Waorani leaders illustrate how, in practice, these two idealized ways of translating become blurred. Their engagements suggest not entirely incommensurable differences, but a shared political space that involves at least partial "pragmatic agreement" between people with different presuppositions about what exists (Almeida 1999, 9; 2013). Conklin and Graham (1995) described alliances between Amazonian peoples and Western environmentalists in the 1980s as "an arena of intercultural communication, exchange, and joint political action"—an ecopolitical "middle ground" that emerged despite differences in understanding (696). The collaborations that constitute this middle ground today—and the conflicting expectations they entail—often require translations across different concepts of land and Indigenous lifeways. There are important stakes in these translations for Amazonian people, environmentalists, and national development agendas that increasingly claim Indigenous concepts within state policy.

As Waorani and other Amazonian peoples become global environmental icons, their ideas about land or territory often remain distinct from extractivist and conservationist approaches. Early ethnography described Waorani as hunter-gatherers who see the forest as an abundant "giving environment" that results in part from past human activities (Rival 1993). While their practices have changed in response to oil and other external pressures (Lu and Wirth 2013), the concept of *wao öme* undermines the idea of land as a natural resource to be extracted, managed, or transacted as property.[6] Here I focus on how *wao öme* figures in the changing context of oil and environmental politics, despite the apparent contrasts between Waorani understandings and the emphasis on resource management in conservation agendas.

Concepts like *wao öme* are often the basis of arguments for Indigenous philosophies that subvert Western categories of thought. The idea of "nature" as a domain distinct from humanity is at odds with many Amazonian contexts in which human and nonhuman beings are understood to share certain social characteristics or concepts (Descola 1994, 2013; Viveiros de Castro 1998).[7] For many young Waorani adults I have spoken with in recent years, it has become clear that outsiders do not generally share their understandings of *wao öme*. Their casual accounts of hunting, gardening, and travel through the forest characterize it as a place where many social beings either share human perspectives or communicate directly with human beings.

However, the opposition of nature and culture, a fundamental principle of modernist thought, is not entirely foreign to many Indigenous peoples. In Amazonia, where ideas of "culture" have long since gained traction in Indigenous politics, "nature" too is a powerful political discourse. This raises questions about how Amazonian people engage with and translate between different visions of Indigenous lands and the people who inhabit them. The politics of nature and its conservation reveals not just differences, but also how Indigenous peoples engage in wider sociopolitical contexts. If *wao öme* is distinct from nature, Amazonian livelihoods are also increasingly embedded in translocal and even global processes in which people have little choice but to think, translate, and work across differences. This involves acts of accommodation, exchange, and contestation where differences change and become expressions of Indigenous autonomy. Translations of these differences point to the possibilities—and limits—of collaboration.

International environmentalism is an increasingly important part of this process, especially for Waorani adults involved in anti-oil activism and conservation projects (K. Escobar 2015; Sempértegui 2019). In Amazonian Ecuador, a shift toward Western discourses of environment, nature, and conservation has contributed to and rewarded Indigenous people becoming environmental citizens whose sovereignty is closely connected to the conservation and the governance of Indigenous territory (Erazo 2013). But such regulatory regimes do not simply remake the identities, values, and beliefs of Amazonian people who participate in conservation partnerships.[8] Amazonian people also put these projects to work for their own purposes and goals, some of which may come into conflict with conventional environmentalist agendas (Cepek 2011).

In recent years a growing number of young Waorani adults have joined state-sponsored and international conservation projects. These include technical training and employment with NGOs involved in environmental mapping and monitoring (Scazza and Nenquimo 2021), international support for the demarcation of territorial boundaries (Lu and Wirth 2013), and participation in a government-sponsored Socio Bosque project promising cash payment to communities for conserving their lands (Erazo 2016, 9). In the early 2000s I also met several young Waorani adults who worked for NGOs, such as the Danish development organization Ibis, which promoted community tourism as part of conservation.[9] The alliances that led to the Waorani Resistance Pastaza campaign are part of this wider context. In at least two villages along the Curaray River, Waorani people have explained to me their efforts to attract tourists by not hunting monkeys, birds, and other animals nearby—an indication that some Waorani people are thinking about conservation beyond specific external projects. These engagements have also taken Waorani activists to meetings on Indigenous rights at the United Nations in Geneva and New York City, and to global climate change conferences around the world.

If these examples evidence Waorani environmental citizenship (K. Escobar 2015), it is less established than among people who have been more closely aligned with Ecuador's national Indigenous movement and environmentalist agendas since the 1980s. A transition from living in mobile longhouse groups to permanent villages since missionization in the 1960s as well as the establishment of Waorani political organizations have contributed to new understandings of Indigenous territory. While ideas of nature, environment, and conservation now resonate among some Waorani people, their everyday discussions tend to emphasize more a distinction between life "inside" and "outside" of their territory and external threats to "living well."

Some Waorani leaders engage in an ecopolitical scene that draws on both *wao öme* and conservation discourses. Since their power in these contexts often depends on them conforming to Western stereotypes, this middle ground is often built precariously from misunderstandings, conflicting expectations, and misleading images of authenticity (Conklin and Graham 1995). Whether in conservation projects (Cepek 2008), ecotourism (Hutchins 2007), or experiences with other agents of development (Ball 2012, 2018), Indigenous practices also challenge external readings of novelty and change as cultural loss (Greene 2009; High 2015a). While stereotypes remain, these interfaces are increasingly characterized by Indigenous people engaging in relationships with nonindigenous people. Whether seeking income to support families or political alliances to protect lands, their livelihoods and desires are often embedded in these relationships, which are as much about Amazonian people working practically across differences as they are about symbolic politics (High and Oakley 2020).

The Waorani Resistance campaign is not the first or only example of this.[10] The novelty here is not environmental politics, or the presence of outsiders, but how technical and political work in environmental organizations is providing young adult Waorani leaders a deeper understanding of global debates—including how their understandings of *wao öme* contradict external interests in their territory. After decades of oil, some of them now communicate effectively across these differences—even when this requires more work than it does for outsiders. Anti-oil politics, in positioning Waorani as environmental subjects, involves strategic translations that are part of what constitutes the contemporary that Waorani people and some *kowori* are coming to share. Even if external images of "noble savages" or "ecological Indians" situate Amazonian people in a different time (Fabian 1983), environmental politics locates them and foreign activists in a shared—or at least adjacent—

temporal frame (Guyer 2016; Rabinow and Stavrianakis 2014). In this context, the young adults I describe are subject to—and engage productively with— seemingly contradictory ideas about oil, *wao öme*, and its conservation.

Rethinking Oil and Living Well

Waorani people have long been known for their conflicts with an oil indus- try that is the primary source of Ecuador's national economy (Rivas and Lara 2001). These conflicts preceded their first peaceful encounters with missionar- ies in the late 1950s,[11] when many Waorani were relocated from areas earmarked for oil extraction to what became a "Protectorate" led by US missionaries from the Summer Institute of Linguistics (Kimerling 1993). While most Waorani re- located to the Protectorate in subsequent years, some—including those who refused contact with outsiders—remained to the east, an area targeted by ex- tensive oil drilling. Despite granting a larger Waorani Ethnic Reserve in 1992 covering around a third of their ancestral territory (Finer et al. 2009, 8), the state's selling of oil concessions on Indigenous lands is indicative of a country that has embraced oil exports as a path to development since the 1970s. Despite increasing GDP, becoming a "petro-state" (Karl 1997) has brought increased national debt and ecological damage resulting in a multi-billion-dollar lawsuit against Texaco/Chevron (Sawyer 2022), with Amazonian communities affected by oil pollution receiving few benefits.[12] Extractive economies have also con- tributed to violent conflicts between Waorani, outsiders, and groups living in voluntary isolation within their territory (High 2015a).

In recent decades Ecuador's national Indigenous movement has made In- digenous self-determination and territorial sovereignty central to establishing a plurinational state (Whitten and Whitten 2011). The Confederation of Indig- enous Nationalities of Ecuador (CONAIE) and its regional body, the Confed- eration of Indigenous Nationalities of Amazonian Ecuador (CONFENIAE), have become increasingly aligned with international environmental concerns (Erazo 2013, 142; Hutchins and Wilson 2010). Environmental NGOs and In- digenous territorial governments have replaced the state in providing public services in some areas, leading to a form of environmental citizenship shaped in part by Western understandings of conservation (Erazo 2013, 5). Although the primary Waorani organization (NAWE) has been relatively marginal in national Indigenous politics, collaborations with environmentalists have a growing presence for a new generation of Waorani leaders, some of whom now work independently from NAWE.

The growing emphasis on environment and conservation in struggles for Indigenous rights should be understood in relationship to a broader shift in Latin American politics in the 2000s. In Ecuador, the election of President Rafael Correa in 2007 promised a radical alternative to the social, economic, and environmental crises of a neoliberal petrostate. His "citizen's revolution" (*revolución ciudadana*) promoted a post-neoliberal vision of state sovereignty and development premised on "well-being" (*bienestar*) and "living well" (*buen vivir*). Investing in public services and benefits to address inequalities, Correa explicitly linked this revolutionary rhetoric to Indigenous concepts. His government's 2008 constitution made Ecuador the first country to formally recognize the rights of nature, embracing the terms *pachamama* and *sumak kawsay*—from Kichwa—as part of a national development agenda, translating them as "nature" and "living well." Despite the pretense of incorporating Indigenous cosmovision into a "socialism for the twenty-first century," the citizen's revolution repackaged oil-based governance in ways that have exacerbated social and ecological conflicts (Lu et al. 2017, 24). The Waorani Resistance campaign should also be understood in the context of the 2017 election of President Lenin Moreno—Correa's former vice president—which marked a return to a more explicitly neoliberal agenda resulting in widespread civil unrest.[13]

Like elsewhere in Amazonian Ecuador, the oil-based economy has become part of everyday life for many Waorani people (Bravo Díaz 2023). As production intensified on their lands from the late 1980s, some Waorani incorporated the obvious wealth of oil companies into a strongly egalitarian economy.[14] Around 90 percent of adult Waorani men worked for oil companies between 1985 and 1992, usually as unskilled laborers on short-term contracts (Rival 2000, 248). In the late 1990s, I asked several men about this work. While some lamented noisy oil platforms, overflowing pools of chemical waste and leaky pipelines, few were wholly against the industry that appeared to be destroying their lands. In contrast to my concern that oil was affecting their lives negatively, men and women described how they hoped to benefit from *la compañía* (the company). Much as Laura Rival (2000) observed a decade before, their main criticism was that oil companies greedily hoarded large stores of food and manufactured goods. They often described oil in terms of relationships they hoped to benefit from materially, whether from using discarded items from abandoned oil camps, wage labor, or blocking roads to demand items. It appeared to me that they were accepting low temporary wages, bags of rice, or the occasional off-board motor in compensation for the damage of an industry generating immense revenues from their lands.

During my subsequent fieldwork in the early 2000s, several older men living in the former Protectorate described to me their work for oil companies in previous decades, such as trips with seismic testing crews, with a sense of adventure. Their accounts emphasized how oil work allowed them to meet people from distant villages or visit places previously inhabited by their ancestors (see also Rival 2002). In our discussions of "*la compañia*," some of them, now elders, reflected on long days spent toiling with friends, the remarkable distances they walked, features of the land they encountered, and the food they ate in camps after long periods of hunger. Alongside accounts of large oil machinery they observed for the first time, several men described *kowori* people they met through oil work, whether Kichwa people or company managers.

By then Waorani relationships with oil had changed considerably since my initial fieldwork. While older men described their previous work primarily clearing paths for seismic testing and oil roads, some younger men now had relatively professional positions as truck drivers or "community relations" personnel. The latter were short-term roles to negotiate access to drilling sites near Waorani communities, often specifically to prevent them shutting down roads or interfering with oil installations. As villages became dependent on cash for medicine, food, and school supplies, several parents described how money from oil work allowed them to buy items from urban areas. Though contracts were still temporary, some men earned wages exceeding a typical income in Ecuador. In some villages, oil work was also intertwined with the trend toward marriages with Kichwa people. In 2002 young men from eastern and western parts of the territory routinely explained to me their plans to marry a Kichwa woman by earning money to buy gifts for her family. In this way oil work became part of an emerging form of masculinity and interethnic relations (High 2010, 2015a).

At that time there was little hope of a population of around 2,500 Waorani halting a billion-dollar multinational oil industry. But even in the early 2000s, few Waorani people I knew appeared to understand the consequences of oil to the extent some do today. Young people and elders alike proudly described *wao öme* as a vast and seemingly inexhaustible territory.[15] This was perhaps not an entirely unreasonable view for a small population living on a reserve of around 7,000 square kilometers. Their discussions focused more on how to populate and defend their land against colonists than to conserve it for its own sake, emphasizing efforts to demarcate it as necessary to support a specifically Waorani quality of life. For many Waorani living far away from the noise and pollution of oil installations, the oil industry did not appear to prevent them "living well."

More recently, these discussions have shifted among some adults who describe their territory as more limited and under threat from oil (Lu and Wirth 2013). While the perceived need to defend *wao öme* comes in the context of changes related to schooling and oil work, multiple Waorani generations today appear to share ideas about *wao öme* and their place in it. Throughout

FIGURE 3.5: An oil road with pipelines extends through Waorani territory in the province of Orellana. Photo by author.

my fieldwork elders and young people have talked about "living well" in reference to the qualities of life they say forests, rivers, and human interactions ought to provide. Here living well is part of a place-based sensory ecology in which Waorani conviviality and ecological practices generate "healthy people and thriving households" (Bravo Díaz 2023, 44).

Waorani people describe diverse beings in this socionatural world, where—much like themselves—peccaries, anacondas, jaguar spirits, and trees, among others, highlight both mutual interdependence and autonomy. Whether in reference to their size, quantity, intelligence, or social lives, animals are thoughtfully measured, interpreted, admired, laughed at, and at times feared. While mutually interdependent, the relative autonomy attributed to these beings is much like the autonomy Waorani themselves express. Rather than a conservationist logic, Waorani describe themselves in dynamic and sometimes antagonistic relations with nonhuman beings, much as relations between Waorani people can erupt into violent conflict. Jaguars and other predatory animals, for example, are part and parcel to assault sorcery (High 2012a), and peccaries raid manioc gardens, much as human thieves do. Such conflicts, whether in hunting or intergroup violence, illustrate how life in *wao öme* contradicts certain conservationist images of Indigenous people in harmonious relations with their environments—and thus have little presence in ecopolitics.

If these ideas resonate with the ways anthropologists contrast Amazonian and Western concepts, for some young Waorani adults *wao öme* is also entangled with environmental politics, where ideas of nature and conservation situate Amazonian people as environmental citizens in specific ways. In Ecuador, international actors have at times romanticized the Amazon as a natural wilderness devoid of human presence and at others positioned Indigenous people as integral to its conservation (Erazo 2016). Despite ideas of nature becoming more central to Indigenous identity, some Indigenous leaders embrace conservation without entirely opposing extractive economies (7). In this context, since *wao öme* and "living well" are distinct from global discourses of nature, culture, and well-being, Waorani activism against oil involves strategic translations—whether in international collaborations or in reference to the rights of nature in Ecuador's constitution.[16]

The Yasuní and Waorani Environmental Politics

Ecuador's 2008 constitution marked an important milestone for the country's Indigenous peoples. It also indicated a crisis with respect to neoliberal regimes of development and the nature/culture distinction at the core of modernist imagination (Blaser 2013; de la Cadena 2010). Yet it remains to be seen how much Indigenous people or *pachamama* stand to gain from their formal presence in state politics. Even as many Indigenous Ecuadorians supported the Correa government's commitment to social and economic reform, their agendas were marginalized in the constituent assembly that drafted the constitution and 2009 National Development Plan (Becker 2011). If the inclusion of Indigenous concepts in the constitution is, as de la Cadena (2010) suggests, an "insurgence of Indigenous forces and practices" into state institutions (336), it is also a translation that equates *pachamama* or *sumak kawsay* with nature and "alternative development." Rather than a translation that "allows the alien concepts to deform and subvert the translator's conceptual toolbox" (Viveiros de Castro 2004, 5), these translations presume a common ground between what the government and Indigenous people are talking about.

While the constitution embraces concepts from the Kichwa language, Waorani people and lands have also become a key reference point in this new politics of nature. The centerpiece of the government's development plan was the Yasuní National Park, which, combined with the Waorani Ethnic Reserve, comprises the Yasuní Biosphere Reserve. One of the world's richest areas of biodiversity, the park includes vast expanses of forest inhabited by Waorani and groups living in voluntary isolation. It also contains Ecuador's largest oil reserves. In an initiative supported by the United Nations Development Program in the late 2000s, the government proposed protecting the park from oil drilling if compensated by the international community for half the estimated value of the oil (Ecuador Yasuní ITT 2010). Prioritizing investment in conservation, renewable energy, scientific research, and social development, the Yasuní Initiative called for "a new cooperative model between developed and developing countries" to address climate change by preventing the emission of 400 million metric tons of carbon dioxide that would result from the burning of fossil fuels (3).

As part of President Correa's "citizens' revolution," the Yasuní Initiative made Amazonia an integral part of an ecopolitical agenda placing nature, Indigenous people, and well-being at the center of national development. It had important implications for Waorani people who live within the Yasuní

Park and claim it as part of their ancestral lands. Framed as conserving nature and addressing historical inequalities, it presented Indigenous rights as part of a new vision of development. Promotional materials emphasizing "respect for the cultures" and "ancestral rights" in the park included photographs and videos of Waorani people (Ecuador Yasuní ITT 2010, 5). In proposing to protect groups in voluntary isolation, the rights of Indigenous people, like the rights of nature, were presented as part of a sustainable future.

The government ultimately abandoned the Yasuní Initiative in 2013, citing the international community's failure to commit sufficient financial support. In August of that year, I traveled with three Waorani language researchers to Quito, where we joined a predominantly mestizo crowd of protestors in front of the national palace to hear President Correa announce his decision. Despite previously warning of the Yasuní's fragility, Correa now insisted that new oil drilling would affect less than 1 percent of the park and generate billions of dollars to develop the country. After decades of experience with oil, my Waorani companions were not convinced. One of them, Nemonte Nenquimo, warned that new drilling would bring further destruction to *wao öme* and pressurize already strained relationships between Waorani and isolated groups. Having come to the protest wearing street clothes and feathered crowns, they appeared amused and encouraged by the solidarity they had come to expect more from foreign environmentalists than from other Ecuadorians. They were soon busy explaining to news reporters their sadness and anger at the prospect of further drilling on Waorani lands.

The failed Yasuní Initiative led to a wellspring of concern about conservation and cultural rights in Ecuador. This included protests calling for a national referendum to stop oil drilling in the Yasuní—which Ecuadorians would vote into law a decade later in 2023. Just as Waorani are often imagined in Ecuador as warriors and in the Yasuní campaign as being close to nature, their "uncontacted" neighbors—whom Waorani refer to as Taromenani or Tagaeiri—became part of a broader narrative of conservation for their assumed natural state of isolation. The long-standing association of Waorani people with violence in Ecuador shows that this symbolism is not strictly positive. After large-scale killings of Taromenani by Waorani men in 2003 and 2013, national media presented them as murderous, stone-age savages—an image also evident in government responses to the violence as a purely "Indigenous issue"—rather than a result of encroaching extractive economies (High 2015a).

My companions at the 2013 protest—two of whom later became leaders of the 2019 Waorani Resistance Pastaza campaign—are part of a Waorani generation who have gained deeper understandings of oil as well as ideas of indigeneity, conservation, and cultural rights that frame contemporary environmentalism. Some have close working relationships with international activists, including employment with NGOs and the coordination of a project to supply drinking water systems to Waorani villages affected by oil. In contrast to the oil-dependent official Waorani organization that took shape at the turn of the twenty-first century—premised on external expectations of male leadership (High 2007)—Waorani environmental politics today involves international collaboration and women leaders.[17] This includes growing international attention to Nemonte Nenquimo and the Association of Waorani Women of Amazonian Ecuador (AMWAE) in environmental activism.

By 2019, the Waorani Resistance Pastaza movement was linking the struggle against oil to broader questions of Indigenous rights, conservation, and Waorani environmental knowledge. After the Block 22 court ruling, Nemonte Nenquimo was quoted in an article in the *New Yorker*:

> Our territory is our decision, and now, since we are owners, we are not going to let oil enter and destroy our natural surroundings and kill our culture. . . . We have shown the government to respect us, and other Indigenous people of the world, that we are guardians of the jungle, and we're never going to sell our territory. (May 15, 2019)

Such appeals to recognize territorial rights, protect nature, and respect Waorani ancestral knowledge are oriented as much toward international audiences as they are Ecuadorian laws and institutions. Nenquimo's work on the lawsuit led to her winning the 2020 Goldman Environmental Prize, and in the same year she was named one of *Time* magazine's 100 most influential people. As Nenquimo's statement about refusing to let oil "kill our culture" illustrates, these new leaders increasingly engage in environmental politics through discourses of "culture" associated with what they call being "like the ancestors." For wider publics, such language can evoke enduring colonial imagery of the "wild" Amazonian warrior or the "ecologically noble savage" (Redford 1991). In contrast to earlier conservation initiatives premised on nature as wilderness (Erazo 2016), international organizations working in Ecuador evidence a shift toward recognizing Amazonian people as "stewards of the forest" (Amazon Watch 2020) and supporting the revival of ancestral cultural practices in "Indigenous-led conservation" (Amazon Frontlines 2020).

While Indigenous rights and conservation are central to environmental citizenship, we should not assume that Waorani people and their allies are always talking about the same things. Framing differences in terms of Western concepts can delimit the space afforded to conflicts that have persisted for centuries in South America (de la Cadena 2010). In this context, the more Amazonian people become fluent in European languages and concepts, the more easily they translate differences as equivalences. For years, Waorani youth have participated alongside other Indigenous groups in urban festivals where animals and plants are presented as "nature," and Waorani spears, food, and shamanism as "culture" (High 2009b). Such translations are an important part of Waorani social and political life—even when unnoticed by *kowori* allies. While central to international collaborations, they also point to different understandings of land, people, and what is ultimately at stake in conservation. Translations in environmental politics are part of an ever-changing middle ground in which Waorani and *kowori* activists are challenging the dominance of oil.

Defending Land

Even with closer involvement in environmental politics, Indigenous understandings of *wao öme* remain distinct from the categories through which many Waorani and outsiders talk to and about each other. While my interlocutors distinguish between different spaces within *wao öme*, such as the forest (*omaëre*), manioc gardens (*kenëkori*) and being in a house (*ökone*), their descriptions do not position Waorani people as separate or alienable from the "land" or "territory" (*öme/ögïpo*)—of which all of these domains are part. Nor, as their accounts of peccaries, jaguars, and other animals suggest, is having gardens or houses exclusive to human beings.

If concepts like *wao öme* evoke something distinct from conventional ideas of nature, conservation, and culture, they should help us see how Amazonian people understand the changing socionatural and political dynamics in which they live. Waorani from several villages have expressed to me their concerns about oil from the point of view of animals that flee noisy oil installations, are poisoned from pollution, or are targeted by poachers along oil roads. Many of them express deep concerns that oil and other extractive economies pose an immanent threat to the animals, forests, and waterways on which their livelihoods depend. In a recent study of Waorani life along an oil road, Andrea

Bravo Díaz observes how young people translate their concerns about the effects of oil into the language of "rights"—emphasizing that the needs of animals and other forest beings are similar to those of Waorani people (2023, 55).

In this way oil and the encroachment of *kowori* people pose a threat to the socionatural dynamics of *wao öme*. Reflecting on the prospect of oil roads extending into his hunting grounds, my host father, Amowa, explained that "oil kills the animals, and [when] the road comes, they leave." Another man described how, while hunting, he discovered dead animals and birds stuck in a thick sludge overflowing from a former oil-drilling site. He explained how each species came there seeking different forest fruits, and how, after heavy rain, the sludge seeps into a river known for its plentiful fish. He and his family lamented this not for the violation of a pristine environment in need of conservation but as something that threatens their own livelihood. While idealizing *wao öme* as a place of abundance, they emphasize how different plants and animals interact and depend on each other within it. Just as the ideal of plentiful animals and forest fruits is mirrored by an emphasis on the growth of their human communities (Rival 1993, 2016), the depletion of human and animal populations is closely linked in discussions of how oil and *kowori* people threaten the prospect of "living well."

Several years ago, a young Waorani woman told me a story that made clear how she experiences oil as a threat to Waorani people and to specific animals. She described how her kinsmen encountered an abandoned camp near a river in oil Block 16 in the Yasuní Park, where poachers had shot large numbers of monkeys, birds, and other animals with rifles and simply left them to rot. Upon discovering this strange scene, they were horrified that the animals, which Waorani see as making "living well" in *wao öme* possible, were needlessly killed. This concern mirrors elders' accounts of past spear-killings I have recorded that emphasize close kin suffering as a result of excessive and needless killing (High 2015a). The fate of the animals in the woman's account evokes a broader social identity as victims or "prey" often expressed in Waorani accounts of *kowori* outsiders (High 2009b; Rival 1998, 2002).

These stories convey how oil and *kowori* people have the potential to undermine the qualities of "living well" within *wao öme*. Some Waorani have become concerned about social and economic changes leading to a scarcity of animals. Oil work and the growing size of villages have made some Waorani, as hunters, gardeners, and forest trekkers, ever more aware of themselves as part of the socionatural dynamics of their lands. Alongside concerns about animals, gardens, and rivers effected by oil, adult men have explained to me how they adjust their hunting practices according to the depletion of monkeys, deer, and other animals near overpopulated villages. These practices do not imply the conservation of animals for their own sake, nor do I suggest they are entirely new. Hunters describe how, even in areas with plentiful game, they decide when and where to hunt in part based on their knowledge of fluctuating animal populations.

Just as Waorani people do not normally describe *wao öme* as something independent from human engagement, my initial interest in how oil was affecting Waorani "culture" was at odds with what many of them say is at stake with oil. Rather than worrying about losing their culture—as a distinct way of life to be distinguished from others against a backdrop of nature or environment—they described threats to the qualities of "living well" that they understand to be inseparable from *wao öme*. In contrast to conventional ecopolitical perspectives that construe Indigenous peoples having a special role in protecting nature, Waorani envision their lives as the product of a different socionatural world, one where what it means to be a Waorani person inheres in the land—rather than being apart from it. This is as apparent in Nenquimo's assertion at the 2019 protest that "our land is our life" as it is in her subsequent references to "nature" and "culture" in describing Waorani people as "guardians of the jungle."

While Waorani activists sometimes engage in struggles against oil through the language of nature, culture, and conservation, I rarely hear them adopt environmental discourses in everyday life. Elders, in particular, find such ideas either quite abstract or reflecting external interests in controlling Waorani practices. One elder, for example, who speaks little Spanish, used the Spanish term *medio ambiente* (environment) to describe, with a mixture of horror and comedy, how state authorities would prevent him transporting live forest birds from his home to the village where his adult daughter lives. For him, it seemed, "environment" had little to do with *wao öme*; it instead referred to specifically *kowori* claims to authority, which he found absurd. This understanding of environment stands in stark contrast to *wao öme* and Waorani descriptions of the autonomy of their elders, ancestors, and isolated groups. Both young people and elders often use the Spanish term "*libre*" to emphasize Waorani people living "free" in their territory. This ideal, alongside that of mutual interdependence of kin and other beings, is integral to what it means to "live well."

However, an increasing emphasis on demarcating *wao öme* and defending animals that suffer from the encroachment of oil companies suggest an understanding of their territory as scarce and bounded.[18] What is new is not the recognition of interdependent socionatural relations, but how *wao öme*—and the quality of living well it enables—needs defending. Some of the Waorani banners at the 2019 protest contained the phrase *öme gompoke*, which can be translated as "defending" or to "care for" the land (Bravo Díaz 2023, 169). Defending *wao öme* also involves adopting discourses of culture and conservation that confirm Waorani environmental citizenship in protecting the rainforest. These terms signal as much an openness to collaboration as they do resistance to state policies and extractive practices. Waorani livelihoods may depend in part on young leaders successfully navigating between their home communities and relationships with outsiders with diverse ideas of nature, Indigenous people, and conservation. As they become adept at working with and translating differences, young adults in particular appear keenly aware that such a world exists outside of *wao öme*. The distinction I hear them routinely draw in Spanish between distinct *mundos* ("worlds")—one denoting life "inside" (*adentro*) and the other "outside" (*afuera*) of their territory—is now as important as that between Waorani and *kowori* people.

This distinction, rather than implying that life on the "outside" is inherently alien or unimportant to them, points to what is at stake in translating *wao öme* as "nature" or "environment." This became clear when I interviewed two leaders of the Waorani Resistance Pastaza campaign after the 2019 protest in Puyo. I asked one of them, a man in his early thirties from a village along the Curaray River, about his work with an NGO making digital maps of Waorani territory. He first described, in Spanish, the benefits of working in collaboration with international activists and other Indigenous nationalities to defend Waorani lands against oil. He then reflected on how, for him, learning digital mapping—which involved locating plants, animals, and culturally significant sites in the landscape, was very different from how Waorani people know *wao öme*. Switching between Spanish and Wao-terero, he called mapping a "*kowori* technology" that outsiders could understand, but that only Waorani people, in contrast, "know *wao öme* directly" through experiences that cannot be conveyed in maps. Although he struggled to communicate the precise distinction, it was clear that his reference to mapping as a *kowori* technology was not a critique, but a recognition that Waorani and outsiders know *wao öme* in distinct ways, both of which he values.

Despite striking generational changes, Waorani and *kowori* people may still not be talking about the same things, even when speaking the same language and working toward shared political goals. If the stakes appear small in these translations, colonial history in the Americas reminds us that formal treaties based on assumed equivalences have often ignored or manipulated fundamental differences in understanding between Indigenous peoples and settlers. Whether thinking about *pachamama* as "nature" or an Indigenous person who signs agreements with oil companies as having the authority of a "chief," these translations—or uncontrolled equivocations—can have major consequences. And yet, the Waorani Resistance Pastaza movement demonstrates that translating *wao öme* as nature and culture can effectively challenge oil interests. Some Waorani are achieving a degree of success in an emergent middle ground that, though still steeped in essentialisms and divergent understandings, is also constituted by enduring collaborations with outsiders.

*

Whether defending *wao öme* through a shared language of nature and conservation or adopting discourses of culture to express differences, Amazonian people communicate beyond their communities in diverse ways. In this chapter I have described how, in their work in environmental politics, some Waorani are engaging successfully from within a *kowori* world they describe as radically "other." Their actions, as Nemonte Nenquimo's statements illustrate, are not simply based on automatic or innocent translations but thoughtful reflection on how to survive, speak, and "live well" as environmental citizens with both *wao öme* and diverse external interests in Indigenous people and territory. Whether unconsciously, consciously, or even in outright deception, relations between Waorani and *kowori* often involve (mis)translations that appear to be at the very heart of collaboration.

Strategic translations occur on all sides of this middle ground, whether in situating Indigenous concepts and the "rights of nature" in national development plans, promoting Amazonian people as environmental citizens, or Waorani leaders adopting conservationist discourses to defend *wao öme*. If these translations appear to depart from the insistence on difference sometimes observed as a key principle of Indigenous thought, they also illustrate that people inhabit multiple "worlds" (Hage 2015; Blaser 2016; de la Cadena 2015; A. Escobar 2018). While there are no doubt limits to the idea of people inhabiting incommensurable realities (Graeber 2015; Nadasday 2021), Amazonian environmental politics shows how engaging in a dominant *kowori* world—in Ecuador and beyond—does not prevent Waorani people also dwelling in and fighting for other, less familiar realities.

Inhabiting such differences involves multiple forms of translation. Waorani people are not just becoming more adept at translating different concepts; their lives are in many ways the product of such differences, whether in school, NGO offices, or the streets of frontier towns. Young adults often proudly explain that, "like the ancestors," they learned to hunt, garden, and walk skillfully in *wao öme*, a place they have never known without oil companies. Some of them also engage in collaborative work with *kowori* people in part by talking about nature, culture, and conservation—whether in environmental politics or in mapping their territory. This work, like of the Waorani Resistance Pastaza movement, is a dynamic international space where they assert distinctly Waorani ideas of life and land and communicate their struggles through the dominant language of multiculturalism and environment.

"Living well" increasingly depends on Waorani collaborations across distinct understandings of their territory. This work holds hope for a new Amazonian middle ground based on projects that reflect long-term personal commitments and shared concerns with not only Indigenous-led conservation but also Indigenous livelihoods. In this context, some Waorani people are becoming skilled at translating worlds as they move within and speak from the "outside" in new ways to challenge oil and defend their lands. Concepts like *wao öme*, beyond simply presenting a contrast to conventional Western thought, can be integral to these engagements, even when rooted in age-old stereotypes and convenient translations. After decades of accommodating and protesting oil, some Waorani are finding significant potential for collaboration and solidarity across such differences.

FOUR

. . .

COP26 AND THE LIMITS
OF COLLABORATION

ENVIRONMENTAL POLITICS ILLUSTRATES the exciting potential some Waorani are finding in new forms of collaboration. As we have seen, this involves not just large-scale mobilizations of Waorani communities but also alliances with various *kowori*. Whether inside or outside their territory, these relationships are an increasingly important part of their contemporary world. Whether in language research, political activism, or other activities, this contemporary evokes new hopes and desires—especially for a generation of young adults who are asserting the value of Waorani people and land in new ways. The expanding imaginative horizons that come with these new opportunities are only part of the story. We have already seen how, despite the gains made by the Waorani Resistance movement, environmental politics can constrain the terms of their engagement. Waorani language researchers and leaders understand well that claiming autonomy and defending land requires a tricky combination of asserting how their way of life is distinct while at the same time engaging familiar ideas of nature, culture, and indigeneity. In this context, the identity that many elders assert as being "civilized" is less salient than imagery of Waorani people as a timeless culture of "warriors" and natural conservationists.

In this chapter I focus on how Waorani collaborations with outsiders, despite the many possibilities they afford, also have certain limitations. This becomes painfully obvious to my interlocutors in some situations. These limits sit awkwardly against the promise of a contemporary context that celebrates collaboration as a seemingly limitless ethical imperative to work cooperatively toward a shared goal. If collaboration promises a more democratic world in which fulfilled, empowered people work together to transcend previous divides or even erase differences altogether (Riles 2015, 154), Waorani experiences in language documentation and beyond illustrate how their interactions with *kowori* people are about much more than the common ground often envisioned in these projects.

Waorani collaborations also involve conflict. As they lay bare different understandings of what are assumed to be shared goals and values, the limitations in these projects are perhaps as typical as the ethical goals they embrace.[1] We may learn as much from conflicts as we do from assessing the apparent successes or failures of specific projects. While collaboration—whether in academic research, environmental politics, or international development—is often assumed to be a value in its own right, in this chapter I explore how Waorani engagements in these arenas also complicate ethical questions. Anthropologists involved in this work must recognize and grapple with ethics as something that is not just "our" problem to deal with. Waorani researchers and environmental leaders often have much more at stake than the anthropologists, linguists, and other *kowori* with whom they work. After all, they are defending their territory and survival against a powerful oil industry and a state that has historically marginalized Indigenous people. Perhaps less obvious is the ways language documentation and environmental politics expose Waorani researchers and activists to new risks within their own communities. Here an emphasis on autonomy and responsibility that limits Waorani political authority also has implications for how collaborations are conceived and what they might achieve.

Autonomy, Responsibility, and the Limits of Politics

Collaboration presents specific challenges for Waorani people who work in projects outside their territory. In language documentation, being researchers and videographers in part defines their status in the communities where they live and work. Just as the linguist, who led the project had to innovate ways of managing the work of young Waorani adults with little previous experience in paid hourly work or caring for expensive equipment, and I struggled to become proficient in the technical demands of parsing and glossing Waorani texts, Waorani language researchers have learned to navigate the challenging terrain of Indigenous politics at a time when the role of new media technologies is becoming increasingly unpredictable. This process not only creates new opportunities to engage in a *kowori* world but also subjects them in new ways to the expectations and moral evaluations of their home communities.

The possibilities and conflicts that come with this novelty have as much or more to do with relations between Waorani people—and their specific social values—as they do with engaging outsiders. Even as simplified images and narratives of a shared Waorani "culture" are easily digestible to external audiences, such an implicit notion of unity and consensus is not something any Waorani person can expect their kin or wider community to accept. Those involved in language research or Indigenous politics become especially aware of this, as any claim they make to represent or speak for "Waorani people" as a whole is likely to be met by their peers with, at best, a degree of skepticism, and at worst, outright hostility. This reflects less a concern with the politics of representation than it does a specific emphasis on personal autonomy and responsibility that is as evident in everyday life as it is in Waorani politics.

Since the start of my fieldwork I have been struck by the autonomy and cooperative solidarity of the Waorani households with whom I have lived. My experience resonates with previous writing about their sharing economy and strong identity of the *nanicabo* (household group) as well as the broader lack of interpersonal authority to undermine individual autonomy.[2] Much of daily life, while attached to a wider community defined principally in terms of the local school, involves members of a single household (or small number of closely related households). Everyday interactions, whether sharing food, caring for children, joking, or simply conversing or gossiping within the home, constitutes much of what my hosts often describe as "living well." While most Waorani carry out daily tasks on their own from a young age, living together implies a high degree of mutual care, such that the bodies and vitality of household members are interdependent and require collective acts to maintain its health (Bravo Díaz 2023). "Living well," rather than a static or transcendent marker of Waorani identity, implies a contingent state of plentiful food, relative peace, laughter, singing, and ideally, a growing household with many children. As we have seen, *kowori* people too can become part of this social ideal.

But such a state of affairs cannot be taken for granted. "Living well" stands in stark contrast to statements about the moral failures of others. Responsibility for transgressions—and their consequences—is often attributed beyond a single individual, even when a specific person is understood to have carried it out. For example, when a shaman is said to practice sorcery, his coresidents may also be deemed responsible, as speaking or joking in the presence of a shaman whose body is inhabited by a jaguar-spirit can, even unintentionally, lead to a sorcery attack (High 2012a).[3] Living well is often contrasted to these practices as an ideal measure of humanity, such that specific actions are morally evaluated as reflecting more or less than human practices, rather than different "cultures" (Ewart 2015; Walker 2015). However, despite the "strong speech" one hears at some public meetings (Bravo Díaz 2023), in everyday life Waorani rarely confront each other to attempt to hold each other to account (High 2015a). The apparent lack of accountability for most unwelcome behavior reflects the recognition of both personal autonomy and the high stakes of confronting others evidenced in prominent memories of past violence.

As elsewhere in Amazonia (Overing 2003; Walker 2012), aspects of dependency and autonomy figure strongly in Waorani understandings of personhood. While the bodies of specific people are mutually constituted over time through living together (Rival 1998), there is also an emphasis on an autonomy that, in certain contexts, is highly individualized from a young age (High 2016; Rival 1996). For example, while parents have shared with me criticisms of their teenage children for poor school attendance or for drinking alcohol, I have rarely seen parents directly confront them or attempt to change their behavior (High 2015b). This was a major point of complaint among mestizo schoolteachers in the early 2000s, who routinely called on parents to do more to discipline their children. Some teachers observed this lack of coercive authority, even across generations, as evidence of a lack of Waorani "civilization."

Autonomy, mutual interdependence, and the body all figure in Waorani understandings of responsibility at multiple scales. Elders, who do not shy away from sharp moral evaluations of others, often acknowledge that other people—whether their own kin, *kowori*, or certain nonhuman beings—will ultimately act according to their own initiative.[4] This reflects more than simply an egalitarian ethos against hierarchical authority. In contrast to external imaginings of Indigenous peoples as unified communities (High 2015a; Stasch 2009), Waorani ideas of autonomy imply a world constituted not by consensus, democracy, or a transcendent notion of justice, but by often irreconcilable differences in perspective (Walker 2015). As Joanna Overing observes, in Amazonia "the very idea of society being based on juridical foundations, and built through legislative, juridical and bureaucratic procedures, would be too dangerous, too repellent, too violent—and indeed not thinkable" since "power usually pertains not to the group but to the individual—each in relationship to other individuals" (2012, 56).[5] In contrast to an "inwardly" Western individualism rooted in the Protestant reformation (Dumont 1985), Waorani understandings of autonomy, mutual dependence, and responsibility offer alternative ways of thinking about politics and practices of collaboration.

In this context Indigenous politics has presented something new. It establishes elected *presidentes* (presidents) and *dirigentes* (directors) of a Waorani nationality made recognizable to the state and other external interests in specific ways. This structure of political authority—based on democratic representation and hierarchical positions—has often led to criticism, misunderstanding, and outright opposition in Waorani communities (High 2007). Elected leaders are routinely denounced as much for not visiting Waorani villages as they are for their perceived access to external wealth or interactions with powerful *kowori* in distant, unknown locations. As "living well" is most often understood in terms of presence and immediacy, rather than abstract future goals, it is difficult to reconcile absent leaders making decisions on behalf of a collective "community" or "nationality" with Waorani ideas of responsibility.[6] Frequent criticisms of their own leaders illustrate how, for many Waorani, politics is inseparable from a specific ethic of care and autonomy.

In the early 2000s, I often heard Waorani people voice concerns about their leaders signing lucrative deals allowing oil companies to operate on Waorani lands far from their home villages. Such accusations in Ecuador are not unique to Waorani politics, especially in areas where personal gain and clientelism are understood as part and parcel of conventional political practice (Villavicencio 2017). It appears that, beyond their specific criticisms, it is individual political authority itself—the practice of being represented by (and subjected to) such authority—that many Waorani find troubling.[7] Leaders are routinely described as "lying" and acting on their own behalf to access money rather than helping the communities they represent. These are more than simply moral criticisms of specific leaders; it does not appear as any surprise to many Waorani that their leaders would act relatively autonomously according to their own interest, rather than in the interest of a "Waorani nationality."

In a world of democratic representation, Waorani leadership positions are frequently contested, with constant turnover and lengthy debates about who can legitimately occupy—or be removed from—a position. This is all the more complicated by the long distances between dozens of Waorani villages, which makes inclusive voting at a single meeting practically difficult. Formal Indigenous politics highlights the sharp contrast between, on the one hand, a Waorani emphasis on individual autonomy that restricts political authority, and on the other, the problem of representation as moral authority in a context where external sources assume—and benefit from—a misleading notion of ethnic unity. On the whole, Waorani leaders have been left to struggle between these two conflicting expectations of what their role should be. Many resign or are ousted from their elected positions long before their scheduled terms finish, and prolonged debates about which leaders are legally recognized by the state are not uncommon.

This internal limit to Waorani political authority, and the ideas of autonomy and responsibility it reflects, points to some of the challenges and risks other Waorani face when they engage in collaborative work. This is especially the case in projects involving travel and work outside of Waorani communities, whether to Ecuadorian cities or abroad. Language documentation and environmental politics involve the kinds of relationships, dislocations, new technologies, and resulting suspicions that many Waorani associate with political leaders. For foreign academics and Waorani researchers, these collaborations offer important opportunities to document their unique ways of speaking and living, or to assert Waorani autonomy as Indigenous people. And yet, for many of their peers, they also appear to involve a relatively small number of young adults engaged in activities oriented toward a *kowori* world in which most Waorani have little power. This is why, despite growing support for such projects across many Waorani villages, they also become sources of uncertainty, speculative rumors, and conflict.

Technologies of Risk and Accountability

The use of video, which many Waorani associate with a *kowori* world outside of *wao öme*, has become entangled with questions of autonomy and responsibility that can expose Waorani researchers and activists to new risks. In this way it has become a technology that creates new possibilities and new conflicts (Sneath et al. 2009). This became clear several years ago when Uboye described his recording of a political meeting in a village where a transition in leadership of the primary Waorani political organization was contested. When a leader was denounced and agreed to vacate his position, some Waorani in attendance met Uboye's video camera with suspicion. He was soon embroiled in a debate about whether he should be allowed to record—and potentially expose to outsiders—an event defined in terms of Waorani political autonomy. Despite threats from those who challenged him, Uboye later described to me how he and other Waorani saw video as a way to make leaders more accountable to people from distant villages not in attendance.

More recently, he has come to see political accountability as part of the value of language documentation, identifying videos as a form of evidence to hold leaders to account for what they say.[8] In contexts like these, Waorani researchers are less interested in the priorities of documenting an Indigenous language than they are recording what they describe as the "truth." Uboye made his own choices about recording encounters like these. Situations where Waorani people insert themselves as participant observers into these political contexts reveal how the open-ended nature of collaboration makes the ethical implications of this work seemingly intractable. This is because it involves a move from conventional academic concerns with research ethics and the politics of representation to the personal projects of Waorani people themselves. It illustrates how collaboration engenders new conflicts and possibilities between Waorani people as videographers, researchers, and as witnesses.

As we have seen, language documentation is not the only way that Waorani use visual media in their own ways. Beyond mediating relations with outsiders, these technologies have become part of long-standing conflicts. In 2013, videos circulated on social media of a Waorani woman dying from spear wounds after an attack by a neighboring isolated group. One recording showed the victim's kinsman at the scene angrily announcing he would avenge her death. Not long after this, a group of Waorani men used digital photography to document a revenge attack that resulted in the massacre of dozens of people (Cabodevilla 2013). It is striking how, after documenting an event that the killers defended against state intervention as a purely "Indigenous issue," these images were distributed to outsiders, including national media (115). This indicates how visual media is as enmeshed in conflicts between Amazonian people as it is in relationships with outsiders. Waorani researchers cannot help but be drawn into these conflicts, especially when their communities associate them with such technologies. One described how peers speculated that he was selling videos or photographs of them to outsiders. These suspicions reflect tensions that, like foreign researchers, Waorani researchers must answer to.

Even as language videos move beyond the essentialist images that characterize their sociopolitical relations with outsiders, I would not describe any of the Waorani language researchers with whom I have worked as politically disengaged. I doubt they could be. As we have seen, some have since become prominent environmental activists. Whether as researchers, filmmakers, or Indigenous leaders, they have no choice but to simultaneously negotiate the expectations of outsiders—including academic researchers—and relationships with other Waorani. The challenges of this position became clear in the aftermath of the heated political meeting Uboye recorded in 2013. Although some Waorani spoke against him filming the meeting at the time, Uboye described to me how the newly elected president of the organization later became interested in the recording as evidence that the previous president had publicly agreed to vacate his position. In the context of ongoing internal political conflicts, some Waorani proposed to use the video to demonstrate the legitimacy of the subsequent president to government authorities.

These are the kinds of ethical minefields most anthropologists would hope to avoid in research design. But to what extent, and for whom, is this really an ethical problem? If the idea of collaboration is taken seriously, should we be surprised or concerned by how people like Uboye, as research partners, use their new skills and insights to advance their own ethical agendas? Examples like these illustrate the novelty and the conflict that collaborative projects generate, especially when they link powerful technologies to specific Waorani people in new ways. They demonstrate the potential—and the limits—of collaboration in research and beyond. I am convinced that anthropology should embrace projects that complicate divisions between researcher and participant, the observer and the observed. But this work also requires reconsidering its ethical implications beyond debates about coauthorship and intellectual property. It should be of little surprise that the agendas of our epistemic partners are not always those we share or find admissible within conventional research ethics. This is part of why research that collapses the boundaries of conventional ethnographic fieldwork has the potential to create something new.

This work also has painful limits and consequences for people like Uboye, who experience age-old stereotypes in more personalized ways as researchers. These consequences are different from and potentially more serious than those for the foreign researchers with whom they work. As they live in urban areas for extended periods while working on transcriptions, Waorani language researchers find themselves entangled in a seemingly contradictory world of which anthropology is part. Despite efforts to recognize and elevate the status of Waorani intellectual contributions in collaborative research, their positionality remains subject to power inequalities in Ecuador and in relation to academics. This became clear in Uboye's description of how he filmed a conference in Quito, Ecuador's capital, organized to discuss concerns about groups living in voluntary isolation within the Waorani reserve. He explained that, after publicly voicing his disagreement with the views of an anthropologist at the conference, the anthropologist responded by questioning his credibility, accusing Uboye of not being a "real Waorani" person because he had a video camera and was living in a house in the city built of concrete blocks.

I was not at the event, but it was clear in Uboye's description that he was upset by the public nature of this exchange and what it implied. It had not been obvious to him that being competent in video recording, working as a researcher in the capital, or being able to address academics at a conference in Spanish, would make him less Waorani. For him and most of my other interlocutors, being Waorani is understood less as identity that one might "lose" than an ideal form of human sociality (Gow 1991, 285). And yet, such stereotypes, like the ideas of cultural authenticity in which they are embedded, were also surely familiar to him. Waorani who engage in this work are not alone in experiencing the contradictions and prejudices of urban environments where they are as likely to suffer discrimination for being Indigenous people as they are of being accused of not being "real Indians" when they fail to meet the expectations of outsiders (High 2015a). Although collaborative work often aims specifically to address these enduring and multifaceted questions of inequality, it inevitably remains entangled with them.

As products of interactions with outsiders, such projects point to the multiple ways that Waorani researchers envision "culture" beyond popular stereotypes of indigeneity in contemporary Amazonia. As a result of generational or personal experiences, or simply intellectual curiosity, people like Uboye have come to view their language and culture in ways that are different from many of their peers. It should not be a question of whether their ideas are more or less accurate or "traditional" than those of an Indigenous politician or elder. Nor is it a question of whether language documentation contributes to new Waorani understandings of culture or simply reveals them. The same can be said of concepts like nature and conservation in environmental politics. The collaborations I have described are part of an ever-changing contemporary in which Waorani people reflect on their experiences and relationships. Language videos have become a technology for imagining difference as well as engaging creatively and politically in this context.

Even if the most ambitious attempts to overcome inequalities between anthropologists and their "others" seem bound to fail, deliberately collaborative work can lay bare a certain epistemological continuity between "us" and "them." This does not imply that anthropologists see things in the same ways as the people they study, or that they even share a common purpose (Viveiros de Castro 2003). Rather, assuming an approximate procedural equivalence between different ways of thinking as distinct "anthropologies" can help us see how people conceptualize and engage in new technologies and relations in ways anthropologists may not anticipate. We might thus envision collaborative anthropology not only as a methodological or ethical innovation but also as fertile ground for producing and revealing unanticipated possibilities (Pandian 2019). Rather than obscuring the structural inequalities in which it is embedded, this work, however fragile, complex, and contested it becomes, may prove useful in conveying concerns about such inequalities.

Anthropologists must take seriously the seemingly intractable ethical issues that come with this work. But the very nature of collaboration inevitably—and perhaps ideally—also relocates ethics to a terrain that may ultimately be outside our control. As these projects become more central to anthropology, we should acknowledge that some ethical issues emerging from them are not entirely "ours" to resolve. Whether envisioned as a cost or benefit of deliberately collaborative anthropology, this may reveal the innovative potential of this work. We might see the role of anthropologists less as authorities who explain and represent others and more as partners with different skills and perspectives engaged in a process of creating something new in the world. Even as our skills increasingly overlap with those of our interlocutors, we may also find that we have very different questions about, understandings of, and uses for the same technologies, images, and knowledge we produce. In this way, turning the ethnographic lens onto this very process affords new insights into a changing lived world.

COP26: Collaboration on the Move

Early in 2021 I received word from Uboye that he would attend the United Nations Climate Change Conference (COP26) in Glasgow later that year. I was initially skeptical about his plans, in part due to the COVID-19 travel restrictions then in place and his not having been vaccinated at the time.[9] I was also surprised because, apart from his recording of the 2019 Waorani Resistance protest, to my knowledge he had little role in environmental politics up to that point. Having become an expert on ideophones in Wao-terero, he was able to travel to academic conferences in Colombia and the United States to present his work on the language documentation project. However, my previous attempts to secure a visa for him to attend a linguistics workshop at the University of London was rejected by the UK Border Agency—a glaring example of the limits of our collaboration. But COP26 was different. He was invited as part of a large delegation of Indigenous people from South America who came to explain to global leaders how climate change and the extraction of fossil fuels and other resources from their lands was affecting their lives. His trip was sponsored by an international group of activists hoping to bring as much participation and recognition of Indigenous people as possible to COP26.

After months of uncertainty about the trip, Uboye arrived in Scotland with his wife Marci and one-year-old son to take part in what became one of the largest-ever gatherings of environmental leaders from around the world. I was as excited to see his presence on such an international platform as I was at the opportunity to host his family at my home in Scotland for a week after the conference. For years, his family has generously hosted me in their home and supported my research and personal well-being in many ways. And yet, until now I was unable to even receive them in my home for a short visit. While people like Uboye are very much aware of the difficulties of securing visas, this situation reflects the kind of structural inequalities that limit the depth and quality of the collaborations we often seek.

In our conversations during and just after COP26, Uboye explained to me some of his encounters with other Indigenous people and environmentalists he met in what he described, with a mix of excitement and exhaustion, as a relentless schedule of meetings, speeches, and protests in Glasgow. Several Indigenous leaders attracted intense media attention for their speeches about the importance of recognizing Indigenous knowledge, land management, and the urgent need for international bodies to finance Indigenous projects to cope with environmental problems. Other Indigenous leaders not in attendance at COP26 used the amplified attention to environmental issues to highlight how extractive economies are placing Indigenous lands and lives under threat. Waorani leader Nemonte Nenquimo, for example, released the following statement through the organization Amazon Frontlines:

> To the presidents of the 9 Amazonian countries and all of the world leaders who share responsibility for the plundering of our jungle. My name is

Nemonte Nenquimo. I am a Waorani woman. I am a mother and leader of my Amazonian people. Amazonia is my home. I am writing this letter because the fires continue to burn, because the companies are spilling oil into our rivers, because the miners are stealing gold as they have been doing for the past 500 years, because the landgrabbers are cutting down the forests so that their cattle can graze and their plantations can grow, so that the white man can eat. As Indigenous peoples we are fighting to protect what we love, our form of life, our rivers, the animals, our forest, and life on earth. And it's time for you to listen to us.[10]

Much as environmentalists were disappointed with the lack of new global commitments to combat climate change at COP26, the Indigenous delegates seemed skeptical about achieving their own specific goals. Uboye reflected on the new friends he made, including Indigenous people from elsewhere in Latin America who helped feed his family at the conference as well as donors whom he described giving money to Waorani and other groups who performed songs and dances. The politics of recognition in which Indigenous identities and political platforms are enmeshed appeared, in his description of the event, to literally involve cash (and card) payments. But when I asked Uboye what prospects for change might come from COP26, he expressed little hope that world leaders would support the projects of Indigenous people. In contrast to the speeches of some well-known Indigenous environmental leaders, Uboye seemed to have less to say about climate change or the environment than about questions of responsibility, as well as the kinds of relations with outsiders and the qualities of life he hopes to see in the future. He was particularly concerned with the fate of Waorani elders.

During COP26 Uboye appeared on Channel 4, one of the leading UK television networks, to speak in response to public criticism of the lack of adequate support Indigenous people received on their arrival in Glasgow. Then, on November 7, a video of him speaking (in Spanish) at the conference, with his infant son in his arms, circulated on social media. In it he said:

I want you all to listen. I want the governments to guarantee our "buen vivir" [translated as "way of life, our well-being"] of the family . . . that they guarantee health, education, and buen vivir. That's why we are here, to ask for this for our future generations. While our elders, our leaders, are disappearing every day. That's why we've come here. So that you hear us; not our politicians, but the voice of the guardian [translated as "the guardians of mother earth"].

In this speech Uboye used the Spanish term *buen vivir*, which was translated by the COP26 translator as "way of life" or "our well-being." This concept, widely embraced as an alternative ideology of development and citizenship in Latin America,[11] is closely linked to the "rights of nature" and "sumak kawsay" as guiding principles of Ecuador's 2008 constitution. Here Uboye, in a quint-essentially international context, effectively translated Waorani concerns into the language of international development and conservation. His speech also included a critique of what he sees as the failure of political leaders—both Waorani and *kowori*—and his concern about the fate of elders. When he insisted that people should listen to Waorani elders, rather than politicians, the translator assimilated his use of the word "guardian" to the discourse of Indigenous people as "guardians of mother earth"—a phrasing that circulated widely at COP26. Here again, the translations in which Uboye and the official translator were involved speak to a wider sociopolitical framing that unites environmentalism and Indigenous rights in specific ways (Albert 2002).

After two busy weeks at the conference, Uboye and his family stayed at my home in Edinburgh for a week before returning to Ecuador. When I arrived to pick them up at the house where they stayed in Glasgow, I was shocked at the massive amount gear they had accumulated during the conference. Marci explained that donors had distributed these items to Indigenous people attending COP26. In addition to high-end outdoor clothing, baby clothes, and other items, Uboye received a professional camera as a gift from a British activist. They also had a bundle of about forty small hardwood feathered spears made by their Waorani relatives, which they had brought from Ecuador to sell. They explained that, although people at the conference offered them large sums of money for the spears, there was no time to sell them with all of the activities going on. The night before their flight home, I recorded an interview with Uboye, in my living room, where I asked him to reflect on his experiences at COP26 and what it meant for Waorani people:[12]

> I am a young Waorani man who lives in the Ecuadorian Amazon . . . in the depths of the forest . . . who is dedicated to territorial defense, to his culture, to his language, to keep our mother tongue alive and known by the whole world. . . . I am helping a lot in my territory to defend it from the destruction of oil companies, loggers, and farmers who cut down primary forest. That is how the world is increasingly destroying human beings. And seeing this, some friends have supported me to come . . . to speak, so that the large, advanced countries that are polluting a lot,

listen. And above all, we have come because we are the true guardians who protect the forest. It is us, not the leaders of the world; they do not protect [the forest], they only destroy it. That is why we have come here, so that they know that we are the ones who protect it. The forest is not only for us, but for all human beings on the planet.

I then asked him to explain who Waorani people are:

We Waorani are those who live in the forest and have always lived there, from generation to generation, even though people used to think that the forest was without people, only trees. But we have always lived there because it is our territory. Before contact with outsiders our territory was very large. And every time, with contact with outsiders, we have been losing it, and every time with the business the government does, it is harming Waorani families. . . . They pressure us to live within the limits of boundaries today. And they are also putting pressure on our uncontacted families, the Tagaeri and Taromenani, but we are protecting . . . our territory. And every time they are destroying us. In other words, whoever it is, the leaders of the State, they do business with the oil companies, because they have an immense debt in our country. That is why we are worried today.

When I asked him what he thought would come of the COP26 meeting, Uboye responded:

We, as true guardians, we wanted to talk with world leaders to protect our forest. But everything has been [decided] between the governments that did not want to listen. They only wanted to negotiate among the great leaders of the whole world. And they wanted to negotiate in another way to save the world. But everything is a lie. The same thing is going to happen. . . . Today they say they want to do things without polluting. They want to create cars, planes, new technology. But I don't think it will save the world. It will always be the same. It is something other than what they say. It is yet another idea to deceive the people, because it will always be the same.

Then I asked if any good might come from COP26:

No . . . I just think they were [doing] what they have always been doing. The politicians, the big leaders, were negotiating among themselves to destroy the world more. I don't think it's any more than that. I think it was just talk . . . because it has always been like that; they will never save the world, because it was just talking and doing business, and it is the same as doing nothing will.

When I asked him about the environmentalists at COP26, he said:

> I already knew some people, through the internet . . . some friends who wanted to save the planet. I don't know if they're environmentalists or not. I've been trying to understand things they say, like this . . . I don't know what it means [he picks up a paper and attempts to read it in English].

After I responded "neither do I," Uboye handed the paper to me and told me to read the English. I explained that it was a proposed agreement called the "Fossil Fuel Non-Proliferation Treaty Initiative." He then continued:

> Many people, they are creating things like this to receive benefit for themselves. Because [they] want to use Indigenous people, saying "we are going to support them." But they have always done it this way. . . . And how are they going to save things? Some organizations were talking like that, and Indigenous people themselves too; sometimes they are corrupt today. They always talk about "Indigenous people," but what Indigenous people? Who are they? In other words, they don't know, they were talking about Brazil, Peru, Bolivia, Venezuela, Ecuador. . . . They talk about Indigenous people, but what they really want is to take advantage . . . of the agreement they made in Paris.[13] Saying that they were going to protect the Amazon. They wanted to receive money and they knew very well that they wanted all the money to enter that organization . . . to take it, and only to deliver . . . part of it.

When I asked what kind of support Waorani people need from foreign allies, he said:

> The Waorani today need to defend territory, to delimit and maintain it, and also to keep a living culture and not lose it. And also maintain the rivers, with clean water, and not allow more oil companies to enter the territory . . . that is, to keep it there, and no longer cut down the trees, to maintain it for the future, because sometimes, the donors, they don't really know where that money goes. They think that . . . the leader of a big organization will send them the results [of a project], telling lies that "here's a photo" [showing what was done with the money]. They show it. It's just so others think it's true. But everything is backward.

I then asked him how he thought this problem could be solved:

> For one thing, it's better to work directly with the community. Not with organizations that are in the cities, but more directly with the communities that benefit, those working or taking care of nature. This is better

because every time money arrives in the organization it is already lost . . . [we need] less politics, and working more directly in the community. In other words, then there will be support for the communities . . . so they can buy medicine, have education.

When I asked about what help international environmental activists at COP26 might provide in this process, he said:

Those activists, I was just watching them, and I know they want to be this, but really, they do no more than just talk. It is different, living in the city, and actually living in the forest . . . [those of us] who truly protect. . . . The international ones, I think they are only talking, nothing more . . . the environmentalists only talk about how to protect the forest and how to maintain it. But the leaders of the forest [Waorani people] actually do protect it. In other words, how can I say it, I take care of something, while other people who live in the city just talk.

When I asked what was important to Waorani elders in COP26, he said:

Thinking about [me] coming here, the elders thought that many people have already said things like "We are going to support you," but . . . failed. Leonardo Di Caprio donated a lot of money. And it turns out they never benefited. I don't know what they've done, but that's why the elders got angry . . . yes, that's why I came here, to bring support to the community. The elders expect a response, and hope that if I manage to take on some projects, it will help them. They also want to benefit because they are the real ones who protect [Waorani lands].

I asked what benefits elders want to see:

Economic benefits, [for those people] working, taking care of the forest. Doing their everyday work. Yes, [support] for their basic needs.

When I asked about climate change in the Waorani territory, he said:

It's changed a lot because there are some communities where it doesn't rain and sometimes it's sunny for one, two, three weeks . . . because they [Waorani people] know a lot about what the year is like. They know perfectly. And sometimes the river grows big, where it should never grow so much.

When I asked what change he hoped to see as a result of COP26, he said:

In the next [climate change] event . . . I want to take the opportunity to say "After everything you talked about, what happened? I mean, where is the result? Where did it go? What did they do?" That is what I want to say, so that people know that what they are saying is all lies; that is why they have to listen to a person who does know the truth about what is happening, and we have to do things in another way to conserve the world.

Near the end of our interview, Uboye referenced the apocalyptic visions of Waorani elders in response to my question about what he thought the future would hold:

It's going to get worse, little by little. Yes, the forest is going to be finished one day . . . from my perspective. There are visions that the elders have seen, that one day in the Waorani territory, the families will kill each other and be finished. There is going to be a war for money and the oil companies.

*

The interview to some extent reflected many previous conversations I have had with Uboye and several other young Waorani adults in recent years. But it was also quite different, not least because it was recorded in my living room and followed Uboye's participation at a global environmental summit in Scotland. I was struck by how his commentary at once embraced much of the environmentalist (and cuturalist) discourse I have described in this book, while at the same time offering a critical perspective on environmental politics and Indigenous leadership. Specifically, he contrasts Waorani elders as the "true guardians" or "protectors" of the forest to the failure of environmental activists, organizations, and political leaders. He describes foreign environmentalists and "city people" more generally as "just talking" about protecting the forest, whereas it is the "leaders of the forest," that is, Waorani people—and elders in particular—who actually protect it. Since foreign activists don't know what it is like to live in the forest, he suggests, they should work "directly" with Waorani communities who do.

For Uboye, this critique applies as much to Indigenous leaders as it does to foreign activists and politicians. His observation that foreign donors do not really know where their money goes supports his suggestion that leaders use the money for their own purposes, and that little of it goes to supporting Waorani elders. This perspective, much like the criticisms of Waorani leaders I have heard during my fieldwork, reflects what I have called a "politics of egalitarianism" that severely restricts the authority and legitimacy of leadership positions (High 2007). Uboye's description of what Waorani people need appears broadly consistent with the concerns of a global environmental politics: to defend their territory, not lose their "living culture," prevent oil polluting their rivers, to stop logging, and protect the forest for the future. But his emphasis on circumventing organizations and working directly with Waorani communities situates elders as the answer to many of these problems. For Uboye, it is Waorani elders—not politicians, environmental activists, or even "Indigenous people"—who know this world and how to protect it. Yet they become angry when externally funded projects fail to support their basic needs.

Uboye's reflections on COP26 and environmental politics more broadly point as much to the possibilities as to the limits of collaboration across what he describes as different "worlds." For him, the meeting was mostly a failure because world leaders only negotiate among themselves, and ultimately their mere talk will do little to stop the world's destruction. But a global meeting such as this also creates new opportunities for solidarity among the Indigenous people who participate. In the days that followed, Uboye and Marci described several activists, donors, journalists, or simply new friends they met in Glasgow, many offering different kinds of support for the Waorani struggle against extractive industries. Some provided winter clothes to keep them warm during their stay, while others offered cameras to document their anti-oil activism or discussed projects involving international funding. As a short-term host, long-term friend and anthropologist, I was inevitably recruited into some of these discussions. As we shall see in the following section, however, these new collaborations were in some ways also limited for much the same reasons that Uboye suggested in the interview.

New Possibilities, New Limits

During the week Uboye and his family stayed with me, they were surprised that they were unable to sell the bundle of spears they had brought from home. In contrast to the amplified international platform for Indigenous people they described at COP26, the COVID restrictions and cold, wind-swept streets of Edinburgh in November offered little opportunity to sell Amazonian crafts. Uboye inevitably left the spears at my house, putting me in touch with one of several new friends he met at COP26 who offered to help find buyers for them. This man, who was involved in a small charity based in the United Kingdom and was inspired by Uboye's speeches and conversations in Glasgow, explained to me on the phone his interest in supporting future projects with

Waorani people. Though I had previously acted, in a very limited capacity, as an intermediary to help market Waorani crafts for the Waorani women's organization (AMWAE), this was quite different. Now I found myself being asked to vouch for the character of Uboye, while at the same time translating between very different understandings and expectations of what this proposed project was for.

The spears were relatively straightforward, with the charity worker asking for video of Waorani people making them—which he hoped would help generate a higher selling price. But this collaboration soon turned to bigger ambitions, with Uboye proposing larger projects requiring donor funding. His counterpart, the British philanthropist, was also passionate about protecting Waorani land and ways of life. It was here that their communication revealed differences and misunderstandings about what their potential collaborations should entail. The philanthropist appeared kind and thoughtful and had considerable experience in finding funding for small-scale projects elsewhere in Latin America. He recruited me to help make sense of his subsequent dialogue with Uboye and to better understand the wider context of Waorani communities. He hoped to support a project that would make an impact on their lives in such a way that could be documented. It was soon clear that, not entirely unlike my own applications for academic research grants, his prospects for securing funding for Uboye's project would depend largely on practical questions about intended goals, methods for delivery, accounting for the budget, potential impact, and subsequent reporting back to the donors.

My identification with this approach likely reflects how academic research, international development, and philanthropy share common ground with regard to the value and qualities expected of collaboration. And yet, my involvement in this conversation also included being asked to vouch, somewhat awkwardly, for Uboye's character and his intentions. Though I was happy to explain my relationship and previous work with him positively, it soon became clear that there was a major gap between Uboye's plans and his counterpart's expectations. Soon after arriving back in Ecuador, Uboye requested funding to distribute directly to Waorani elders at a large meeting, with little explanation of the context or purpose. This of course was met with questions about what the money would be used for, how it would help protect Waorani land or support cultural preservation, and how all of this could be reported and justified to donors in the United Kingdom. The philanthropist explained this, and the need for a precise proposal and budget, in a series of clear and sincere emails to Uboye in Spanish. He also called me, somewhat exasperated, wondering how one could expect any donor or organization to provide this kind of support without such assurances.

Uboye's project to bring money directly to Waorani elders is consistent with the concerns he expressed in our interview after COP26. It reflects his insistence that environmental activists should not "just talk," but instead "work directly" with Waorani communities to make sure they, and especially elders, receive benefits. For him, the point of this prospective collaboration was not to do anything particular for these elders, much less ask them to do anything differently. It was to ensure they receive direct benefit to support their basic needs. It was unclear to my British interlocutor how such a proposal would support the transmission of "ancestral knowledge" or the struggle to defend Waorani territory from oil. For Uboye, it involved a perfectly sensible suggestion that *kowori* people with access to money should help the specific people who defend Waorani territory. His vision of collaboration, even if it falls well short of conventional development or political goals, evoked exactly the kind of relationship he sees missing in most engagements with *kowori*—whether oil companies or international activists.

I do not highlight this gap in understanding to endorse Uboye's project, or to criticize his counterpart's expectations as reflecting conventional "Western" values. In my conversations with both of them, I suggested the possibility of a project to incorporate videos of elders speaking from the language documentation project into village schools. This of course, was entirely viable for someone invested in the ideas of Waorani elders as a source of cultural preservation and environmental knowledge. Uboye was not against this idea, but it did nothing to address his expressed purpose of directly supporting the elders he sees rarely receiving any benefit from the projects of *kowori* and Waorani leaders. In fact, during his most intense period of work in language documentation years before, he had told me that one of the things he liked most about the research is how speakers were paid directly for their involvement. Though it was not a large sum, Uboye seemed proud to be involved in an activity that brought at least some direct benefit to Waorani communities—and particularly to elders.

Uboye ultimately failed to gain the support he hoped could bring money to Waorani elders. I do not suggest that his exchanges with his UK-based ally simply indicates a failed collaboration, nor I do I want to imply that language documentation research is an ideal alternative. Instead, this example illustrates the new potential Waorani people are finding in environmental politics, and also the limitations that emerge when people work from very different assumptions about the purpose of such work. As with language research and conventional ethnography, we simply do not know where these interactions and relationships will go and what novelty they will bring. In this case, after coming to understand the philanthropist as yet another outsider who "just talks," Uboye later sent him a proposal to create an ecotourism project that would bring together Waorani elders and young people to host foreign researchers and tourists in their home community. Although the proposal, requesting tens of thousands of dollars of support, was well beyond the small grants Uboye's new friend worked with, he sent links to larger organizations that might support such a proposal in the future.

*

Whether in language research, protests against oil, or COP26, Amazonian people are finding diverse opportunities to work across worlds. They may have better prospects in this regard than previous Waorani generations whose relations with *kowori* were primarily defined by missionization, oil companies, and less than sympathetic state institutions. The harsh power inequalities reflected in these early relationships have certainly not disappeared. And yet, in an emergent Waorani contemporary, some young adults are finding new possibilities to advance their personal and collective interests. These collaborations inspire new and expanded imaginative horizons that insist on the value of Waorani people and territory and also embrace more varied relationships with a *kowori* world than their elders would have known. But I also hope to have shown that the shared ground on which this work sometimes appears to rest is also limited in certain ways. This has as much to do with structural inequalities and enduring stereotypes of Amazonian people as it does Waorani understandings of autonomy, responsibility, and political authority.

All of this is complicated by the fact that Waorani people, foreign activists, and global leaders tend to hold different ideas about land, environment, and conservation—and the place of Indigenous people in it. What I have described in this chapter illustrates how translations can bridge such differences and also how they can lead to certain misunderstandings. While enabling new forms of solidarity between Waorani and *kowori* people, translations also point to some of the challenges of collaboration. These projects can disappoint the expectations of Waorani and other people invested in them, and they may fail entirely. Anthropology is perhaps an illustrative example of this, as I have certainly felt the prospect of failure in fieldwork, my evolving relationships with Waorani people, and my efforts to write a book that does not betray the premise of our collaboration. Anxieties about failing to find a sincerely shared ground, in my own experience, only intensify when deliberately collaborative projects—whether language documentation or environmentalism—raise the personal and political stakes of participation.

In contrast to what is often assumed, collaboration is no easy solution to the world's problems, whether climate change, poverty or protecting Waorani lands from oil companies. Nor is it a simple remedy to the ethical, political, and epistemological problems of an academic discipline like anthropology. It is less a solution than a starting point that, at the very least, implies multiple participants with stakes in achieving something. Both language research and environmental politics envision Waorani people as protagonists in this process, rather than mere participants, research subjects, or passive observers of a world beyond their control. Of course, being protagonists does not liberate Waorani people from the inequalities, material needs, and injustices they face. Nor does it simplify or resolve the ethical challenges we all face in trying to get something done. I hope to have shown that, for people like Uboye and other young Waorani adults, collaboration involves both risk and promise. The unpredictable consequences they experience in becoming researchers, videographers, and environmental leaders indicate how we might rethink not only the concept of collaboration in anthropology but also the ethical dimensions of this work.

FIVE

. . .

HOW ANTHROPOLOGISTS LIE

ONE AFTERNOON, DURING A recent fieldwork visit, I found myself explaining to some of my oldest Waorani friends some details about my life in Scotland. We sat in hammocks around my host family's *durani öko*—a traditional open-plan house, with its rounded, thatched roof extending down to the ground. Its loosely braided leaf walls to the opposite sides allowed the light breeze and sounds and smells from the surrounding gardens to flow through the house. I was talking about what Waorani people call *kowori öko*, a term that translates most directly as "the outsider's house" but that most commonly refers to life in the city or the world outside their territory. My hosts often ask about my family back home and are keenly interested in hearing about people, objects, and the techniques for making them that seem so distant from their own lives. While my stories about *kowori öko* are often met with a degree of skepticism— indicated by smiles and whispers among those listening—on this occasion I was confused when everyone exploded into an uproar of laughter. I thought, what did I say that was so funny or unbelievable? Like many anthropologists, I think, I have always measured—and doubted—my linguistic and social competence in fieldwork at least in part based on how well I can follow the humor around me. Living for extended periods with a Waorani family offers many opportunities for this. But on this occasion, I had clearly missed the point; I had no idea what was going on.

As my confusion became evident to those around me, one of my hosts explained, between bursts of laughter, "Iniwa,[1] you are lying." "What?" I said, "No, what I say is true, *nawäga*, it really is like that in Scotland." In response, I heard people say *onöke* ("it's not true") and *babe* ("liar"). Then someone explained that my account had been interrupted by the *geñëta* bird, whose call, "*tïka*," which everyone present except for me had heard in the gardens surrounding the house, clearly contradicted what I was saying. I was again reminded that this particular call, for Waorani people, means "untrue" or "lie." As we saw in chapter 2, if I had been speaking "truthfully" or "seriously" (*nawäga*), as I claimed, the *geñëta* bird's affirming call would have been "*titititi*." That the bird's accusatory call intervened so directly in response to my statement about a distant, foreign place made this a particularly funny occasion—perhaps even more so as my ignorance of what was going on became obvious to everyone present. My insistence that I was indeed telling the truth surely only added to the comedy, and probably joy, that Waorani people often find in such absurdities.

Comedy aside, the idea of deceiving people, or not telling the truth, is the kind of thing that would make just about any anthropologist uncomfortable. Such accusations can, in other contexts, be very serious—both for anthropologists and the people we work with and write about. In fieldwork and well beyond it, the whole endeavor of anthropology rests on multiple and complex forms of trust (Marcus 2001), some of which inevitably break down. Even as anthropologists have long since dismissed the idea of being detached, objective scientific observers of other worlds, most of us like to think that we do our best to at least tell things as we see and experience them. I present this final chapter about lying not as an attempt to make my efforts in collaboration appear more reflexive, introspective, or even humble, but to highlight what I suggest is an important aspect of a changing Waorani lived world. Specifically, my interlocutors' understandings of what "truth" is and what it is to say something that is untrue, are closely linked to a specific theory of knowledge and language that can help us better understand their engagements at home, in Ecuadorian cities, and abroad. Waorani concerns about lying—whether by their neighbors, agents of the Ecuadorian state, or anthropologists, give shape to the possibilities and limits of collaboration.

Here I draw on my analysis in the preceding chapters of Waorani language research and environmental politics—and the translations they involve—to identify a distinct epistemology that associates "truth" with direct, embodied experiences rather than more abstract forms of representation. In this context, despite an emphasis on the mutual constitution of bodies, persons, and households in everyday social life, the experiences or thoughts of one person are often understood to be inaccessible to others. Such an understanding of autonomy, and its link to the body, helps makes sense of Waorani moral evaluations of environmental politics, whether in reference to their own leaders or *kowori* people. This is also why *kowori* anthropologists too "lie" when we attempt to describe the lives of Waorani people. Rather than concluding that such a contention renders any collaborative anthropology futile in this and other Amazonian contexts, I suggest that it points to the distinct form and purpose anthropology might come to have for Waorani researchers themselves.

Truth and Lies

I am sure that even my closest Waorani friends at times doubt the things I say to them. Their reaction to the *geñëta* bird's call, even in a joking context, was the first time I had been accused directly of lying during fieldwork. But it was certainly not the first time that someone cast doubt on the kind of academic work I do. Several years ago I visited a young Waorani man, whom I knew well, at a university near Quito. He was one of a handful of Waorani students who, in the early 2000s, received scholarships provided by an oil company to attend Ecuador's most exclusive private university.[2] As I spent the day with him, he seemed excited to be living and studying among so many other young people in *kowori öko*. However, I had also heard from mutual friends in his home village that he was struggling with his studies, and he now explained that he was having a hard time finding the money he needed to cover the costs of living in the city—expenses that his scholarship did not cover. As I asked him about his studies for a degree in tourism, which included an internship working at a bar in Quito's city center, he spoke with some confidence about the subjects he studied.

When I asked him about anthropology specifically, I was surprised to hear him casually say "anthropologists lie." Initially absorbing this as a criticism directed at me personally, I asked him to explain what he meant. He responded that "anthropologists, they write books about the Waorani, but they don't really know. They just lie." Though I had not yet published my own book about Waorani people at the time, I had recently finished my PhD and was eager to know what observations or claims he was refuting. But he was unwilling or unable to give examples of these lies, or even specific anthropological texts he had read.[3] My impression was that, rather than having been upset by the claims of a particular author, he was reflecting on what he had come to understand anthropology to be. And strangely, the fact that he knew

I was an anthropologist did not seem to figure in his observation or our conversation. In no way did he seem to imply that I had done anything wrong. He and his family had been, and continue to be, among the most accommodating and supportive people during my fieldwork in his home village. I initially, and somewhat nervously, put this brief conversation down to his exposure on campus to a politics of representation—casting a critical light on the idea of foreigners representing and claiming to know about Indigenous peoples, or Waorani people in particular.

I have since come see this comment that "anthropologists lie" in a different light. Sometime after my first monograph was published in English a few years later, a British woman I know who was working on a Waorani environmental project sent me a photograph of this same young man and his brother holding a copy of the book, smiling, with their thumbs up. Though I took this more as a teasing joke than any endorsement of a book they could not possibly have read, it reminded me of that conversation about lying years before. More recently, I had a similar conversation about anthropology with Uboye, who, despite his relatively cosmopolitan experiences in language research and environmental politics, has not attended university. As we sat in his parents' house talking about language documentation and anthropology, he said something to the effect of: "People write lies about Waorani people because, even if they've been to the communities, they can't really know what it is like to live the way we do." I said I agreed, but suggested that anthropologists don't claim to know "the truth," but just offer our own interpretations and opinions based on our experiences. I offered my own research as an example and explained, probably in a more positivist tone than I would normally adopt, that disagreement, critique, and correcting mistakes are part of the whole point of advancing knowledge. But Uboye was not convinced. He explained that outsiders cannot really access the "truth"; it is only Waorani people who really know this, he said, through "direct" or "physical" experience of *wao öme*.

At first sight, this conversation about lying and truth appears as an example of the kind of impasse anthropologists have reflected on for decades with regard to epistemology, ethics, and representation.[4] We should take the critical insights of people like Uboye—those "interlocutors" who become researchers in their own right—particularly seriously in this regard. And yet, I want to suggest that even this commentary has as much to do with translating between worlds as it does a straightforward critique of anthropology or *kowori* people. Like the university student mentioned previously, Uboye has been incredibly supportive of my research and subsequently took a major role in our collaborative work. As we have seen, he has come to identify himself, through various forms of collaboration, as a linguistic and ethnographic researcher. We should be careful not to assume that his reflections about "lying" and "truth" indicate a kind of Christian or otherwise religious moral judgment with regard to sincerity, nor the adoption of a conventional Western scientific rationale of objectivity in search of a universal truth. I suggest that it instead reflects a specific understanding of autonomy and the limits of what people can hope to truly know (or should say) about the thoughts and experiences of others. In this way, the assertion that "anthropologists lie" reflects a specific theory about the very nature of language, embodied knowledge, and human being.

The Limits of Knowing Others

Understanding this specific epistemology requires further attention not only to a Waorani theory of language and the body but also to the delicate balance between individual autonomy and collective forms of social life. We have already seen that, despite criticisms of moral "others" being a routine practice in Waorani households, people generally place a strong emphasis on individual autonomy in many aspects of social and political life. This is reflected as much in the subsistence activities that children are expected to undertake from a young age as it is in how people deal with what they see as the moral transgressions of their neighbors, political leaders, and *kowori*. An emphasis on autonomy also has important bearing on Waorani concepts of knowledge, truth, and the limits of what people can know about each other.

Despite the moral evaluations one hears in everyday life, only rarely have I seen Waorani people confront each other to hold someone to account or otherwise explicitly challenge their actions. For example, during my longest period of fieldwork, from 2002 to 2004, the teenage children from one end of the village, I was told, had repeatedly stolen clothes that my hosts had hung to dry next to their home. One family was known for excessive drinking—and the moral transgressions elders often associate with drinking alcohol. Other households included Kichwas, whose relatives were accused of making local babies sick through sorcery, and so on. My questions about these situations were often met with sharp moral commentaries, framed as people "doing badly" (*wiwa kerani*), being "crazy" (*dowëta bai*), "lying" (*babe*), or "deceiving" (*onöki*) others. My hosts had much more to say about such objectionable practices than what motivated specific people to do such things. Such attributions of responsibility, evident in daily gossip, are probably familiar to most anthropologists who work in intimate Amazonian contexts. They become particularly intense at times of serious illness, calamity, and death, which are most often understood in some way to be the result of human actions.

While accounts of the moral failings of others are often accompanied by warnings about the dangers they present, I am often struck by how, in a population so often noted for past revenge killings, there is rarely discussion of confronting people associated with such transgressions. For example, when, in response to ongoing complaints about teenage neighbors seen wearing clothes stolen from my host family's drying line, I would ask, "Why don't you go and ask the teenager wearing your shirt to give it back?" The silence or brief, noncommittal responses to these questions made clear that my hosts did not see the prospect of accountability through such direct confrontation as viable.[5] If specific individuals were deemed responsible, this did not appear to imply that they were accountable—at least not without risking violence. Nor did there appear to be any prospect of punishment or resolution at the level of the wider community. On the contrary, practices that Waorani sometimes translate in Spanish as "castigo" (punishment), such as whipping (*pägi*) children after a peccary hunt with a vine, or the past practice of ritually piercing a young person's ears to fill with wood plugs, are not understood as a punishment to discourage or correct a transgressive behavior but instead a method of transmitting desired capacities across generations or from animals to humans (High 2010).

Curious about what has often seemed to me as a strong recognition of individual autonomy in Waorani communities, I have asked young adults what their parents think about their actions—or those of their siblings—that would appear transgressive in their terms. These include questions like, "What does your mother think about your brother arriving drunk?" or "Does your father approve of your little brother marrying a Kichwa woman?" or "What do your parents think about your sister moving to the oil area to live with a *kowori* man?" The most frequent response I hear to such questions is "I don't know/hear" (*iñinamai*). I think that, for most Waorani people, this is an obvious answer to a ridiculous line of questioning—one implying the arrogance of assuming, or worse, claiming to know, the thoughts of others. The reluctance to make such claims about other people reflects what anthropologists have described in diverse parts of the world as a recognition of "the opacity of other minds" (Danziger and Rumsey 2013; Robbins and Rumsey 2008).[6] As Robbins and Rumsey describe in the Pacific, this "opacity doctrine" is often less a matter of personal reflection than something that shapes everyday practice, such that people refrain from speculating publicly about the thoughts of others (408).

This is not to suggest that, in everyday practices, Waorani people—or anyone else—are somehow oblivious to or disinterested in the knowledge and attention of others. But statements of not knowing are closely linked to specific understandings of the nature of language that conceive of communicative practices and their relation to thought in particular ways. So even as all human beings share the capacity to infer the mental states of others, or a "theory of mind," language ideologies can limit (or promote) the extent to which such inferences are openly recognized, deemed acceptable, or actualized in speech (Robbins and Rumsey 2008, 414). Even in contexts where opacity statements are explicit or strong, people engage in everyday social interactions in ways that are implicitly orientated toward the knowledge and thoughts of others (Danziger and Rumsey 2013, 247). In Waorani social life, claims to such knowledge, or open speculation about it, appear to have little credibility. It is these claims, distant from the words and deeds of the people in question, that I think people like Uboye associate with anthropology and its limited truth-value. As Robbins and Rumsey (2008) point out, such statements of opacity challenge the epistemological basis of anthropology and conventional Western thinking:

> Pacific assumptions about the impossibility of knowing the minds of others fundamentally contradict social scientific models that assume such knowledge is possible, and that further assume that gaining such knowledge stands universally as a regulating ideal for human beings in engagement with their fellows. (408)

Much as Rumsey (2013) has described among the Ku Waru people of highland Papua New Guinea, Waorani statements about not knowing the thoughts or intentions of others suggest less an abstract philosophical concern about the nature of minds than an emphasis on deceit as an ever-present possibility in social relations. For many Waorani people, it seems, a claim to such knowledge is the kind of speculation or deception that Uboye contrasts to the "truth" he identifies with the speech of elders. In contrast to reported speech or the "truths" embodied by the words of Waorani elders, claiming to know the thoughts and motivations of others—in the absence of their own words—is understood to be all but impossible. Making such a claim, which for Waorani people is closely associated with intentionally deceiving others, is precisely the sort of thing they translate as "lying."

If responding in their own language to questions about the thoughts of others, the specific way to express not knowing such things is typically *iñinamai*—"to not hear"—as opposed to not knowing something on the basis of "not seeing" it (*aramai*). Where responses extend beyond explicit statements of not knowing, my interlocutors tend to refer directly to quoted speech, such as "my father says 'Wareka will do what he will do'" or "my mother said 'the manioc does not grow large in the oil area.'" But even responses to my questions, for example, about what a parent has said about someone's seemingly contentious decision, rarely report claims to authority over them—even if regarding their own children. So even as adults have a keen sense of the conduct they associate with "living well" and express strong opinions about what they see around them, they understand that other people will ultimately act—and speak—for themselves. Similarly, if openly inferring the thoughts of others is a form of lying, it is not something I have heard Waorani people tell each other (or me) not to do.

Whether describing a recent hunting trip, a visit to another village, or retelling a well-known personal biography or myth, Waorani conversations often report the speech of others who articulate their own views and experiences. Similarly, skilled speech includes expressions that mimic the sounds of animals and human beings as they move through and experience their surroundings. In contrast to the "lies" constituted by speculating about the thoughts or motivations of others, or in acts of deception, the speech of elders is associated with a "truth" that comes with the direct experience of hearing and seeing the world around them. For people like Uboye, elders present an ideal model of bearing witness to "truth" in a way that he and others see as antithetical to anthropology and other "lies" about Waorani people. Much as this theory of knowledge expands the boundaries of what is understood as lying in many Western contexts, it also presents a distinct understanding of "truth." Here, the value associated with Waorani elders is not some universal or transcendent theological notion of "truth" that can or should be accessed by everyone but one contingent on the singular experiences of individual beings—experiences that are not generally understood to be accessible to others.

This epistemology, premised on the singularity of experience and its opacity to others, has been observed elsewhere in South America. Marcelo González Gálvez (2015) describes a Mapuche philosophy in southern Chile premised on "an inextricable link between personal experience and truth" such that reality is "different for each specific person" (143). His description of how Mapuche recognize an incongruence between this autonomy of individual experience and how people communicate it socially parallels Waorani statements about lying and what they call the "truth" of "direct" experience. Even if, like the Mapuche, Waorani people can never be sure about what others actually think, the "strong speech" of elders and their extensive use of ideophones appear to partially transcend this opacity. As Waorani language researchers observe, their speech—with its rich sound symbolism and corresponding gestures—is "powerful" and "true" insofar as it establishes some degree of shared perception between speakers and their audience.

Living with Difference

Just as claims about the thoughts of other people tend to have little credibility, insisting on not knowing about the unspoken knowledge of others can be a way of asserting one's own commitment to Waorani sociality. For example, despite frequent complaints about sorcery attacks, which are often—but not exclusively—attributed to Kichwa shamans, few Waorani claim to know very much about the specific knowledge or skills that sorcery entails. I have previously argued that this is in part because, in a context where knowing and being are not entirely separable, having such knowledge is tantamount to being a shaman (High 2012b; 2015b).[7] As envy is understood as a major cause of sorcery, in some ways this presents an exception to the tendency to avoid imputing the thoughts of others. But accounts of this contentious practice focus more on envy as a particular—and potentially dangerous—emotional state. As such, it is a somewhat generic explanation for a wide range of calamities, with victims and their kin left to speculate about what they may have done to make other people envious. They wonder, might I have been targeted for having several healthy young children in my home? Or did they become envious seeing the large manioc and plantains growing in our gardens, or the abundant game meat we have been eating? My interlocutors also explain that rumors about a person receiving unusual wealth from *kowori* sources can cause such envy.

Rather than positing rules or attempting to punish offenses, Waorani and other Amazonian people often understand such objectionable behavior as reflecting a state of being less than human. Elizabeth Ewart (2015) links this observation to a general Amazonian insistence on there being only one way of being human, with differences more often explained in terms of the body (Viveiros de Castro 1998). To some extent Waorani people understand living and eating together to have the power to transform differences into a shared body. But different perspectives, and the recognition of relatively autonomous individual wills, remain a central part of everyday life, whether in interpersonal relationships within Waorani villages, in subsistence activities, or in relationships with various *kowori*.

For example, Waorani often talk about Kichwa-speaking people generally as moral others, even as interethnic marriages and friendships with them have been a key feature of Waorani social life for decades (High 2015a; Reeve and High 2012; Yost 1981). In parallel ways, the behaviors of certain animals, especially jaguars, are described as dangerous and antithetical to Waorani people "living well" (High 2012b; Londoño Sulkin 2005). Kichwas and jaguars can evoke strong expressions of moral otherness, such as envy or a predatory perspective, but my Waorani interlocutors tend to describe their characteristics in terms of essential, almost stereotyped differences. Rather than differences to be transcended, remedied, or addressed by an overarching authority or sense of justice, this alterity is part of the very basis of expressing what it means to be a Waorani person.

As Harry Walker observes among the Urarina in Peru, where "moral shortcomings are attributed to the body rather than the mind," and where people refuse to claim knowledge of others' thoughts, "disputes of any kind are almost impossible to mediate" (2015, 50). Instead of attempting to resolve such differences, moral evaluations of Kichwas, other *kowori*, and certain animals, become points of contrast to Waorani social practices associated with generosity, sharing, autonomy, and the ability to provide for one's household and visitors. These are all facets of "living well," which I often hear Waorani people contrast to greedy and envious Kichwas invading their lands, demanding cash payment for food, and attacking them with sorcery.

So, if *kowori*—whether Kichwas, mestizos, or white people—are so clearly associated with moral deficiency, how can Waorani reconcile this with a desire for relations with them, much less their participation in the collaborative projects I have described in this book? Their evaluations of moral failure can be emotionally charged, such as the helplessness one feels on seeing kin suffering from a sorcery attack. However, outside of these highly charged contexts, my interlocutors often take a seemingly relativist stance, appearing to accept that different kinds of people—and their different bodies—will have different moralities. While practices associated with *kowori* people are routinely—and often jokingly—contrasted to the ways Waorani people "live well," they appear more as markers of inherently different perspectives than individual transgressions to be remedied, controlled, or even understood.

I hesitate to assimilate this understanding to any version of cultural relativism, especially as few Waorani I know normally describe these contexts in terms of "cultural differences." Nor do they shy away from criticizing objectionable *kowori* behavior. Despite decades of exposure to multiculturalist thinking in school and elsewhere in Ecuador, most Waorani use the Spanish term *cultura* almost exclusively in reference to themselves, and particularly their elders. They laugh at the absurdity of my references to the "cultures" of Kichwas, mestizos, and white people, as if "Waorani culture" is a measure of humanity antithetical to other peoples. As others observe, in Amazonia it is often different bodies or "natures"—not cultures—that distinguish one's point of view (Viveiros de Castro 1998).

Kowori present a model of moral failure, it seems, as a result of their particular bodies and the perspectives they entail. But their bodies can, under the right conditions, be remade through living in a Waorani household, where coresidents come to share a body associated with Waorani ways of knowing and being. In this way, rather than positing a racialized theory of bodily difference, Waorani incorporate Kichwa spouses and other *kowori* into their daily lives. If we risk translating across different worlds, we might describe Waorani as moral relativists more than cultural relativists, with different moralities being constituted by different bodies.

Despite quoting the words of others more than inferring their reasoning, the Waorani people I know often appear keenly attuned to the emotional states of others. Such affective conditions, whether being happy/laughing (*tobi/toki*), sad (*tote*), or angry (*pii*), are not purely internal or psychological, but embodied emotional states that can be read in the words, gestures, and actions of others. They often comment empathetically on the pain and suffering of others, whether recounting how ancestors were speared in the past or lamenting the painful cries of coresidents who fall ill. It is not uncommon to hear descriptions of kin as *nägi nätate* (to be in a lot of pain/suffering).

Such recognition can be an urgent concern, especially where the anger, sadness, pain, or envy poses a threat to a household or village "living well." While emotions like rage can be clearly visible and audible, more subtle conditions of frustration can be evidenced by a person's silence or self-isolation. Since anger and solitude are particularly antithetical to "living well" (High 2013), they become a focus of attention among coresidents and neighbors.[8] This sensitivity to others' emotional states is part and parcel to the intimacy of everyday household life, where a person's bodily integrity itself can depend on the actions of others.

In this way everyday social life reflects as much the recognition of autonomous, individual wills as it does the mutual interdependence of household residents. Here "living well" is not conceived or achieved through conforming to a hierarchical authority or even explicit coercion, but by recognizing the ability of individuals to actively contribute to such conditions of abundance, health, and laughter. People belong to a household not because they are descendants of a particular ancestor, or because they are obligated by a powerful elder or leader to be part of it, but because their individual thoughts, decisions, and actions constitute the intimacies of everyday conviviality. Language, or more specifically, speaking Wao-terero, is a potent force in establishing this collectivity—one that is always contingent on the individual decisions and actions of multiple people. Through living together, what appear to be radically autonomous individuals come to share a consubstantial body and the collective qualities of "living well" that come with it.

Speaking Truth

This emphasis on autonomy and the limits of what can be known about the thoughts of others provides important context for understanding what Waorani people mean when the say that politicians, environmentalists, and anthropologists "lie." Recall the interview in the previous chapter, where Uboye repeatedly describes political leaders at COP26 "lying" and international environmental activists as "just talking." He contrasts this "talk"—whether by Ecuador's president, activists, or "city people" generally—to Waorani people, who he describes as the "true guardians" of the forest. What becomes clear in the interview is not just a compelling criticism of corrupt politicians doing business with oil companies rather than working to combat climate change, but the idea that outsiders do not really know the forest—or how to protect it—in the ways Waorani people do. For Uboye, it makes sense that if foreign activists and donors really want to conserve the forest or help Waorani people, they should directly support Waorani elders, as these are the people who truly know *wao öme* in the ways that outsiders do not. In contrast to "lies" or "just talking," Uboye describes the direct experiences of elders in defending their territory and protecting the forest.

Admittedly, like reflections on anthropology, COP26 is a very particular context. It probably indicates more about how Uboye, Nemonte Nenquimo, and other young Waorani adults are increasingly able to engage and translate environmental discourses than it does a specifically Waorani theory of knowledge. These translocal engagements are of course quite different from everyday life in Waorani communities. And yet, even as Waorani environmental leaders translate their struggles against oil into a global rhetoric of conservation, Uboye's critique implies a similar epistemological stance with regard to what it means to "lie" and what constitutes "truth." His comments raise the question: how can a distant politician or environmentalist, even if well-meaning, truly say that they will protect the forest if they do not actually live there or work directly with those people who do? As he said in the interview:

> The international ones, I think they are only talking, nothing more . . . the environmentalists only talk about how to protect the forest and how to maintain it. But the leaders of the forest [Waorani people] actually do protect it. In other words, how can I say it, I take care of something, while other people who live in the city just talk.

The "leaders of the forest" Uboye refers to are Waorani elders. Given the emphasis on autonomy I have described, it should be of no surprise that they are understood less as hierarchical authorities in Waorani communities than people whose prolonged, direct experiences in *wao öme* give them the ability to speak truthfully about it.[9] They know the forests, gardens, and rivers of their territory through such experience, much as their skilled speech demonstrates knowledge of past events, mythic characters, and long-deceased ancestors often identified with specific features of the landscape. As Uboye observes, their ways of speaking reveal much more than "just talk"; their words and gestures skillfully embody—rather than represent—other perspectives.

In contrast to the "lies" associated with attempts to represent other people, or in making speculative assumptions about their intentions, elders' speech is "true" in that it is borne out of the direct experiences that Uboye observes younger Waorani generations to increasingly lack. This "truth" is reflected not just in what elders remember about the past or their commentaries about current situations but also in the weight attributed to their prophecies about the future. Uboye, for example, explicitly contrasts their prophetic words to the "lies" of *kowori* leaders.

Even if elders epitomize this understanding of "truth," it should already be clear that the kind of talk that constitutes "lies" is not exclusive to *kowori* people. Leaving aside the particularly global stage of COP26 and environmental politics, my Waorani interlocutors also routinely apply such critiques to each other, Indigenous organizations, and particularly their own leaders. A general skepticism about claims to represent other people, much less a unified Waorani "nationality," continues to present major challenges for elected Waorani leaders. Since they ostensibly represent Waorani people in a *kowori* world, it should be of little surprise that they are often accused of lying. But lying is not always morally charged in the way it is in critiques of Waorani leaders, *kowori* environmentalists, or Ecuador's president. Lying can also involve outright deceptions that are as likely to be a source of humor as they are serious offense.

One day in 2003 I met a European tourist in Quito who, having recently returned from a trip to a Waorani village arranged by a tourist agency, was interested to hear about my research. I doubt I am alone among anthropologists in observing that encounters with ecotourists tend to reveal very different impressions of the people and places I came to know in fieldwork. After describing her exciting adventure accompanying Waorani people hunting monkeys in the forest, she asked if I knew the Waorani "chief" who had joined her on the trip. I was at first perplexed by the idea of a Waorani chief after coming to know their seemingly anarchic egalitarianism. But when the woman told me the name of the man she met, whom I knew, and who at the time had no formal role in ethnic politics, it started to make sense. I knew that the man, having previously worked for oil companies in the 1980s, had since forged friendships among *kowori* environmentalists, journalists, and filmmakers. As a prominent ecopolitical activist himself, he often takes tourists and foreign activists to visit Waorani villages and is known for his outlandish sense of humor.

Sometime later I described my encounter with the tourist to some Waorani friends, who responded with laughter at the man's self-portrayal. It emerged that, much to their amusement, he was well known for describing himself as "chief" of the Waorani to impress on foreigners his importance, sometimes with romantic intentions. Even if my friends found his lying quite bold in this case, above all they thought the deception was hilariously funny. In some ways there is nothing extraordinary in this example. Such deceptions, whether received jokingly or judged seriously as a moral transgression, are just one of many ways Waorani people communicate beyond the boundaries of their own communities. This can involve anything from attempts to draw approximate equivalences between *wao öme* and "nature" or "environment," to emerging discourses of "culture" in public performances, to spurious claims to status according to a foreign structure of hierarchy. Whether unconsciously, consciously, or even in outright deception, relations between Waorani and *kowori* people often involve (mis)translations or uncontrolled equivocations that appear to be at the very heart of many relationships in contemporary Amazonia.

It is worth considering how the increasingly dispersed and varied relations in Waorani social life figure in all of this. Whether in prolonged absences from villages, migration to frontier cities, or the expanded political arenas I have described, this involves travel and communication across great social, conceptual, and geographical differences. Living with and engaging these differences evokes concerns about "truth" and "lying"—and the theory of knowledge they reflect—in particular ways. I do not suggest that such processes are somehow antithetical to a "traditional" Waorani epistemology doomed to disappear in the face of a "modern" world. Despite the strong sense of alterity in Waorani moral evaluations, their ideas of difference and change appear less reductive than conventional Western dichotomies. However, traveling to Ecuadorian cities or abroad, representing a Waorani nationality or territory, and forging ever closer relationships with *kowori* people outside of *wao öme* all appear distant from the "truth" many Waorani see in the lives and words of their elders. These practices, and the work of translation they involve, are an important part of an emergent Waorani contemporary at the same time as they are precisely the contexts that lend themselves to what my interlocutors understand as "lies."

Collaboration beyond Text

So anthropologists do lie. But we are not the only liars—much less the most important ones—that Waorani people deal with. Though we tend to think of ourselves, often self-critically, as representing the lives of others in ways that Waorani people would associate with lying, I do not think that this is our most important or visible role to most of them. While some Waorani university students and language researchers may describe anthropologists as liars, few

Waorani people I know, especially elders, have a very concrete idea of what anthropology is. Elders, who are often happy to share with me their knowledge, personal experiences, and reflections on the ways of the "ancient ones" and current issues, appear to have little interest in the "lies" I might write about them. Most Waorani appear to understand people like me in terms of what they see us doing. For some, I am the *gringo* who came to teach English at a local school many years ago; for others I am a coresident who stubbornly—and often clumsily—tries to participate in as many everyday activities as possible; some refer to me by kin terms; others see me accompanying Waorani language researchers on trips with video recording equipment. For some, I am sure, this collaboration reinforces my position as a potential source of external wealth.

The point is, if writing about their lives is a kind of "lying," even for Waorani researchers it does not to appear to be a particularly important activity. Some of them recognize the professional status of anthropologists, but I do not think that many would understand us as people with the authority to represent Waorani people or "culture." Even their own elected leaders would struggle to claim such authority. But if I am right that anthropological writing is currently of little consequence to most Waorani, it is also the case that some young adults are becoming keenly interested in some of the same processes, questions, and observations that we are curious about as ethnographers. They ask, for example: What is distinct about the way Waorani people live and speak? How has life changed since the time of the "ancient ones"? What can the words and experiences of elders tell us about how to defend *wao öme*? How can Waorani people manage to "live well" alongside *kowori* and oil companies? Of course, some of their concerns extend well beyond conventional ethnographic questions, such as when Uboye looks to the words of elders for prophetic accounts of what the future holds for his people.

For some, reflecting on what it means to be a Waorani person in the contemporary world often has more to do with urgent political needs than simply intellectual curiosity. Waorani environmental activists must come to understand very different concepts and assumptions about "nature," "Indigenous people," and their lands. Defending *wao öme* and ensuring the prospect of "living well" requires not just an awareness of such differences but also the ability to translate, communicate, and successfully navigate across them if Waorani people are to have any hope of challenging powerful external interests. And operating in these translocal contexts, like so many other aspects of contemporary Waorani life, often requires money. If some of their questions are coming to share common ground with anthropology, their purposes are often more concrete and immediate than those of ethnographic writing.

While translating across worlds is an important endeavor for many Waorani people, this process also raises pressing questions about relations within their communities. Language researchers like Uboye, for example, reflect not just on the "lies" of politicians or oil companies but also key changes and problems within their own communities. His ethnographic lens tends to focus not on generalized questions of Waorani identity, but on the words of his elders, specific generational differences, and changes he sees undermining the ability of Waorani people to live well. With diverse experiences in *wao öme* and *kowori öko*, young adults like him increasingly feel they can engage productively in a contemporary they see constituted by these different worlds. At times this involves criticizing other Waorani people, whether for "lying" or failing to support the elders.

At first glance, Uboye's interests as a researcher appear to be aligned with those of many conventional anthropologists and linguists. However, if we identify Waorani researchers and environmental activists as para-ethnographers engaged in a form of "reverse anthropology" (Kirsch 2006; Wagner 1981), we should also acknowledge the distinct priorities and epistemological issues foregrounded in Indigenous modes of analysis. People like Uboye bring their own analyses to changing relationships within and beyond their communities, and they do this based on specific understandings of the nature of language, the body, and knowledge. For many of my interlocutors, there are limits to what *kowori* can know about Waorani people, much as there are limits to what any human being can know or should say about the thoughts of others. Whereas speaking has the power to transform relations and embody different perspectives, individual thoughts and experiences remain relatively opaque to others beyond what people say about themselves.

And yet, the traditional anthropological mantra of participant observation, involving long periods of coresidence, learning local languages, and engaging in everyday activities, seems to at least approximate what Uboye describes as the "truth" of "direct" experiences. Even if, for Uboye, what anthropologists write are lies, I do not think he doubts the veracity of my own experiences in Waorani communities or the knowledge I have gained from them, not least those we have shared as coresidents or as coinvestigators. This is in fact the opposite of what he and his family have often conveyed during my longest periods of fieldwork. Their comments about me as a new resident speaking and becoming more like them is probably more a positive statement about the health and vitality of the household than about any specific person. It is rather the conceit of knowing the lives of others—perhaps epitomized by abstract textual representations of "the Waorani"—that appears deceitful. For them, I think, what I call my "fieldwork" constitutes the "truth" of my own singular experience, not "Waorani culture." For people like Uboye it is elders, not *kowori* anthropologists, environmentalists, or even Waorani youth, who "truly know" the world of *wao öme* and how to defend it. They are, as he suggests, the "true guardians" of this socionatural world because this is the life they live.

Such comments on anthropologists and elders, and the notions of lies and truth associated with them, raise important questions about the possibilities and limits of anthropological collaboration with Waorani people. Why, for example, would they even want to be involved in collaborative research with "liars"? It also allows us to imagine what a specifically Waorani anthropology might be for people like Uboye. After all, from the point of view of Waorani language researchers and probably most other Waorani people I know, writing ethnography is a relatively small—and often invisible—part of what anthropologists do. I consider them to be ethnographers in their own right not because they share the epistemological commitments of conventional anthropology but to highlight their interest in observing, listening, documenting, and interpreting the words and lives of diverse Waorani speakers. Perhaps it should be of little surprise that their ethnographic interest is not primarily in authoring texts to be read by *kowori* or their own communities,[10] much less in generating a complete picture of "Waorani culture," but recording videos that show the knowledge of individual Waorani and specific features of their language.

For Waorani language researchers, these videos do not simply constitute a growing corpus of linguistic data, nor an archive of Waorani culture, but the words of specific Waorani people who recall events that are often temporally and spatially distant. Whether narrating personal experiences, quoting the words of others, or gesturing and mimicking the sounds of an encounter in the forest, the videos contain the kind of "truth" they see lacking in textual representations or conjectural claims about other people. Recordings of elders, particularly those who have since passed, appear to have particular value in this respect. Their stories, commentaries, and ways of speaking offer Waorani language researchers the opportunity to learn new knowledge. This is because their speech reflects the personal experiences of people who truly know.

*

In this chapter I have described how ideas of "truth" and "lying" figure in Waorani engagements with—and moral evaluations of—a range of social and political contexts. This implies a specific theory of embodied knowledge that prioritizes autonomy and the mutual constitution of household life in ways that distribute responsibility beyond individual people. We have seen that this epistemology has important bearing on the current challenges of Waorani ethnic politics, as well as the possibilities—and limits—of collaborations with *kowori* people. It helps makes sense of why Waorani people often see the purposes of language documentation and environmental politics in ways that are different from outsiders.

It should be clear by now that, in contrast to some of my interlocutors, I continue to see value in ethnographic writing. Some Waorani adults are becoming more interested in publishing texts, whether about their unique history and current situation, or as a call to global action against extractive industries (Ima 2012; Nenquimo 2011, 2014). For years I have talked with Uboye about the prospect of him writing about his own experiences or coauthoring a text. While he appears to have little interest in becoming a writer, his identity as an ethnographer of his own people has led to an interest in publishing his own words. For him, I think, the forthcoming publication of our interview after COP26 as a chapter in a reader about Lowland South America is as much an opportunity to demonstrate his expertise as an author as it is to share his critical views on environmental politics. This is perhaps as good an example as any of how Uboye's interests both intersect with and remain distinct from those of *kowori* people like me.

As questions of collaboration continue to change in challenging and fascinating ways in anthropology, I am convinced that we should think and write more about these contexts. This is in part because such processes—and prevailing discourses about them—are an increasingly recognizable feature of the world well beyond our specific fieldwork sites. But I am also suggesting that we should think with our "research participants" or "interlocutors" cum "epistemic partners" about collaboration beyond texts or even questions of conventional ethnographic representation. In Waorani communities, I am not so sure coauthorship, even when desirable, represents the common ground many of us seek. Maybe sharing such a purpose is not the point. Perhaps it is just the opposite—the unpredictable shapes, forms, and directions collaboration often takes—that makes it interesting. As we have seen in language documentation and environmental politics, some Waorani people are bringing their own political and epistemological concerns to bear on diverse forms of collaboration in ways that are both anthropological and distinctly Waorani.

CONCLUSION

. . .

UNFINISHED BUSINESS

ONE OF THE DEFINING features of the collaborations I have described is that they remain unfinished and ultimately open-ended. Years after the language documentation project formally ended, many of the video recordings are still yet to be deposited in the Endangered Languages Archive. My discussions with Waorani researchers about what use they might have for their communities— whether in education, remembering deceased relatives, politics, or marketing crafts to European consumers—are ongoing and likely to follow unanticipated directions. The linguist involved in the language documentation project, Connie Dickinson, is currently working with Waorani communities to find new ways of integrating language materials in Wao-terero into local schools. Uboye continues to record people and contexts that have less to do with documenting language than with making a "true" record of events that matter to him.

Likewise, Waorani environmental politics at home and abroad involves ongoing projects without obvious conclusions or predictable outcomes. Solidarity and collaboration with an international network of environmentalists and Indigenous rights activists will surely have an important role in ongoing struggles for Waorani territorial autonomy. Even as a new generation of leaders like Nemonte Nenquimo is gaining international attention, and their demand for free and prior informed consent regarding oil extraction on Indigenous lands has been acknowledged by Ecuador's legal institutions, the state's continued ownership of subsoil rights and dependence on oil revenues illustrate the challenges that remain.

The unfinished character of collaboration should be especially clear—and sometimes painfully so—to anthropologists engaged in long-term fieldwork. In most cases, I suspect, including my own, these collaborations have as much to do with ongoing personal relationships and commitments as they do specific research agendas. Even when designed to address the inequalities embedded in academic research and beyond, such projects are more likely to lay bare these problems than to resolve them. Being involved in a project that situates Waorani people themselves as researchers was a major turning point in my fieldwork. It has deepened my relationships with certain people and forced me to engage with them as something more than informants, friends, or Indigenous people living in remote Amazonian villages. And yet, this is not a simple or inherently positive process of making research more engaged, equitable, or ethical for everyone involved. I have come to see that the more collaborative anthropology endeavors to be in this respect, the more unfinished it tends to feel for everyone involved. The open-ended character of collaboration illustrates the tensions between foreign researchers and Indigenous communities that some see as a key site of productive work in settler-colonial contexts (Jones and Jenkins 2008; Fine 1994; McLaren 1995; Morris 2017).

In my experience, in contrast to older models of anthropology premised on participant observation confined to a specific time frame, there is ultimately no turning back from genuinely collaborative work in which our research partners have clearly defined stakes beyond simply accommodating a foreign researcher. Once our interlocutors become researchers and environmental activists, how can they be anything less than epistemic partners who—like us—bring their own agendas, needs, and desires to such collaborations? These relationships, and the evolving expectations that come with them, are not somehow contained in time and space—even when we might want them to be. Nor is the production of anthropological texts—and the sense of boundedness or completion they imply—necessarily at the center of these expectations. This is not a critique of ethnographic writing, much less of an innovative field of collaborative ethnography that recognizes the importance of dialogue and solidarity beyond coauthorship. And as feminist scholars and those committed to decolonizing research have long argued, we need to think about the stakes, consequences, and possibilities of anthropological engagement beyond the assumed value of research in the academy.

Much as it would be unusual today to limit an ethnography to local contexts alone, the young Waorani adults at the center of my description in this book extend their expectations of collaboration well beyond their engagements as researchers. This reflects as much the unfinished, indeterminate nature of this kind of work as it does the potential limits of anthropological collaboration. Toward the end of chapter 5, I described the frustrated exchanges between Uboye and a new UK-based ally he met at the COP26 climate change conference in 2021. They clearly brought different values and expectations to what initially appeared as a shared project of protecting Indigenous lands and reviving Waorani ancestral knowledge, and their collaboration ultimately broke down as a result. I too felt certain limitations particularly acutely in the aftermath of COP26, an event that appeared to sharpen Uboye's expectations of what his engagement in academic research, environmental activism, and international donor organizations might bring. When he asked me: "How can we do another project?" or stated that he wanted to do more work as a researcher, I was as pleased by his interest as I was nervous about not being able to give him any simple assurances. His reflections were often connected to questions of how to bring monetary support to Waorani elders or how to pay school and medical expenses for family members. My explanations about the many months needed to prepare research grants, the review process, and the uncertain outcomes of grant applications, much less my limited ability to cover the costs of health and education, disappointed his hope for immediate support that COP26 appeared to inspire.

As an old friend, a host-brother, and the primary investigator for the grant that employed him for more than three years, I am an obvious person for him to approach about all of these things. And yet, the more tangible (and concretely monetary) these potential collaborations have become for some of my interlocutors, the more limited I have come to feel in my capacity to support them. This has less to do with my own romantic concerns about monetizing my relationships with Waorani people than it does the practical matter of how to meet their needs and expectations as skilled researchers, leaders, and friends who have limited access to money. For some of them whose families have generously supported not only my research but also my safety and well-being during years of fieldwork, it is probably obvious that our collaboration should extend well beyond the formal arrangements of a particular research project. It has never really been otherwise. But deliberately collaborative work—whether in language research, anthropology, or environmental politics—intensifies the possibilities and expectations of these relationships in complex ways that I am only beginning to understand.

Even if Waorani researchers value documenting their language and culture, they do not appear to separate their engagements as researchers—or as political activists—from the immediate needs of their families and communities. Whether to do with health, education, or the desire to buy consumer goods, these needs increasingly require money—a commodity that remains scarce in remote Amazonian villages and among recent Waorani migrants to frontier cities. As we have seen in Uboye's nuanced commentary on *kowori* environmentalists at COP26, for him protecting *wao öme* and Waorani ancestral knowledge is not simply about rescuing "Waorani culture" but supporting the material needs of elders who he sees at risk of disappearing. His suggestion speaks to what is probably a major concern for most Indigenous peoples of Amazonia today: the need for cash and the marginal position from which many Indigenous people are able to acquire it. This reflects another layer of inequality that is sometimes lost in a global-facing environmental politics focused on Waorani cultural and territorial autonomy in the face of oil. We might wonder whether, in the context of recent generational changes that include urban migration and relocation to work for oil companies, is such autonomy enough to make a living?

I suggest that these questions are just as important as—and closely connected to—those about how Waorani people translate and work across different ideas about their land, language, and what it means to "live well." Although concerns about money are probably no less important to Indigenous people than they are to other economically marginalized groups in Latin America, ethnographies of Amazonia rarely address this issue as a problem in everyday social life.[1] There is instead a strong tendency to highlight the agency and autonomy of Amazonian people and their distinct lived worlds (High 2015c). Of course, one of anthropology's established strengths has been in recognizing how diverse forms of marginality and injustice—often linked to colonialism and empire—in no way preclude Indigenous expressions of autonomy and agency (Day et al. 1998; Gow 2001; Janeway 1980; Scott 1985). But it is worth considering why descriptions of alterity in Amazonia tend to focus on relations between humans and nonhumans, shamanic cosmologies and myth, rather than the extreme political and economic inequalities in which the lives of many Amazonian peoples have been embedded for centuries. Is it that such inequalities are too obvious, or do they risk undermining what is assumed to be a more authentic and redeeming sense of difference? Or would such a recognition get in the way of theorizing difference in more provocative, abstract ways?

In a very general sense, I think many anthropologists who work in Amazonia implicitly approach expressions of Indigenous autonomy—and the radical alterity we see in Indigenous peoples—as a more authentic form of difference than complaints about elders lacking access to money or medicine. And yet I suspect that anyone who works closely with Amazonian people— whether as researchers, activists, or local schoolteachers—knows reasonably well that what makes their worlds distinct is not just a question of cosmology. Long-term collaborations, particularly those seeking to complicate and exceed the subject-object model of conventional anthropological research, present exactly the contexts where less exotic differences become more difficult to ignore. For example, it would be all but impossible to involve Waorani communities in language documentation without seriously addressing the material needs of Waorani researchers who relocate to urban areas with little money or prospect of other employment. Even if Indigenous politics presents a growing platform for expressing differences in terms of "culture" and territorial autonomy, such differences are of course not enough in themselves to address the diverse needs emerging in Waorani communities.

If the kinds of collaboration I describe are part of an emerging Amazonian contemporary, it is important to remember that enduring inequalities remain part of them. This is not to suggest that Amazonian people define themselves primarily in terms of these challenges, or that anthropologists should ultimately understand them simply as subaltern victims. In some Amazonian contexts today, Indigenous people have much more political clout—and access to land—than their neighbors. But accepting Amazonian people as part of the same temporal frame—a contemporary we share with them—requires recognizing inequalities as relevant forms of difference, among others.[2]

Such an approach implies a kind of responsibility that can be more challenging than identifying Indigenous philosophies that challenge Western thought. This responsibility should not imply paternalism, much less a sense of guilt on the part of foreign anthropologists, but a more reflexive and rounded view of the complex lives we aspire to understand. Deliberately collaborative work lays bare certain inequalities, but it also inevitably pushes researchers like me to rethink and address our particular place within these inequalities. Even if we are ultimately unable to achieve the horizontal relations of solidarity we seek as activist scholars, this kind of work requires deeper engagement with long-standing anthropological questions of relative power, positionality, and the situatedness of our ethnographic descriptions.

Translating Worlds in an Amazonian Contemporary

For some observers, it is in part questions of unequal power—and the broader historical processes that have integrated many Amazonian people into a capitalist economy—that place them firmly in the domain of modernity. In challenging colonial imagery of premodern "primitive" societies and emphasizing Indigenous agency in relation to nation-states and global economic forces, they identify the kinds of novelty and creative tension I have described in this book as expressions of "Indigenous modernities" (Halbmayer 2018; Whitten 2008).[3] Ernst Halbmayer, for example, observes that "modernity creates experimental ritual practices, creative tensions and transformative actions" (2018, 12), and that alternative modernities "reconnect expressions of modernity with the past and embed it in local culture" (14). Much as I have argued with regard to Waorani collaborations in research and politics, these approaches emphasize the translocal processes and relations in which contemporary life in Amazonia is embedded (Oakdale 2022). They make clear that Indigenous social worlds are coeval with those of nonindigenous peoples, rather than exotic relics of an imagined prehistoric past.

We should remember here that the very idea of indigeneity emerged through colonialism and the modernist ideologies of nation-states, even as marginalized groups today embrace Indigenous identities in diverse ways— often to challenge these same structures of power (de la Cadena and Starn 2007; Kenrick and Lewis 2004; Merlan 2009; Warren and Jackson 2002).[4] And yet, I question the extent to which we should understand any or all of the novelty, creative experimentation, tension, and transformation in Amazonia today as an expression of modernity—in whatever form we might imagine it.[5] Modernity, of course, means many things, and its connotations in Western thought have changed significantly from classical notions of progress, historical epochs, individualism, or a "heroic" attitude toward discontinuity (Foucault 1991). Today, concerns about climate change, conceptualizations of the Anthropocene, and the introduction of Indigenous terms into national laws, all indicate that the nature/culture distinction at the heart of modernist imagination and neoliberal development regimes is in crisis (Blaser 2013; de la Cadena 2010; A. Escobar 2007, 2018). And yet, in many postcolonial and other contexts around the world, being "modern" is an identity by which people situate themselves in relation to the past and assert their place in the world.[6]

Modernity clearly remains a powerful mode of historical imagination in much of the world today, including Latin America. But I am struck by how the Amazonian people I know seem to so rarely talk about their lives in these terms. Even as their environmental politics increasingly evokes nature and culture—key terms of the "modern constitution" (Latour 1993)—I cannot think of a context in which my Waorani interlocutors have asserted their desires, differences, or political goals as a specifically modernist project. Of course, other Ecuadorians and international travelers routinely comment on them in precisely these terms: whether as praise or sincere concern, they describe Waorani people wearing typical American jeans and t-shirts on the streets of frontier towns as signaling a break with seemingly archaic cultural traditions. For some of these observers, not entirely unlike salvage ethnographers of the past, money and popular consumer goods in the hands of Waorani people evokes a sense of nostalgia for a timeless, authentic Amazonian world on the brink of being irrevocably lost. For others, it is a welcome sign of "primitive" people—or their country—achieving progress toward modernity.

While such modernist imagination is surely familiar to many of us, my ethnographic account in this book suggests that Waorani people tend to see something else in these contexts. Over the years I have heard many of my interlocutors distinguish between the lives of their ancestors—"the ancient ones"—and the younger generations. They are keenly aware of how the experiences of monolingual elders—who grew up in the relative isolation of highly mobile longhouses—are distinct from those of younger adults today who go to school, speak Spanish, and spend more time in urban areas. As we have seen, sometimes these generational differences are a point of concern and critique in Waorani communities. But what these observations seem to lack is a distinctly modernist sense of nostalgia that sees such changes as either a form of irreversible loss or a progressive path that should fundamentally undermine the ways of "the ancient ones" (High 2021; 2023).

I have often heard young adults who, having lived most of their lives as students in large villages or towns, express little doubt that they will someday establish their own longhouse in a remote area of *wao öme*. They assert a connection to land, whether actual or not yet realized, that is integral to what it means to be Waorani. For many of them, there is nothing fundamentally contradictory about being a Waorani person and being a researcher, a videographer, or an environmental activist, much less someone skilled at navigating urban areas, state bureaucracies, and relations with nonindigenous peoples.[7] These processes do not present a kind of identity crisis we might be tempted to read into them based on our own assumptions. Many Waorani—including language researchers and activists—are keenly interested in novelty, change, and the increasing prospect of mobility beyond their territory. But in contrast to a notion of Indigenous modernities that assimilates their lives into a *kowori* historical framing, we might well ask why it is that their assertions of identity and difference do not describe such processes in terms of being or becoming modern.

We should be careful about what we assume to be shared in these contexts, even when my Waorani interlocutors adopt the vocabularies most familiar to *kowori*.[8] The Amazonian contemporary I have described is as much about questioning this common ground as it is highlighting how people speak and engage across what they often understand to be stark differences. Halbmayer (2018), who identifies Indigenous modernities as "a process emanating from joint becoming that allows communication with and mutual awareness of the Other" (20), suggests that we should "ask from an ethnographic perspective what Indigenous modernities as lived realities are about" (19). But why not ask just the opposite: to what extent are such lived realities reflective of what we call modernity at all? And if not, what *does* make a difference to our interlocutors, in their own terms, and in their own lives? That is, who or what do they see themselves becoming, and how might their "awareness of the other" depart from our own understandings—whether modernist, Marxist, feminist, or whatever? These are the kinds of questions that are as important to understanding Waorani engagements as researchers and environmental activists as they are kinship, gardening, wage labor, and everyday village life.

At stake for my Waorani interlocutors is not their imagined place in an alien temporal narrative that fetishizes their culture as "tradition," but what they sometimes describe as the different "worlds" of Waorani and *kowori* people. Much has been made of the sharp contrast they draw between themselves (as "real" people) and non-Waorani people (*kowori*)—a term that has in various past contexts denoted enmity, subhuman behavior, and even predatory cannibalism (Rival 2002; Robarchek and Robarchek 1998; Yost 1981). After decades of schooling, interethnic marriages, and Indigenous politics, this *waorani/kowori* distinction remains a routine expression of difference for my younger and older interlocutors alike. And yet, as we have seen in the emphasis on defending their territory from colonists and oil, many of them also express such differences in spatial terms. In chapter 4 I noted how *wao öme* ("Waorani land"), one of the rallying cries of the Waorani Resistance Pastaza campaign, also evokes a key contrast between life "inside" and "outside" Waorani territory—a distinction I have heard repeatedly during field-work. Younger people in particular, who tend to be more fluent in Spanish and regularly engaged with *kowori*, tend to link this spatial distinction to what they call "worlds."

In distinguishing between what they describe in their own language as *wao öme* ("Waorani land") and *kowori öko* ("the city") or what they call in Spanish *mundos diferentes* ("different worlds"), some young Waorani adults highlight not just fundamental differences between themselves and *kowori*, but also how they understand the limits of knowing others. It is a lack of direct experience in *wao öme* that makes it impossible for *kowori* to know such a world in the ways Waorani people—and particularly elders—do. This is as clear in their critiques of politicians and foreign environmentalists as it is in the observation that anthropologists "lie" when they claim to understand or represent Waorani people. But the keen sensitivity to difference in this theory of knowledge is not nearly as confining or essentialist as it might first appear in these expressions. Nor does it typically imply a temporal distinction akin to that between tradition and modernity.

The Waorani collaborations and translations I have described complicate the suggestion that any group of people inhabit or should be defined by en-tirely incommensurable worlds (Nadasday 2021). And yet, such approaches are important for thinking about differences beyond ideas of culture at the heart of modernist thought. As de la Cadena (2015) observes, these worlds are par-tially connected (Strathern 1991) in various aspects of social and political life. Similarly, the translations in Waorani environmental politics, whether draw-ing equivalences between *wao öme* and "environment," or between *waponi kiwimonipa* (living well) and "Waorani culture" or *buen vivir*, demonstrate that these worlds are not completely separate or incommensurable in practice. I hope to have made clear some of the differences that can be erased in these translations—whether on the part of Waorani people, Western environmental activists, or Ecuador's constitution. But I have also shown how, whether in lan-guage research, politics, or elsewhere, Waorani people operate—sometimes quite skillfully—across these differences. Rather than being restricted to a single ontology, concept, or understanding, it is the ability to translate, com-municate, and collaborate across seemingly incommensurable worlds that de-fines their Amazonian contemporary.

The different worlds I have described only appear to be incommensurable in the abstract. As Paul Nadasday writes of hunting in the Yukon, we must recognize that the same Indigenous person may be as invested in cultivating a social relationship with a moose (as a sentient being) as they are in their work at a wildlife-management office that regulates moose populations (2021, 361). This kind of multiple engagement is—often by necessity—an increasingly common feature of life in contemporary Amazonia, whether in conservation, politics, or health services. The diverse and challenging ways in which Amazonian people think and work across such differences is itself a significant part of their reality, and it is in the complexity and creativity in these lived experiences that we might best focus our ethnographic attention. This is why it is as misleading to think of Amazonian people as simply "animist" as it is to represent urban Europeans as a "modern" population, somehow purified from the shackles of tradition. Thinking through ontological differences is useful for understanding many contemporary Amazonian contexts (Blaser 2010; Kelly 2011), but we should not assume that such differences simply determine (or define) the people, processes, and practices we encounter in this contemporary.[9]

Regardless of what anthropologists or Waorani people mean by "worlds," the actual practices of engaging across differences reveal their indeterminacy in a shared contemporary. The collaborations I have described, despite all of the miscommunications, equivocations, and deceptions that come with them, illustrate how people are able to do this without entirely sharing a single understanding of what constitutes land, language, and what it means to be a Waorani person. As we have seen, even when Waorani and their *kowori* allies talk about very different things, their alliances can still achieve certain shared goals. Of course, given the colonial and global inequalities in which these relationships are embedded, some translations have much more power than others (de la Cadena 2010). But here translating worlds is not just about state authorities, elites, or anthropologists assimilating Indigenous people and concepts into their own narrative—modernist or otherwise. I hope to have also shown how Waorani engagements in translation have afforded them power in certain contexts, even when this involves thinking and working with ideas that seem so different to—or even irreconcilable with—the ontological or cultural particularities anthropologists describe.

Possibilities in Collaboration

These collaborations reveal more than just skill in translating and moving between different understandings. They are also reflective of a deeper familiarity with these differences, particularly on the part of young adults, for whom environmental politics and academic research are not their first exposure to new or foreign concepts. In this book I have emphasized how young Waorani adults, most of whom have spent many years in school learning an Ecuadorian curriculum orientated toward *kowori öko*, have never known a world without oil companies, mestizos, missionaries, and the occasional anthropologist. To at least some extent, the differences often attributed to "Western" and "Amazonian" thought are internal to their world, even as Waorani people draw contrasts between themselves and *kowori* and between the worlds within and outside *wao öme*. And after all, like any minority group subjected to enduring discrimination, they must do a disproportionate share of the interpretative labor in their relations with a dominant national society that does not speak their language and usually has little interest in their concepts and values. This is easy to forget in fieldwork with communities for whom autonomy is a central expression of identity.

All of this suggests that Waorani people may have as much to teach us about how to live with differences as about particular socioecological concepts. We might then ask not just what makes their culture and politics distinct, but also what they can tell us about the possibilities (and limits) of collaboration. The diverse ways in which my interlocutors live and think with differences suggest a collaborative anthropology beyond projects oriented toward conventional development or academic goals. This involves approaching ethnography not just as a source of new concepts and theories but also of methods and possibilities for collaboration in a world rife with differences, mistaken assumptions, and inequalities. For example, the collaborations I have described evoke ideas of language, land, and knowledge that challenge conventional modernist imagination. But rather than simply dwelling on the assumed incommensurability of the different worlds in which they understand themselves to be engaged, they work with and translate across these differences without pretending to overcome all of them. Rather than comparing or explicitly reconciling abstract conceptual differences between *wao öme* and discourses of nature, environment, and conservation, what is at stake for most of my interlocutors in these collaborations is the urgent matter of defending land and engaging with *kowori* in ways that allow for "living well" on their own terms.

We might wonder whether such a method for dealing with differences—without trying in vain to reconcile, obliterate, much less essentialize them as cultural objects or abstract philosophies—is something badly needed well beyond the particular Amazonian context I have described. Whether in the polarizing "culture wars" of current US politics or wider geopolitical impasses around the world today, a willingness to engage with our counterparts in a substantive way—rather than presenting them simply as extreme social and political "others"—might present a valuable skill. Perhaps somewhat ironically, if I have learned anything from living with Waorani families only a few decades removed from relative isolation and intense intergroup violence, it is how a strong sense of identity in contrast to moral others in no way precludes a deep interest in meaningful engagement with these same others. Even as they protest passionately against extractive economies and the state, most Waorani people continue to engage in and value amicable relationships with many *kowori*, including mestizo Ecuadorians and even oil workers.

This will be of little surprise to anthropologists working elsewhere in Amazonia. Regional ethnographies are replete with accounts of Indigenous peoples who define themselves as "real people"—a yardstick of humanity encompassed by a world of dangerous "others" who are also valued as a source of social reproduction, exchange, and desire.[10] In various processes of transformation, including rituals and even warfare, very rarely is the point to extinguish differences entirely (Fausto 2012); in many cases a ceaseless process of "opening to the Other" (Lévi-Strauss 1995, xvii) or "other-becoming" (Viveiros de Castro 1992, 270) is a key value. This is a place where people are understood to be transformed more through bodily processes, often by living, eating, and drinking together in everyday life (Overing and Passes 2000), than through abstract ideological questions of becoming "modern" individuals. While few Waorani people I know would accept the idea of "becoming *kowori*" as anything but negative, the *kowori* world they identify themselves against is as much a site for productive social engagement as it is a source of danger, greed, and destructive oil companies. In this way, even as outsiders often appear as moral others, collaboration with them is not only possible, but often desirable.

For many of my interlocutors, these collaborations create something new. But engaging with differences, whether working closely with foreign researchers and Indigenous rights activists or appearing at climate change conferences abroad, in no way appears to undermine a sense of what it means to be a Waorani person. I suspect that, if anything, these emerging collaborations cultivate a more nuanced awareness of what makes their world distinct. As we have seen, in language documentation Waorani researchers sometimes describe their language as something that distinguishes them "culturally" from others. In environmental politics, some Waorani leaders contrast their own notions of land and "living well" to conservation at the same time as they communicate their world to outsiders in terms of "nature" and "culture." These observations are simultaneously assertions of differences and translations that claim a common discursive ground with powerful *kowori*. So what might these engagements mean for rethinking the methods, goals, and possibilities of a collaborative anthropology fit for contemporary contexts like those I have described?

Anthropology has a strong tradition of engaging precisely these questions—whether with regard to method, epistemology, or ethics in fieldwork and writing. Feminist scholars, among others, have long argued for an anthropology that embraces not just questions of difference but also the social, intellectual, and emotional connections that constitute ethnography as a sympathetic practice (Behar 1996, 14). In complicating the conventional distinction between the observer and the observed—an important methodological consideration of any collaborative anthropology—we might think of anthropology's primary method as being, as Anand Pandian (2019) describes it: to "give yourself over to the circumstances of some other life, hoping to find yourself taken beyond the limits of your own" (6). For him, such methods are an essential part of "anthropology's pursuit of humanity as a field of transformative possibility" (Pandian 2019, 6).

Like Pandian's formulation of *A Possible Anthropology*, the collaborative anthropology I have argued for in this book seeks this transformative potential not just in conventional anthropological theorists, but others who "have nurtured affinities with anthropology from beyond its professional bounds" (10). In the collaborations I have described, these affinities tend to be less explicit or abstract than they are embedded in Waorani practices, goals, and reflections on what is at stake in defending their lands, working with *kowori* colleagues and allies, and "living well" in the world of *wao öme* and beyond. They also emerge in the processes of Waorani people becoming researchers, videographers, and environmental leaders. While these people have little interest in anthropological theory, or even the writing of ethnographic texts, their observations contain important critiques of the epistemological basis of conventional ethnography. They imply a certain method for engaging differences that we should accept as no less ethnographic or anthropological than those written by professional academics.

When Uboye contrasts the "truth" he sees in the words of his elders, "the ancient ones," to foreign environmentalists and other *kowori* who "just talk" or "lie," he evokes something more than a conventional politics of recognition premised on indigeneity. Having learned the language of nature, culture, and conservation, he and other young Waorani adults also challenge the common ground outsiders often seek with them in activism and research. The differences they highlight, however, whether describing distinct cultures or worlds, are as epistemological as they are ontological. If, as they suggest, it is only through "direct" experiences in *wao öme* that Waorani people know and speak truthfully about a world in which a person's thoughts and experiences remain relatively opaque to others, then politicians, foreign environmentalists, and anthropologists can hardly avoid being liars when they talk about Waorani people and land.

Such a theory of embodied knowledge implies a method and an ethics that is as radical as it is probably familiar to many academic anthropologists. It points to the limits of collaboration and what my Waorani interlocutors expect of this kind of engagement in an emerging Amazonian contemporary—a world defined as much by debate and conflict between Waorani people as it is alliances with outsiders. Perhaps not entirely unlike their parents, who insisted that their children go to school to become familiar with the power of *kowori* ways, they value what these collaborations enable and create—whether socially, intellectually, politically, or materially. This book no doubt falls short of their expectations of this work, not least insofar as it is read as an authoritative claim to know about or represent Waorani people. But it is equally clear that the collaborations I have described are still worthwhile to many of them.

. . .

BETWEEN HOPE AND APOCALYPSE

An Epilogue

SOME IMPORTANT EVENTS HAVE occurred in Ecuador since I wrote the first draft of this book. On my last visit in July 2023, I was jolted by the changes I saw in the country. Whether in Quito or the Amazonian provinces, everyone seemed to share a palpable sense of insecurity. I was constantly warned of the growing risk of violent crime. In the capital, friends were wary of even meeting at a restaurant for a meal, for fear of being robbed at gunpoint, kidnapped, or worse. Only a few years removed from President Correa's consolidation of state authority in the "citizen's revolution," now Ecuadorians described themselves living in a country controlled more by criminal gangs than any stable government. Long spared the civil wars and violence witnessed in neighboring countries, Ecuador has in short order become the leading exporter of cocaine to Europe while its murder rate has increased fivefold since 2016. As international cartels exert growing influence over political and legal institutions, as well as the prison system, everyone seems to have a frightening story to tell. Many businesses have little choice but to pay regular bribes—what Ecuadorians call *vacunas* ("vaccinations")—or face the threat of violence, while many police appear powerless or complicit.

This insecurity, though worse in coastal areas, has extended to Amazonian Ecuador. I arrived in Puyo—previously a vibrant and relatively safe frontier city—to find it almost silent after dark, its central plaza seemingly abandoned. On the outskirts of the nearby town of Shell, home to a military base and regional airport that services many Amazonian communities, a growing number of Waorani families have built houses on small plots in recent years. Easily mistaken for just one of many sprawling neighborhoods of makeshift houses of rough-cut wood planks and sheets of corrugated metal roofing, the area is now home to dozens of Waorani families. I first met many of the adult residents when they were schoolchildren in remote villages in the late 1990s. I had visited these semi-urban neighborhoods before, but on this occasion was taken aback by the number of Waorani living there. Some families stay in Shell intermittently, continuing to also maintain houses, gardens, and other connections with their distant home villages. For others I spoke with, particularly adults married to mestizo or Kichwa spouses or those with children attending schools in town, Shell appears to be a more permanent home.

In July 2023 I had come to this outskirt area of Shell, which Waorani people jokingly refer to as "Shellpari," to visit Uboye, his wife Marci, and their three children. "Shellpari" combines the name of the town—founded by Shell Oil Company in 1937 as a base for oil exploration in Ecuador—with -*pari*, a place-

FIGURE E.1: A house built by a Waorani family on the outskirts of Shell in 2023. Photo by author.

marker in Wao-terero often used in reference to Waorani villages. Uboye and Marci had recently built a single-room house there, which, despite limited access to public utilities, had a working light bulb hanging from the ceiling and an open pipe spitting up water from the ground next to the house. I had not seen them since the COP26 meeting in Scotland in 2021, and, due to the COVID-19 pandemic and the birth of my son in 2020, this was my first trip to Ecuador since 2019.

Having spent most of my previous fieldwork in Waorani villages, I was struck by the relative precarity of life in Shellpari. With few opportunities for regular paid work, just feeding and clothing children—much less buying medicines and school supplies—was an everyday struggle. Gas cylinders for cooking, among other urban necessities, required cash, which was in short supply—especially since even the salaries of Waorani political leaders at NAWE had not been paid in full for months.[1] Many women I encountered showed me collections of colorful palm-fiber bags they had crafted in hope of selling for cash. Their houses were not dissimilar from some of those built today in Waorani villages, but the minimal fruit trees and other plants around them does little to hide the reality of urban life: here families live without the gardens and forests for hunting and collecting wild foods that they find in *wao öme*. My hosts explained how their material insecurity was amplified by the constant risk of their possessions being stolen whenever houses are left unattended.

During my visit Uboye and Marci made clear that these insecurities were not strictly material or economic—at least not in the way they are for many other Ecuadorians. For years I have heard Waorani people lament the witch-craft attacks they attribute to neighboring Kichwa people. These concerns, it appears, are heightened in urban neighborhoods, where some Waorani plots are directly adjacent to Kichwa or mestizo households. Uboye's father, Amowa, who was suffering severe illness as a result of such attacks, was now living in a Waorani village located along an oil road a few hours south of the city of Coca, a long day's travel by bus from Shell. One of my priorities on this trip, along with reviewing the text of a previous interview with Uboye for publication, was to visit his father. A respected elder who has spent a great deal of time looking after me and teaching me about Waorani life over the years, Amowa lost his wife Ñai to illness only two years prior and was staying in the home of his daughter and son-in-law, too weak to hunt.

After traveling with Uboye's family to visit Amowa, we found him in better health than expected. Amowa attributed his improvement to treatments from a shaman, including a strict diet prohibiting game meat. Though still weak, before long he was eagerly telling us stories about "the ancient ones" as he sat in his hammock. Given the prominent place of elders in Waorani discussions of environmental politics, I was interested to hear what Amowa thought about these issues. He responded with a detailed account of ancestors who defended *wao öme* from outsiders and traveled much farther afield than the present boundaries of Waorani territory. While I have had the privilege of hearing Amowa speak like this many times in the past, I was struck by how this particular story challenged what outsiders—including anthropologists— tend to think about Waorani people. He described not a once-isolated people discovered by missionaries in the twentieth century, nor a lack of genealogical depth often observed in Amazonia. Amowa named ancestors across several generations who ventured as far north as rivers in Colombia. These were stories of violence, leadership, and excessive bravery, invariably culminating in the demise of a famous warrior. Perhaps more importantly, in this context, they asserted an expansive vision of what constitutes *wao öme* and the ability of Waorani people to defend it.

Much as Waorani environmental leaders look to their elders, the *pikenani*, as a model of territorial autonomy and knowledge, elders like Amowa point to the past deeds of ancestors who defended *wao öme*. Even if their stories are not easily translated into a wider sphere of environmental politics in Ecuador and beyond, their words are part of an emerging Waorani territorial politics that is being carried forward more directly by young adult activists. These stories are political, even if not in the ways Waorani leaders and their allies sometimes talk publicly about Indigenous autonomy or conservation. As we have seen, some elders today turn as much to the future as they do the past in addressing the great challenges of oil, the *kowori* world, and changes they see occurring all around them.

As we sat with Amowa, Uboye and Marci talked about the prophetic statements many elders have been making about the future. Marci was particularly interested in her grandfather's account of what she described as "how the world will end," which she summarized in Spanish:

An orphaned Waorani boy will grow up and become familiar with the outside (*kowori*) world. Then he will return to try to unite all Waorani people, but he will be killed by other Waorani who are suspicious and envious of him. Then a huge road will be built through the Waorani territory, passing through the village of Toñampari and arriving at the hillside visible from the village of Damoïtaro. But it will stop there. Waorani people will fight among themselves over oil and money, reviving past divisions between rival families. Then *kowori* people will invade Waorani territory (*wao öme*) and kill all the Waorani, chopping off their heads and taking them like trophies.[2] Then they will dance and sing right there where Waorani people once lived, danced, and sang, and tell stories about the Waorani just as we tell stories today. Then the world will end with a big explosion. But just before this, the Waorani elders, anticipating what would happen, will tell two twin girls to flee the violence. They will turn into birds and fly to faraway places like the United States and Europe, never to return.

My hosts described other elders sharing similarly apocalyptic predictions. In this story, the "world" that comes to an end—which Marci described in Spanish as "el mundo"—refers not to the planet as a unitary whole, but the world of *wao öme* that "explodes," with the twins surviving in faraway places.[3] Much as young adults reflect on the powerful speech and knowledge of elders, Marci and Uboye were fascinated by what they called the "truth" of these prophecies. Uboye described how an old woman had predicted that he would one day have a house in Shell. He noted current conflicts between Waorani people over oil and money as another example of this "truth." Marci described how she, while nearly succumbing to illness a few years ago as a result of witchcraft, was suddenly able to "see" a future world where "everything is destroyed." Much as the ability to see things hidden to others—and surviving near-death experiences—are central to Waorani shamanism, the "truth" of elders' predictions appears to stem in part from their association with firsthand visions of the future.

As we sat there with Amowa, the discussion of prophetic visions soon turned to the issue of roadbuilding. Unbeknownst to me, I had arrived only days before a big meeting to discuss a new road being built through a major swath of the Waorani territory in Pastaza—the same area protected from oil drilling in the successful 2019 lawsuit. A municipal government project, the proposed road would extend from the town of Arajuno, located in a predominantly Kichwa area about two hours by bus east of Puyo, into the western part of Waorani territory, ultimately passing through the village of Toñampari. This is the community where Amowa and Ñai raised their ten children and where I first began my fieldwork with them some twenty-five years ago.

Uboye and Marci were quick to point out that elders had prophesized the road as well as the conflicts that emerged between Waorani people over its construction. Their discussion was in some ways familiar to me. Since my first visits to Toñampari I have heard speculation about a road connecting their community to the outside world. Though not as isolated as some Waorani villages to the east, trips to provincial cities require either an expensive thirty-minute flight by small aircraft to Shell, a trip of several hours upriver by canoe, or a long day's walk in the forest to reach a road to the city. Over the years many people in Toñampari have expressed concerns that a road would bring the problems long observed along oil roads: the colonization of Waorani lands by *kowori*, strains on gardens and game populations due to stolen produce and poaching, the pollution of rivers, and concerns about witchcraft. Others worried that it would lead to young people spending too much time in the city.

I had also previously met Waorani who embraced the idea of a road allowing easier travel to urban areas. But now the discussion appeared to be different. My hosts complained of what they saw as outside interference in the road project. For many of those I spoke with the central concern was one of autonomy. Specifically, there were concerns that, with the support of foreign environmentalists, some Waorani leaders were undermining the decisions of people in Toñampari, and particularly elders. They described how, years before, village elders approved the proposed road and now, after much of it was already built, some Waorani leaders had convinced the municipality to halt construction on the basis of community resistance and environmental impacts. So, while elders have become a focal point in Waorani environmental politics, here the priorities and alliances at the very base of this politics were also accused of undermining their decision.

As we have seen, the idea of outsiders or other Waorani people making decisions on behalf of others—whether claiming authority or acting in their name—is a familiar concern in Waorani politics. This concern, along with elders' prophetic statements about roads, indicated to me the possibility of a major conflict at the upcoming meeting. Some people framed it as a conflict between the overarching Waorani organization (NAWE) and a regional organization (OWAP) with close ties to environmental activism. Uboye and I decided on a whim to make a two-day trip to the Waorani village of Obepari— near Arajuno—to attend the meeting. I admit being horrified by the thought of a road extending into the communities I know best, so I was personally invested in attending, even as a mere observer. Uboye, in contrast, wanting to ensure the voices of elders were recognized, planned to make a recording of the meeting—which was conducted in Wao-terero.[4]

Despite the rumors and tensions surrounding it, what struck me most about the meeting was its inclusion of diverse voices and the apparent consensus that emerged. Of the more than one hundred people who attended, including representatives from around twenty Waorani villages, dozens of people took the floor of a covered outdoor public area to speak. A large majority supported the road being built. Some noted the need for quicker access to hospitals—particularly for elders, while others described how a road would allow them to more reliably attend meetings and other events outside their villages. Others identified its economic benefits in allowing Waorani people to bring their garden products and handicrafts to wider markets. One speaker later took me to see a peanut-growing project he was developing to market specifically Waorani products in the capital, explaining his hopes to expand it once the road is finished.

The main point of contention, it appeared, was not whether the road should be built, but who was responsible for suspending it. Responding to concerns that some leaders were more committed to external environmentalist agendas than the decisions of Waorani communities, an OWAP representative emphasized that her organization was not responsible for the decision. She insisted that government authorities had raised legal concerns about the environmental impact of building the road. Even if this did not entirely dispel concerns, I was struck by the emphasis on Waorani unity at the meeting. All of the speeches were followed by collective applause. Many spoke critically—whether about the poor quality of the road sections already built, the lack of Waorani employed in it, or the area it covers—but rarely identified specific people as responsible. In their speeches, several women repeatedly shouted phrases like "It is Waorani land!" (*Waorani öme ïpa*) "It's our land!" (*monito öme ïpa*). or "It's ours!" (*monito ki*), insisting that only Waorani people should be involved in the decision.[5]

While there was some discussion of roadbuilding damaging local ecology, complaints were directed more at questions of Waorani autonomy and economy than conservation. Uboye, for his part, spoke of the importance of foreign donors working directly with Waorani communities rather than through intermediary organizations that he sees taking money for themselves. This suggestion—an implicit critique of some Waorani representatives in attendance—was consistent with his comments about environmentalism in our interview after COP26 two years before. However, like others who spoke at the meeting, he did not frame his suggestion in terms of nature, culture, or conservation, but in the importance of respecting Waorani autonomy and the views of elders. In contrast to public speeches orientated toward *kowori* audiences, this was, after all, a meeting of Waorani people about what they wanted to see happen in their territory.

Given the references to elders in debates about the road, I was surprised that few attended the meeting. When one of the oldest men from Toñampari finally spoke, the audience listened attentively as several people gathered close to record him with mobile phones. He said he agreed with the road, explaining the difficulties of travel he experienced, but also warned against cutting down too many trees along it, which he feared would cause the earth to dry out. The meeting also indicated misunderstandings between people of different generations or those with more or less experience with projects originating beyond the boundaries of *wao öme*. The most contentious moment occurred when a middle-aged man spoke angrily in favor of extending the road to his own village, located several hours walk beyond Toñampari. Appearing not to understand that the meeting was specifically to discuss the existing road plans, the discussion of legal processes—including untranslated Spanish terms like "environmental assessment"—was opaque to a man who sought better access to sell his family's garden products. As young adult leaders tried to explain the limited scope of the meeting, he abruptly stormed off into the bush carrying several spears over his shoulder.

Despite recent success in defending land, Waorani environmental politics is as contentious and prone to misunderstanding as it is productive. Whether fighting against external oil interests, working closely with *kowori* allies, or trying to explain an environmental impact assessment to someone from a distant village, efforts to translate worlds can fail. But at this meeting, divergent views and misunderstandings did not prevent a formal agreement. Those present spent hours discussing the specific wording of a written resolution, which called for the roadbuilding to be resumed and completed. It also called on the local prefecture to ensure that at least 70 percent of the employment to build it come from the affected communities and that vehicles be prevented from using the road for logging, hunting, and fishing. Printed in Spanish from a computer connected to a generator, the resolution also named Waorani organizations (NAWE and OWAP) as responsible for ensuring that these stipulations are followed—particularly to control the environmental impact of the road.

As the meeting finished, several young adult Waorani activists—some linked to OWAP—passed out leaflets and posters in support of an upcoming national referendum to halt oil extraction in the Yasuní National Park. These were Waorani people who had joined the "Yasunidos," a broad-based environmentalist movement in Ecuador that had been campaigning for the protection of the Yasuní park for more than a decade. Another group then took to the floor passing out materials in support of a presidential candidate in the national election only weeks away. All of this culminated with several Waorani leaders in attendance—notably those pitted against each other in the meeting—playfully chasing and hurling manioc beer pulp at each other. As with so many other Waorani political events I have attended, laughter was never far from the surface. Before long a celebratory atmosphere of singing, joking, and dancing transformed the event into one of play.

Much happened in Ecuador in the weeks following my visit in 2023. On August 9, Fernando Villavicenicio, a presidential candidate running on an anticorruption platform, was assassinated after openly denouncing the influence of cartel gangs in the country. This placed an international spotlight on the decline of security less than two weeks before a national election. At the same time, Uboye and other Waorani people traveled around Ecuador with the Yasunidos movement, in hope of convincing a predominantly urban mestizo public to vote against oil and for conservation in Amazonia. On August 20, the same day as the first round of presidential elections, Ecuadorians shocked much of the world when a majority voted in favor of the Yasuní referendum, requiring that oil drilling cease in the Yasuní within one year and prohibiting the sale of new oil concessions in the park.[6]

If the 2019 Waorani Resistance Pastaza campaign and 2023 Yasuní referendum suggest hope for the future, they also indicate that the fate of Waorani people and *wao öme* is increasingly tied to wider sociopolitical processes in Ecuador and beyond. Even with the dynamics between Indigenous rights, extractive economies, and conservation changing in a positive direction, I am not entirely surprised that the young Waorani adults I know take such an interest in the apocalyptic prophecies of their elders. After all, they know all too well from stories of "the ancient ones" and their own experiences what oil, roads, and a *kowori* world can bring. It remains to be seen how Ecuador's descent into violence—perhaps its own version of apocalypse—will figure in the efforts of Waorani people to live well and defend their land.

NOTES

Introduction

1. Some prominent examples include Boyer and Marcus (2021); Fleuhr-Lobban (2008); Holmes and Marcus (2008); Lassiter (2005); and Rappaport (2008).

2. This emphasis stands in contrast to collaboration's "darker" definition as an immoral appeal, betrayal, or submission to power.

3. Ingold's proposal has parallels with feminist anthropologists who suggest that research is as much about cultivating relationships as it is describing, documenting, or translating them (di Leonardo 1991; Ginsburg 1998; Riles 2015, 175).

4. Such an "agonistic" approach to collaboration (Heffernan et al. 2020) resonates with what has been described as the "agonistic-antagonistic" mode of interdisciplinarity (Barry and Born 2013).

5. Examples of this work include Kirsch (2006); Rappaport (2008); Strathern (1991); Viveiros de Castro (2002); and Wagner (1981).

6. Several anthropologists address questions of possibility, whether specifically in Amazonian environmental politics (Cepek 2012), or anthropology more broadly (Graeber 2004; Pandian 2019).

7. Examples of critical writing on the politics of recognition include Bessire (2014); Clifford (1988, 2013); Coulthard (2014); Graham (2005); Povinelli (2002); and C. Taylor (1992).

8. Video is an emergent "technology of imagination" (Sneath et al. 2009, 19) that, for Waorani researchers, brings about indeterminate effects in social life.

9. In linguistic anthropology the study of language ideology explores how such beliefs about language affect the ways people speak (Kroskrity 2000; Woolard and Schieffelin 1994).

10. Acts of interpreting, reporting, paraphrasing, and explaining the words of other people—"intracultural translation"—have a constitutive role in social life, even when not explicitly comparative (Hanks 2014, 18).

11. Such translations are as likely to create equivalences and connections as they are to produce disjuncture, inequality, and incommensurability (Gal 2015, 226).

12. Unlike typical Western ideas of "land," Waorani people do not generally understand *öme* as a form of alienable property (Rival 2016).

13. Examples include Descola (1994); Viveiros de Castro (1998); Cormier (2003); and Kohn (2013).

14. For examples of environmental citizenship linked to territorial sovereignty in Amazonia and elsewhere, see Agrawal (2005); Erazo (2013); and West (2006, 2016).

15. Critics argue that the idea of multiple worlds flattens the complexity of social life in order to theorize radical differences (Erazo and Jarret 2018; Nadasday 2021; Vigh and Sausdal 2014), ignores shifting understandings and multiple engagements (Cepek 2016, Graeber 2015), and ultimately presents Amazonian people as an exotic contrast to modernity (Bessire and Bond 2014; Ramos 2012). While some promote such ontological approaches as integral to decolonizing thought (Viveiros de Castro 2014), others see them as reflecting a colonial practice that fails to acknowledge—and lays claim to—what Indigenous people have long known (Todd 2016).

16. For examples of how Indigenous peoples negotiate such multiplicity, see De la Cadena (2010, 2015); High and Oakley (2020); and Kopenawa and Albert (2013).

17. For discussions of how colonial power is linked to processes of othering in Latin America and elsewhere, see Mignolo and Walsh (2018); Quijano (2007); and Said (1978).

18. Feminist anthropologists offer diverse approaches to the possibilities and limits of what can be shared in collaboration (Abu-Lughod 1990a, 2002; Behar 1996; Riles 2015; Strathern 1987).

19. Anthropologist have often failed to adequately recognize the contributions of research assistants, ignored the unequal relations with their interlocutors, and assumed a mutual interest in research (Lassiter 2005, 88). This includes those who applied anthropological knowledge to the service of colonial or national institutions and those who envisioned themselves simply gathering ethnological data (Deloria 1969, 99). These critiques have important bearing on questions of collaboration, whether regarding authority in ethnographic writing or struggles to decolonize anthropology and related fields (Allen and Jobson 2016; Harrison 1997; Quijano 2007; Smith 1999).

20. For Lassiter, collaborative ethnography "invites commentary from our consultants and seeks to make that commentary overtly part of the ethnographic text as it develops" (2005b, 16). Recognizing the complexity of producing such texts, he argues for making all stages of research more collaborative.

21. Different parts of the world, such as Latin America, have their own traditions of research collaboration that challenge the division between the observer and the observed (Rappaport 2008).

22. As Riles observes, "like happiness or health, collaboration would seem to be

something no one can really argue against but about which very little can be said" (2015, 149). Whether in business or research, it may insulate those in charge from criticism by sharing responsibility and the burden of knowledge. As expertise gives way to collaboration experts, it has become—like interdisciplinarity (Strathern 2006)—a key measure of academic value (Shore 2020; Heffernan et al. 2020).

23. Linguistic and anthropological research can become ethically fraught or unviable in these contexts (Errington 2003; Debenport 2015), as ethnography can have a damaging connotation, tantamount to stealing knowledge (Brown 2003; Smith 1999; Whiteley 2003).

24. This has parallels with international development, where an emphasis on "participation"—as a form of empowerment—often fails to recognize relative power (A. Escobar 1995; Kothari 2001; Moss 1994).

25. The desire for collaboration can present "an unwitting imperialist demand" on Indigenous people (Jones and Jenkins 2008, 2).

26. Even engaged or activist research should not assume too firm a common ground in collaboration. Writing on decolonization warns against the erasure of difference in political solidarity (Fine 1994; Jones and Jenkins 2008; McLaren 1995; Mohanty 1997; Morris 2017).

27. This is despite decades of anthropologists writing against stereotypes of static cultural homogeneity (Abu-Lughod 1991; Clifford 1988; Stasch 2009).

28. Rather than situating anthropology and its object in different times, the contemporary asserts a "coevalness" (Fabian 1983) whereby self and other are "adjacent" to each other.

Chapter 1

1. As elsewhere in Amazonia (Alexiades and Peluso 2015; Padoch et al. 2014), these families regularly circulate back to their home villages.

2. This relative isolation is not a primordial condition but the result of wider social and economic processes that threaten their livelihoods (High 2013). As elsewhere in Amazonia, groups living in voluntary isolation struggle to maintain autonomy—often in response to encroaching extractive economies (Cabodevilla 2013). The Ecuadorian state's failure to protect the human rights of isolated peoples has led Indigenous rights advocates to bring a legal case on behalf of these groups against Ecuador to the Inter-American Court of Human Rights (see Rival 2022). Many Waorani people describe these groups—whom they call Tagaeiri or Taromenani—as distant kin who became isolated near the time of missionization (High 2013; Nenquimo 2014), an example of how, in Amazonia, isolation and contact are often understood as temporary and reversible (Viveiros de Castro 2019). For an extensive literature on Waorani relationships and violent encounters with these groups, see Narváez (2018); Narváez and Trujillo (2020); Trujillo (2011); and Rivas (2003, 2020).

3. Since the 1990s, the Confederation of Indigenous Nationalities of Ecuador (CONAIE) and its regional grouping, the Confederation of Indigenous Nationalities of Amazonian Ecuador (CONFENIAE), have organized protests against the govern-

ment in support of land rights and other issues (Whitten 1996; Whitten and Whitten 2011).

4. Examples of this work include Beckerman and Yost (2007), Cabodevilla (1999), Rival (2002), Robarchek and Robarchek (1998), and Yost (1981).

5. Waorani elders describe how a Waorani man was fatally wounded by the gunshot of a missionary during the attack—a detail often omitted in the missionary literature (see High 2009a).

6. Since the 1970s the oil road has brought much tension and conflict to Waorani people in the area, including frontier violence and repression by the Ecuadorian military (see Alban 2015; Almeida and Proaño 2008; Narváez 2022; and Tassi 1992).

7. In August 2023 Ecuadorians voted in a national referendum to halt oil extraction in the Yasuní Park.

8. In recent years criminal gangs linked to international drug cartels have led to a major rise in violence in Ecuador. As security has deteriorated in Ecuador since I wrote the initial draft of this book, I describe how this situation relates to Waorani communities in the epilogue.

9. The lives of Waorani people and their ancestors have been deeply affected by colonialism and more recent developments that threaten their way of life and contribute to violent internal and external conflicts (High 2015a).

10. NAWE replaced the previous Waorani organization, the Organization of Waorani Nationalities of Amazonian Ecuador (ONHAE), which was established in 1990.

11. OWAP was previously called the Coordinating Council of the Waorani Nationality of Ecuador-Pastaza (CONCONAWEP).

12. More recently, Cawetipe Yeti Caiga (2012), a Waorani man, published a grammar of Wao-terero.

13. At the time of the research ELDP and the Endangered Languages Archive (ELAR), was based at the School of Oriental and African Studies, University of London.

14. Speakers who featured in the videos were also compensated on a consistent hourly basis.

15. Although the primary research period ended in 2014, the documentation project continues today, with Dickinson occasionally receiving Waorani researchers to work at her home to develop language materials for Waorani schools.

16. Salvage anthropology was problematic for a number of reasons, such as its representation of Indigenous people as if they were already in the past (Clifford 1989; Fabian 1983).

17. Video is a technology through which some Amazonian people come to see themselves as members of a "culture" or "ethnic group" and claim a more powerful voice (Turner 1991, 70). It is part of how new political identities are taking shape in contemporary Amazonia (Brown 1997; Graham 2002, 2018; Jackson 1995; Oakdale 2004; Veber and Virtanen 2017), where some Indigenous peoples have come to understand "culture" in terms of iconic images that mediate their relationships with Western environmentalists, tourists, and other outsiders (Conklin 1997; Conklin and Graham 1995; High 2015a).

18. This reflects an ideology of "interculturality" that has taken center stage in Ecuador (Santos and Jimenez 2012; Whitten 2008).

19. Although boys and girls often participate in gardening, hunting and gathering forest products from an early age, school leaves them little time for such practices (Rival 1996, 2002).

20. The "hyperbolic valorization" of endangered languages converts languages into objects of preservation in ways that may be at odds with the interests of speakers (Hill 2002, 120), particularly in Indigenous communities that resist the production and circulation of texts as a form of potential appropriation (Whitely 2003, 717; Errington 2003).

21. This resonates with Pierre Clastres's (1974) observation that speaking is integral to leadership in Amerindian societies.

Chapter 2

1. Birds are a recurrent theme in Amazonian ethnography, whether as having social characteristics similar to human society (Crocker 1985; Lévi-Strauss 1966), in association with shamanism and ritual (Belaunde 1994; Rival 2002; Uzendoski et al. 2005) in relation to song (Brown 1984; A. C. Taylor 1983) or as a form of language and communication (Fiorini 2011; Gutierrez-Choquevilca 2010; Walker 2010).

2. Along with Keith Basso's (1996) study of Western Apache stories attached to place names, similar observations are evident in discourse-centered approaches in South America (E. Basso 1995; Graham 1995; Sherzer and Urban 1986).

3. This is a feature of Indigenous languages in diverse areas of the Americas (Course 2012; D. Smith 1985, 1998; Whiteley 2003; Witherspoon 1977). As linguists and philosophers have observed with speech-acts generally (Austin 1962), certain utterances demonstrate the performative qualities of language as a form of action that does far more than simply represent the world.

4. Uzendoski and Calapucha (2012) describe how the body defines communicative systems in Amazonia (see also Uzendoski 2012). Hauck and Heurich (2018) adopt the term "linguistic natures" in considering diverse understandings of the nature of language in the Americas.

5. For examples in Amazonia, see Déléage (2009), Seeger (1987), and Townsley (1993).

6. For a more extensive analysis of Waorani shamanism, see High (2012a, 2012b, 2015a, 2015b); Rival (2002), and Wierucka (2015).

7. Encounters with nonhuman beings that appear as human are particularly dangerous, as speaking with them involves adopting their (nonhuman) perspective (see also Lima 1999).

8. This has parallels with the Wari in Brazilian Amazonia who see communication between different human and animal beings to occur "through a bodily transformation enabled by new foods, the proximity to other bodies, and the new relations of sociality as a whole" (Vilaça 2016, 59–60).

9. Ramos argues that the idea of perspectivism simplifies the complexity and diversity of Indigenous thought by inverting a "deeply rooted" Western nature/culture di-

chotomy (2012, 483; see also Turner 2009). Course (2010) observes that descriptions of perspectival cosmologies draw on a rhetorical analogy between subject and object familiar to speakers of European languages, which risks obscuring the ontologies implicit in Amerindian grammars.

10. McCallum (1996), for example, describes how, among Cashinahua people in Brazil, "Knowledge does not appear to have a separable existence outside the body, but rather is an intimate part of each developing body" (355). Smith (1998) similarly describes how Canadian Chipewyan thought is monistic insofar as typical Western distinctions, whether between body and mind, thought and action, human and nature, spirit and matter, are absent.

11. In this way speaking is integral to what has been described as an Amazonian "moral economy of intimacy" (Viveiros de Castro 1996, 189) or "aesthetics of conviviality" (Overing and Passes 2000).

12. Much writing emphasizes how kinship and personhood in Amazonia are constituted less by birth or descent than through living together, a process by which bodies become consubstantial (Gow 1991; McCallum 2001; Overing and Passes 2000; Vilaça 2002).

13. As Vilaça (2016) describes among the Wari: "To them it seems obvious that those who perceive each other as humans, as companions, automatically share the same language" (60).

14. Vilaça makes a similar observation among the Wari, who say that a person will "learn their language by eating their food" (2016, 61).

15. Examples from Amazonia include Carneiro da Cunha (1978), H. Clastres (1968), Conklin (2001), and A. C. Taylor (1993).

16. The term "gringo" refers generally to white foreigners in much of Amazonian Ecuador. As Gow (1993) describes in Peruvian Amazonia, gringos often evoke a strong contrast to local sociality.

17. Praet (2005) describes a similar practice among the Chachi people of northwest Ecuador, who play "funerary games" that involve "utterances that are meaningless in the vernacular" (133). As with my Waorani interlocutors, these practices are meant to "ensure the unambiguous passage of the deceased person from the realm of the living to that of the dead" (139). The reference to "gringos" in this case is an example of what Álvarez (2010) describes as the incorporation of certain aspects of contact with the national society into Waorani funerary practices.

18. Bravo Díaz (2023) provides several fascinating examples of how Waorani people understand bird sounds as a form of communication. She also describes their songs as a "form of sharing energy" that has positive bodily effects on peoples' willingness to engage in "living well" (119).

19. In some Amazonian contexts the language of birds is understood to have "privileged access to truth" as it "establishes a sense that meaning is immanent in the world, merely awaiting discovery, rather than externally produced by human beings" (Walker 2010, 16).

20. This raises questions about the generalizability of Vilaça's (2016) description

that for the Wari "there is just one language through which people who live together could immediately communicate" (57).

21. There is also an increasing emphasis on learning English. See Korak (2015) for a study of Waorani multilingualism and its relation to internal hierarchies in their communities.

22. Language rights discourses tend to reify language as an allegory of ethnic identity, as something "detachable"—rather than integral to—religious beliefs, ritual, and other practices (Silverstein 1998; Whiteley 2003, 716).

23. As Whiteley observes, "when a language becomes thought of as detachable from locality and from an assemblage of cultural codes and practices, it turns into a denatured symbolic system" (2003, 715).

24. See Fawcett (2018) for a linguistic study of ideophones in Wao-terero.

25. Nuckolls's concept of ecological dialogism resonates with Kohn's (2013) proposal—also based on fieldwork with Runa people—that "nonhuman life-forms also represent the world" (8).

26. In communicating the "vivid truths of everyday experience," ideophones have "a lyrical quality that captures the aesthetic appreciation and enjoyment of a perception, rather than an objectively detached version of a perception" (Nuckolls 2010, 44).

27. When Indigenous Amazonian leaders formally address government officials and outsiders their speech is often necessarily simplified or "impoverished" for circulation among diverse audiences (Ramos 1998, Graham 2002). In contrast to intimate contexts where speakers often foreground diverse sensory experiences, there is little place for these perspectives in political speech (Nuckolls 2010).

28. This involves whipping children after a hunt, a practice understood to transfer strength to them (High 2010). Bravo Díaz (2023, 72) describes differences in how boys and girls are involved in this practice.

29. Wrobleswki (2021) describes how "pluralistic discourses" are a key part of Indigenous experience—and alliances with outsiders—in Latin America (34).

30. Some Native communities in North America reject the circulation and teaching of their language beyond private contexts as a threat to their sovereignty (Whiteley 2003, 716).

Chapter 3

1. The organization was later renamed the Waorani Organization of Pastaza (OWAP).

2. Article 57, Section 7 of Ecuador's 2008 constitution states that Indigenous communities are guaranteed "free prior informed consultation, within a reasonable period of time, on plans and programs for prospecting, producing and marketing nonrenewable resources located on their land which could have an environmental and cultural impact on them." Ecuador is also bound to ILO convention 169, the UN Declaration on the rights of Indigenous peoples (2008).

3. The ruling concluded that the right to prior consultation and self-determination had been violated and ordered that, as reparations, officials from the government min-

istries involved receive training regarding these rights. It also ordered the investigation of officials involved in the 2012 consultation. See Scazza (2022) for further details on the ruling.

4. Despite the government's appeals, in July 2019 the Provincial Court of Pastaza upheld the ruling in favor of the Waorani and denied potential future appeals. In May 2020, Ecuador's Constitutional Court adopted the ruling as jurisprudence.

5. This distinction is a conceptual and methodological implication of Amerindian perspectivism, which Viveiros de Castro proposes inverts the modernist premise of multiculturalism. He and others describe how modernist thought relegates or "tames" difference by construing "cultures" as distinct perspectives on a single world of nature (Blaser 2013; de la Cadena 2010, 2015; Kelly 2011). Similarly, as De la Cadena (2010) notes, there is no space for nonhuman actors in what Latour (1993) calls the modern constitution, where cultural differences are permitted only where they do not challenge the basis of state policies.

6. Whereas Rival (1993) observed the absence of individual or collective land ownership, Lu (2001) describes a Waorani "common property regime" where specific groups recognize spatial boundaries and private property (425). Rival, who translates *öme* as "land," "territory," or "forest," describes how they attribute forest cultigens to both human and animal activities, and how food collecting across vast territories makes distinguishing between "extraction" and "management" all but impossible (2002, 81). As Erazo (2013) notes, even the term "resources" itself "indicates a Western-inflected approach to nonhuman living things" (144).

7. As Descola observes, in contrast to the modern concept of nature that "only has meaning when set in opposition to human works, whether one chooses to call these 'culture,' 'society,' or 'history,'" Amazonian cosmologies often do not draw clear distinctions between humans and animal and plant species (2013, 8–9). Waorani ethnography, while illustrating the relevance of these approaches, also highlights contrasting "gendered models of nature" (Rival 2007, 519) and the distinct moral connotations of human and animal perspectives (High 2012a).

8. Studies of conservation initiatives in Ecuador (Cepek 2011, 2012; K. Escobar 2015), elsewhere in Amazonia (Mentore 2017; Oakley 2020; Zanotti 2016), and in Papua New Guinea (West 2006) illustrate how Indigenous people bring their own ideas, expectations, and practices into the process of becoming environmental citizens.

9. Escobar (2015) describes how work with Ibis and other NGOs, such as the Wildlife Conservation Society and Ecociencia, is part of Waorani people becoming environmental citizens.

10. In the early 1990s Waorani leader Moi Enomenga was propelled into the global spotlight when journalist Joe Kane's book (1995) and a documentary film (C. Walker 1996) highlighted Enomenga's struggle against oil on behalf of Waorani people.

11. Already in the 1940s, Waorani attacked workers conducting oil exploration for Royal Dutch Shell. Texaco and other companies subsequently negotiated government oil concessions on Waorani lands.

12. Descriptions of this situation include Cepek (2018); Fiske (2023); Gerlach (2003); Lu et al. (2017); and Sawyer (2004), among others.

13. The 2021 election of president Guillermo Lasso, a conservative, extended this neoliberal political and economic agenda in Ecuador.

14. Rival describes how Waorani people approached oil companies much as they did givers of traditional manioc feasts, as providers of "natural abundance" to be treated "as sources of endlessly renewable wealth" (2000, 257).

15. Rival (2000) and Lu (2001) make similar observations about Waorani seeing their territory as vast and abundant.

16. Bravo Díaz (2023) describes the interface between Waorani ideas of living well and a state discourse of *buen vivir*—premised on an ideal of progress—that encourages Indigenous peoples to conceptualize their needs in terms of productive projects (43).

17. Sempértegui (2019) describes the growing presence of Indigenous women leaders in the context of extractivism in the Ecuadorian Amazon, and their complex relationships with ecofeminism.

18. Lu and Wirth (2013) present survey data indicating Waorani concerns about resource scarcity, biodiversity conservation, and territorial boundaries, analyzing how these processes have led to internal conflicts.

Chapter 4

1. Ball (2018) similarly observes the risks, difficulties, and divergent understandings in exchanges and communications between Indigenous people and outsiders in development projects in the Xingu Park in Brazil.

2. Robarchek and Robarchek (1998) describe Waorani society as "egalitarian in the extreme" (102), and Rival (1998) describes them as "fiercely egalitarian" (63).

3. Accounts of past revenge killings, sometimes aimed at eliminating an enemy group to prevent future reprisals, also evoke this distributed responsibility. A man's coresident kin may contribute to his anger by expressing anguish over losing kin to violence or complaining of his or her group's unwillingness to avenge a death (High 2013).

4. Bravo Díaz (2023) provides a telling example of this Waorani emphasis on autonomy in describing how they did not establish a rule for or against vaccination during the COVID pandemic, instead opting for "a much more egalitarian approach" where "each person and village decides over their own body" (90). She also reports just three Waorani deaths and few hospitalizations resulting from the pandemic (89).

5. Even exchange—perhaps the most prosaic logical form of what we might very loosely call "justice," is difficult to locate as a key value in the context of a Waorani emphasis on unilateral provision, immediacy, and generosity.

6. The Association of Waorani Women of Amazonian Ecuador (AMWAE) was founded in 2005 in part as a response to these issues.

7. This insistence on individual autonomy and resistance to political authority is reminiscent of Clastres's (1987 [1974]) classic argument about the limits of individual leadership in what he called "societies without the state" in Lowland South America.

8. Bravo Díaz (2023) describes how, after giving five Waorani men audio devices to record sounds of the forest, some used them as an "instrument of power" to record

meetings with state institutions and oil companies (117). As with Waorani language researchers, she observed such political motivations alongside the desire to record elders whose knowledge they saw at risk of being lost.

9. Despite a focused drive to vaccinate Amazonian peoples in Brazil, many Indigenous peoples, like other marginalized groups in Latin America, remained unvaccinated during much of the pandemic. Some of my Waorani interlocutors were initially suspicious of COVID-19 vaccinations at least in part because they did not trust their government or those administering vaccines.

10. The text of Nenquimo's statement was also published in an article in *The Guardian* newspaper on October 12, 2020. www.theguardian.com/commentisfree/2020/oct/12/western-worldyour-civilisation-killing-life-on-earth-indigenous-amazon-planet.

11. For an expansive discussion and conceptual genealogy of *buen vivir* in Ecuadorian and wider Latin American politics, see Acosta (2012), Caria and Dominguez (2016), Cortez (2014), Gudymas (2011), Larrea (2011), and Walsh (2010).

12. This is of part of the full interview, which is soon to be published under the title "Amazonian Environmental Activism at COP26: A Conversation with Uboye Gaba" (Gaba and High, in press).

13. He refers here to the Paris Agreement, a legally binding treaty on climate change adopted at the UN Climate Change Conference (COP21) in Paris in 2015. It was agreed by 196 countries and entered into force in 2016 (https://unfccc.int/process-and-meetings/the-paris-agreement).

Chapter 5

1. Iniwa is the name I was given by elders during my first fieldwork and is the name by which I am often referred to in the Waorani villages most familiar with me.

2. These scholarships were one way that Repsol-YPF, the primary oil company drilling in Block 16 at the time, compensated Waorani communities for their continued presence in their territory and the vast profits derived from it. Most Waorani people have found this and other company-sponsored projects to be inadequately supported and in no way commensurate with the damages and profits of these companies.

3. Although it was not clear whether he had read any anthropology books, he had obviously come to understand the kinds of representation anthropology involves.

4. For diverse strands of thinking on these issues since the 1980s, see, for example, Clifford and Marcus (1986), Harrison (1997), Metcalf (2003), Rosaldo (1989), and Vargas-Cetina (2013). Linda Tuhiwai Smith (1999) considers these issues with specific reference to decolonizing research with Indigenous peoples.

5. See High (2015a, 153) for expanded examples and discussion of how people prioritize the avoidance of direct conflict in a particular Waorani village.

6. The tendency not to claim specific knowledge about the thoughts or intentions of others, or to assume the inaccessibility of other peoples' thoughts, has been observed widely in Melanesia (Rumsey and Robbins 2008) and Amazonia (Conklin and Morgan 1996; Ewart 2015; High 2016; Walker 2013).

7. Sorcery accusations have increased significantly over the course of my fieldwork, making the position of shamans quite dangerous and contested in large villages. In part as result of this context, and the history of missionization, there are very few Waorani shamans today, with most Waorani seeking Kichwa shamans for curing (for further analysis of this topic see High 2012a, 2012b).

8. As Alès (2000) describes among the Yanomami, "The members of the community must help the person return to their state of health, happiness and propriety. . . . The main idea is that one should not be suffering and in pain . . . nor should one allow a co-resident to remain in such a state" (135).

9. Recent research describes how, within the Waorani Resistance Pastaza movement, Waorani activists referred to elders as "knowledge leaders" (Scazza 2022; Scazza and Nenquimo 2021).

10. However, some Waorani authors, such as Manuela Ima (2012), have written about their own communities, whether about family histories and myths or current issues affecting them. Fabian Nenquimo published a book about the mythical origins of the Waorani (2011) and another (2014) about past relationships between Waorani families and those living in voluntary isolation. Other Waorani have coauthored journal articles or interviews with academics (Baihua and Kimerling 2018; Borja, Bay, and Davidsen 2021; Gaba and High forthcoming; Scazza and Nenquimo 2021). Waorani environmental activist Nemonte Nenquimo recently published a memoir, with her husband Mitch Anderson, titled *We Will Not Be Saved: A Memoir of Hope and Resistance in the Amazon Rainforest* (2024).

Conclusion

1. Bessire (2014b) develops the idea of hypermarginality to describe how anthropologists often fail to recognize the marginal living conditions of Amazonian populations subject to colonial abuses and, more recently, a neoliberal cultural politics that further stigmatizes Indigenous people who fail to meet conventional expectations of alterity.

2. Buitron (2020) and Heckenberger (2003, 2005) are recent examples of studies focused past and present forms of hierarchy and other inequalities in Amazonia.

3. Halbmayer (2018), for example, draws on the idea of alternative modernities in the work of Comaroff and Comaroff (1993) and Sahlins's (1999) concept of the indigenization of modernity to advance Indigenous modernities as a key framework for understanding these processes in South America.

4. Many scholars today see Indigenous peoples not in terms of a primordial link to place, but as groups who are defined in relation to structures of power (Friedman 2008; Kenrick and Lewis 2004); in this way they can be seen as "co-constituted" by colonial expansion and modern nation-states (Halbmayer 2018, 6).

5. See Englund and Leach (2000) for a broader exposition of how ethnographic research provides the basis for questioning metanarratives of modernity often adopted in the social sciences.

6. Arjun Appadurai (1996), for example, describes how popular imagination is in-

creasingly embedded in global flows in ways that transcend local or national identities.

7. Oakdale (2022) draws on the autobiographical narratives of Indigenous Kaiabi leaders in Brazil to similarly show their cosmopolitan engagements across radical differences in new contexts.

8. Kelly (2011) makes a similar observation regarding the use of homonyms that have led to misunderstanding and conflicts between Yanomami people and Venezuelan state health care.

9. For example, Nadasday (2021) argues for the concept of "indeterminacy" as a remedy to the theoretical and political shortcomings of what he calls the "multiple worlds thesis" (357). He describes how, in implying the incompleteness of any understanding, "indeterminacy does not require multiple worlds, only incompatible material and semiotic practices" that can in fact be complementary (363).

10. This general framework, described in diverse Amazonian contexts, is often associated with the work of Eduardo Viveiros de Castro (1992, 1996) and can be traced to Lévi-Strauss's (1976 [1942]) writing on warfare and commerce in South America.

Epilogue

1. For many years the organization's salaries were paid through an agreement with Repsol, a Spanish oil company whose license to operate Block 16 has expired.

2. Marci used the term "tzantza" to describe the severed heads, alluding specifically to the past practice—associated with neighboring Shuar groups—of ritually preserving the heads of enemies. This imagery has become part of regional lore in Amazonian Ecuador.

3. This prophetic statement has several thematic parallels in Waorani mythology and oral history, such as twins, survivors of apocalyptic events, bodily transformations into animal forms, and mistaken or unjustified killings.

4. The discussion introduced some technical terms in Spanish referring to environmental assessment and local state authorities.

5. The majority of OWAP representatives at the meeting, including its director, were women, whereas all of the NAWE representatives were men.

6. In October of the same year, Daniel Noboa, the thirty-five-year-old son of a prominent politician and banana plantation tycoon from the coast, won the presidential runoff. President Noboa, who ran on a platform addressing violent crime, narrowly defeated Luisa Gonzalez—the candidate supported by former President Correa.

BIBLIOGRAPHY

Abu-Lughod, Lila. 1990a. "Can There Be a Feminist Ethnography?" *Women and Performance: A Journal of Feminist Theory* 5, no. 1: 7–27.

———. 1990b. "The Romance of Resistance: Tracing Transformations of Power through Bedouin Women." *American Ethnologist* 17, no. 1: 41–55.

———. 1991. "Writing against Culture." In *Recapturing Anthropology: Working in the Present,* edited by Richard Fox, 137–54. Santa Fe, NM: SAR Press.

Acosta, Alberto. 2012. *El Buen Vivir: Sumak Kawsay, Una Oportunidad para Imaginar Otros Mundos.* Quito: Abya-Yala.

Agrawal, Arun. 2005. *Environmentality: Technologies of Government and the Making of Subjects.* Durham, NC: Duke University Press.

Ahearn, Laura. 2012. *Living Language: An Introduction to Linguistic Anthropology.* Oxford: John Wiley and Sons.

Ahlers, Jocelyn C. 2009. "The Many Meanings of Collaboration: Fieldwork with the Elem Pomo." *Language and Communication* 29, no. 3: 230–43.

Ahlers, Jocelyn, and Suzanne Wertheim. 2009. "Introduction: Reflecting on Language and Culture Fieldwork in the Early 21st Century." *Language and Communication* 3, no. 29: 193–98.

Alban, Dayuma. 2015. "Teen Pregnancy on the Oil Road: Social Determinants of Teen Pregnancy in an Indigenous Community of the Ecuadorian Amazon." Master's thesis, University of North Carolina, Chapel Hill.

Albert, Bruce. 2002. "O Ouro Canibal e a Queda do Céu: Uma Crítica Xamânica da Economia Política da Natureza." In *Pacificando o Branco: Cosmologias do Contato no Norte-Amazônico,* edited by Bruce Albert and Rita Ramos, 239–76. São Paulo: UNESP.

Alès, Catherine. 2000. "Anger as a Marker of Love: The Ethic of Conviviality among the Yanomami." In Joanna Overing and Alan Passes, eds. *The Anthropology of Love and Anger*, edited by Joanna Overing and Alan Passes, 133–51. London: Routledge.

Alexiades, Miguel N., and Daniela M. Peluso. 2015. "Introduction: Indigenous Urbanization in Lowland South America." *Journal of Latin American and Caribbean Anthropology* 20, no. 1: 1–12.

Allen, Jafari Sinclaire, and Ryan Cecil Jobson. 2016. "The Decolonizing Generation: (Race and) Theory in Anthropology since the Eighties." *Current Anthropology* 57, no. 2: 129–48.

Almeida, Alexandra, and José Proaño. 2008. *Tigre, Águila y Waorani: Una Sola Selva, Una Sola Lucha; Deuda Ecológica de las Transnacionales Petroleras con el Pueblo Waorani y Parque Nacional Yasuní*. Quito: Acción Ecológica.

Almeida, Mauro William Barbosa de. 1999. "Guerras Culturais e Relativismo Cultural." *Revista Brasileira de Ciências Sociais* 14, no. 41: 5–14.

———. 2013. "Caipora e Outros Conflitos Ontológicos." *Revista de Antropologia da UFSCar* 5, no. 1: 7–28.

Álvarez, Kati. 2010. "El Efecto del Contacto de la Sociedad Nacional en las Prácticas Culturales Entorno a la Muerte en los Waorani." Master's thesis, Facultad Latinoamericana de Ciencias Sociales, Quito.

Amazon Frontlines. 2020. Website accessed March 2, 2020. www.amazonfrontlines.org/chronicles/Indigenous-conservation-amazon/.

Amazon Watch. 2020. Website accessed March 2, 2020. https://amazonwatch.org/work.

Appadurai, Arjun. 1996. *Modernity at Large: Cultural Dimensions of Globalization*. Minneapolis: University of Minnesota Press.

Asad, Talal, ed. 1973. *Anthropology and the Colonial Encounter*. London: Ithaca Press.

———. 1986. "The Concept of Cultural Translation in British Social Anthropology." In *Writing Culture: The Poetics and Politics of Ethnography*, edited by James Clifford and George Marcus, 141–64. Berkeley: University of California Press.

Austin, J. L. 1962. *How to Do Things with Words*. Oxford: Clarendon Press.

Austin, Peter, and Julia Sallabank, eds. 2011. *The Cambridge Handbook of Endangered Languages*. Cambridge: Cambridge University Press.

Baihua, Penti, and Judith Kimerling. 2018. "Voces de la Selva: Una Propuesta para Yusuní del Pueblo Huaorani Baihuaeri de Bameno." In *Zona Intangible del Yasuní: Entre el Manejo Territorial y la Geografía Imaginada*, edited by Robert Wassestrom et al., 63–94. Quito: Abya-Yala.

Ball, Christopher. 2012. "Stop Loss: Developing Interethnic Relations in Brazil's Xingu Indigenous Park." *Journal of Latin American and Caribbean Anthropology* 17, no. 3: 413–34.

———. 2018. *Exchanging Words: Language, Ritual, and Relationality in Brazil's Xingu Indigenous Park*. Santa Fe, NM: SAR Press.

Barry, Andrew, and Georgina Born, eds. 2013. *Interdisciplinarity: Reconfigurations of the Social and Natural Sciences*. London: Routledge.

Basso, Ellen. 1995. *The Last Cannibals: A South American Oral History*. Austin: University of Texas Press.

Basso, Keith. 1996. *Wisdom Sits in Places: Landscape and Language among the Western Apache*. Albuquerque: University of New Mexico Press.

Bauman, Richard, and Charles Briggs. 1990. "Poetics and Performances as Critical Perspectives on Language and Social Life." *Annual Review of Anthropology* 19, no. 1: 59–88.

Bauman, Richard, and Joel Sherzer, eds. 1989. *Explorations in the Ethnography of Speaking*. Cambridge: Cambridge University Press.

Beck, Sam, and Carl Maida, eds. *Toward Engaged Anthropology*. New York: Berghahn.

Becker, Marc. 2011. "Correa, Indigenous Movements, and the Writing of a New Constitution in Ecuador." *Latin American Perspectives* 38, no. 1: 47–62.

Beckerman, Stephen, and James Yost. 2007. "Upper Amazonian Warfare." In *Latin American Indigenous Warfare and Ritual Violence*, edited by Richard J. Chacon and Rubén G. Mendoza, 142–79. Tucson: University of Arizona Press.

Behar, Ruth. *The Vulnerable Observer: Anthropology That Breaks Your Heart*. Boston: Beacon Press.

Belaunde, Luisa Elvira. 1994. "Parrots and Oropendolas: The Aesthetics of Gender Relations among the Airo-Pai of the Peruvian Amazon." *Journal de la Société des Américanistes* 80, no. 1: 95–111.

Benjamin, Walter. 1996 [1923]. "The Task of the Translator." In *Walter Benjamin: Selected Writings Volume 1 (1913–1926)*, edited by Marcus Bullock and Michael Jennings, 253–63. Cambridge, MA: Harvard University Press.

Berlin, Brent. 1994. "Evidence for Pervasive Synesthetic Sound Symbolism in Ethnozoological Nomenclature." In *Sound Symbolism*, edited by Leanne Hinton, Johanna Nichols, and John Ohala, 76–93. Cambridge: Cambridge University Press.

Berlin, Brent, and John O'Neill. 1981. "The Pervasiveness of Onomatopoeia in the Jivaroan Language Family." *Journal of Ethnobiology* 1: 95–108.

Bessire, Lucas. 2014a. *Behold the Black Caiman: A Chronicle of Ayoreo Life*. Chicago: University of Chicago Press.

———. 2014b. "The Rise of Indigenous Hypermarginality: Native Culture as a Neoliberal Politics of Life." *Current Anthropology* 55, no. 3: 276–95.

Bessire, Lucas, and David Bond. 2014. "Ontological Anthropology and the Deferral of Critique." *American Ethnologist* 41, no. 3: 440–56.

Blaser, Mario. 2010. *Storytelling Globalization from the Chaco and Beyond*. Durham, NC: Duke University Press.

———. 2013. "Ontological Conflicts and the Stories of Peoples in Spite of Europe: Towards a Conversation on Political Ontology." *Current Anthropology* 54, no. 5: 547–68.

———. 2016. "Is Another Cosmopolitics Possible?" *Cultural Anthropology* 31, no. 4: 545–70.

Bodenhorn, Barbara. 2012. "Meeting Minds; Encountering Worlds: Sciences and Other Expertises on the North Slope of Alaska." In *Collaborators Collaborating:*

Counterparts in Anthropological Knowledge and International Research Relations, edited by Monica Konrad, 225–44. New York: Berghahn.

Borja, Danilo, Juan Bay, and Conny Davidsen. 2021. "Ancianos Amazónicos en la Frontera Petrolera: La Vida y Muerte de Nenkihui Bay, Líder Tradicional Waorani." *Journal of Latin American Geography* 20, no. 1: 238–48.

Boudreau Morris, Katie. 2017. "Decolonizing Solidarity: Cultivating Relationships of Discomfort." *Settler Colonial Studies* 7, no. 4: 456–73.

Boyer, Dominic, and George E. Marcus, eds. 2021. *Collaborative Anthropology Today: A Collection of Exceptions.* Ithaca, NY: Cornell University Press.

Bravo Díaz, Andrea. 2021. "Nangui Tereka, Hablando Duro en la Vida Política de las Mujeres Waorani." *Cadernos de Campo* 30, no. 2: 1–15.

———. 2023. *Between the Forest and the Road: The Waorani Struggle for Living Well in the Ecuadorian Oil Circuit.* New York: Berghahn.

Brown, Michael. 1993. "Facing the State, Facing the World: Amazonia's Native Leaders and the New Politics of Identity." *L'Homme* 126–28: 307–26.

———. 2003. *Who Owns Native Culture?* Cambridge, MA: Harvard University Press.

Buitron, Natalia. 2020. "Autonomy, Productiveness, and Community: The Rise of Inequality in an Amazonian Society." *Journal of the Royal Anthropological Institute* 26, no. 1: 48–66.

Cabodevilla, Miguel Angel. 1999. *Los Huaorani en la Historia del Oriente.* Quito: CICAME.

———. 2013. "La Massacre . . . 'Qué Nunca Existió?'" In *Una Tragedia Ocultada*, edited by Miguel Angel Cabodevilla and Milagros Aguirre, 21–125. Quito: CICAME.

Caria, Sara, and Rafael Domínguez. 2016. "Ecuador's Buen Vivir: A New Ideology for Development." *Latin American Perspectives* 43, no. 1: 18–33.

Carneiro da Cunha, Manuela. 1978. *Os Mortos e Os Outros: Uma Analise do Sistema Funerario e da Noçao de Pessoa Entre os Indios Kraho.* São Paulo: Hucitec.

Cepek, Michael. 2008. "Essential Commitments: Identity and the Politics of Cofán Conservation." *Journal of Latin American and Caribbean Anthropology* 13, no. 1: 196–222.

———. 2011. "Foucault in the Forest: Questioning Environmentality in Amazonia." *American Ethnologist* 38, no. 3: 501–15.

———. 2012. *A Future for Amazonia: Randy Borman and Cofán Environmental Politics.* Austin: University of Texas Press.

———. 2016. "There Might Be Blood: Oil, Humility, and the Cosmopolitics of a Cofán Petro-Being." *American Ethnologist* 43, no. 4: 623–35.

———. 2018. *Life in Oil: Cofán Survival in the Petroleum Fields of Amazonia.* Austin: University of Texas Press.

Cipolletti, Maria Susana. 2002. "El Testimonio de Joaquina Grefa, una Cautiva Quichua Entre los Huaorani (Ecuador, 1945)." *Journal de la Societé des Américanistes* 88: 111–35.

Clastres, Hélène. 1968. "Rites Funeraire Guayaki." *Journal de la Societe des Americanistes* 57: 63–72.

Clastres, Pierre. 1987 [1974]. *Society against the State: Essays in Political Anthropology.* New York: Zone Books.

Clifford, James. 1988. *The Predicament of Culture: Twentieth-Century Ethnography, Literature, and Art.* Cambridge, MA: Harvard University Press.

———. 1989. "The Others: Beyond the 'Salvage' Paradigm." *Third Text* 3, no. 6: 73–78.

Clifford, James, and George Marcus, eds. 1986. *Writing Culture: The Poetics and Politics of Ethnography.* Berkeley: University of California Press.

Comaroff, Jean, and John Comaroff. 1993. "Introduction." In *Modernity and Its Malcontents: Ritual and Power in Postcolonial Africa*, edited by Jean Comaroff and John L. Comaroff, xii–xxxvii. Chicago: University of Chicago Press.

Conklin, Beth. 1997. "Body Paint, Feathers, and VCRs: Aesthetics and Authenticity in Amazonian Activism." *American Ethnologist* 24, no. 4: 711–37.

———. 2001. *Consuming Grief: Compassionate Cannibalism in an Amazonian Society.* Austin: University of Texas Press.

Conklin, Beth, and Laura Graham. 1995. "The Shifting Middle Ground: Amazonian Indians and Eco-Politics." *American Anthropologist* 97, no. 4: 695–710.

Cormier, Loretta A. 2003. *Kinship with Monkeys: The Guajá Foragers of Eastern Amazonia.* New York: Columbia University Press.

Cortez, David. 2014. "Genealogía del Sumak Kawsay y el Buen Vivir en Ecuador: Un Balance." In *Post-Crecimiento y Buen Vivir: Propuestas Globales para la Construcción de Sociedades Equitativas y Sustentables*, edited by Gustavo Endara, 315–52. Quito: Friedrich-Ebert-Stiftung.

Coulthard, Glen. 2014. *Red Skin, White Masks: Rejecting the Colonial Politics of Recognition.* Minneapolis: University of Minnesota Press.

Course, Magnus. 2010. "Of Words and Fog: Linguistic Relativity and Amerindian Ontology." *Anthropological Theory* 10, no. 3: 247–63.

———. 2012. "The Birth of the Word: Language, Force, and Mapuche Ritual Authority." *HAU: Journal of Ethnographic Theory* 2, no. 1: 1–26.

Crocker, Christopher. 1985. "My Brother the Parrot." In *Animal Myths and Metaphors in South America*, edited by Gary Urton, 13–47. Salt Lake City: University of Utah Press.

Danziger, Eve, and Alan Rumsey. 2013. "Introduction: From Opacity to Intersubjectivity across Languages and Cultures." *Language and Communication* 33: 247–50.

Davis, Dana-Aín. 2016. "Collaboration: Provocation." Correspondences, *Fieldsights*, September 26. https://culanth.org/fieldsights/collaboration-provocation.

Day, Sophie, Evthymios Papataxiarchis, and Michael Stewart, eds. 1998. *Lilies of the Field: Marginal People Who Live for the Moment.* Boulder, CO: Westview Press.

Debenport, Erin. 2015. *Fixing the Books: Secrecy, Literacy, and Perfectibility in Indigenous New Mexico.* Santa Fe, NM: SAR Press.

De la Cadena, Marisol. 2010. "Indigenous Cosmopolitics in the Andes: Conceptual Reflections Beyond 'Politics.'" *Cultural Anthropology* 25, no. 2: 334–70.

———. 2015. *Earth Beings: Ecologies of Practice across Andean Worlds.* Durham, NC: Duke University Press.

———. 2019. "Uncommoning Nature: Stories from the Anthropo-Not-Seen." In *Anthropos and the Material*, edited by Penny Harvey, Christian Krohn-Hansen, and Knut G. Nustad, 35–58. Durham, NC: Duke University Press.

De la Cadena, Marisol, and Orin Starn, eds. 2007. *Indigenous Experience Today*. Oxford: Berg.

Déléage, Pierre. 2009. *Le Chant de L'anaconda: L'apprentissage du Chamanisme chez les Sharanahua (Amazonie Occidentale)*. Nanterre, France: Société d'éthnologie.

Deloria, Vine, Jr., 1969. *Custer Died for Your Sins: An Indian Manifesto*. Norman: University of Oklahoma Press.

Descola, Philippe. 1994. *In the Society of Nature: A Native Ecology in Amazonia*. Cambridge: Cambridge University Press.

———. 2013. *Beyond Nature and Culture*. Chicago: University of Chicago Press.

Dickinson, Connie. 2010. "Quand les Tsachila (Equateur) eu-Mêmes Documentent leur Langue et leur Culture." In *Linguistique de Terrain sur Langue en Danger: Locuteurs et linguists*, edited by Colette Grinevald and Michel Bert, 303–22. Paris: Faits de Langues 35.

Di Giminiani, Piergiorgio, and Sophie Haines. 2020. "Introduction: Translating Environments." *Ethnos* 85, no. 1: 1–16.

Di Leonardo, Micaela, ed. 1991. *Gender at the Crossroads of Knowledge: Feminist Anthropology in the Postmodern Era*. Berkeley: University of California Press.

Dingamanse, Mark, and Kimi Akita. 2016. "An Inverse Relation between Expressiveness and Grammatical Integration: On the Morphosyntactic Typology of Ideophones, with Special Reference to Japanese." *Journal of Linguistics* 53: 501–32.

Doke, Clement Martyn. 1935. *Bantu Linguistic Terminology*. London: Longman, Green.

Dumont, Louis. 1985. "A Modified View of Our Origins: The Christian Beginnings of Modern Individualism." In *The Category of the Person: Anthropology, Philosophy, History*, edited by Michalel Carrithers, Steven Collins and Steven Lukes, 93–122. Cambridge: Cambridge University Press.

Ecuador Yasuní ITT Trust Fund: Terms of Reference. July 28, 2010.

England, Nora. 2003. "Mayan Language Revival and Revitalization Politics: Linguists and Linguistic Ideologies." *American Anthropologist* 105, no. 4: 733–43.

Englund, Harri, and James Leach. 2000. "Ethnography and the Meta-Narratives of Modernity." *Current Anthropology* 41, no. 2: 225–48.

Erazo, Juliet. 2013. *Governing Indigenous Territories: Enacting Sovereignty in the Ecuadorian Amazon*. Durham, NC: Duke University Press.

———. 2016. "Saving the Other Amazon: Changing Understandings of Nature and Wilderness among Indigenous Leaders in the Ecuadorian Amazon." *Humanities* 5, no. 60: 1–12.

Erazo, Juliet, and Christopher Jarrett. 2018. "Managing Alterity from Within: The Ontological Turn in Anthropology and Indigenous Efforts to Shape Shamanism." *Journal of the Royal Anthropological Institute* 24, no. 1: 145–63.

Errington, Joseph. 2003. "Getting Language Rights: The Rhetorics of Language Endangerment and Loss." *American Anthropologist* 105, no. 4: 723–32.

Escobar, Arturo. 1995. *Encountering Development: The Making and Unmaking of the Third World*. Princeton, NJ: Princeton University Press.

———. 2007. "Worlds and Knowledges Otherwise: The Latin American Modernity/Coloniality Research Program." *Cultural Studies* 21, no. 2–3: 179–210.

———. 2018. Designs For the Pluriverse: Radical Interdependence, Autonomy, and the Making of Worlds. Durham, NC: Duke University Press.

Escobar, Kelly. 2015. "La Construcción de Sujetos Ambientales: Los Huaorani del Ecuador." *Boletín de Antropología* 30, no. 49: 35–57.

Estalella, Adolfo, and Tomás Sánchez Criado, eds. 2018. *Experimental Collaborations: Ethnography through Fieldwork Devices*. Oxford: Berghahn.

Evans, Nicholas. 2009. *Dying Words: Endangered Languages and What They Have to Tell Us*. Oxford: John Wiley and Sons.

Ewart, Elizabeth. 2015. "Categories and Consequences in Amazonia." In *Legalism: Rules and Categories*, edited by Paul Dresch and Judith Scheele, 205–30. Oxford: Oxford University Press.

Fabian, Johannes. 1983. *Time and the Other: How Anthropology Makes Its Object*. New York: Columbia University Press.

Faubion, James D. 2016. Introduction to "On the Anthropology of the Contemporary: Addressing Concepts, Designs, and Practices." *HAU: Journal of Ethnographic Theory* 6, no. 1: 371–402.

Fausto, Carlos. 2012. *Warfare and Shamanism in Amazonia*. Cambridge: Cambridge University Press.

Fawcett, Alexia. 2018. "Ideophone Integration and Expressiveness in Wao Terero." Master's thesis, University of California, Santa Barbara.

Field, Les. 1999. "Complicities and Collaborations: Anthropologists and the 'Unacknowledged Tribes' of California." *Current Anthropology* 40, no. 2: 193–210.

Fine, Michelle. 1994. "Working the Hyphens: Reinventing Self and Other in Qualitative Research." In *Handbook of Qualitative Research*, edited by Norman Denzin and Yvonna Lincoln, 70–82. Thousand Oaks, CA: Sage.

Finer, Matt, Varsha Vijay, Fernando Ponce, Clinton N. Jenkins, and Ted R. Kahn. 2009. "Ecuador's Yasuní Biosphere Reserve: A Brief Modern History and Conservation Challenges." *Environmental Research Letters* 4: 1–15.

Fiorini, Marcelo. 2011. "Desire in Music: Soul-Speaking and the Power of Secrecy." In *Burst of Breath: Indigenous Ritual Wind Instruments in Lowland South America*, edited by Jonathan D. Hill and Jean-Pierre Chaumeil, 171–97. Lincoln: University of Nebraska Press.

Fiske, Amelia M. 2023. *Reckoning with Harm: The Toxic Relations of Oil in Amazonia*. Austin: University of Texas Press.

Foucault, Michel. 1991. "What Is Enlightenment?" In *The Foucault Reader*, edited by Paul Rabinow, 32–50. London: Penguin.

Friedman, Jonathan. 2008. "Indigeneity: Anthropological Notes on a Historical Variable." In *Indigenous Peoples: Self-Determination, Knowledge, Indigeneity*, edited by Henry Minde, 29–48. Delft: Eburon.

Gaba, Uboye, and Casey High. Forthcoming. "Amazonian Environmental Activism at

COP26: A Conversation with Uboye Gaba." In *The Lowland South American World*, edited by Casey High and Luiz Costa. London: Routledge.

Gal, Susan. 2015. "Politics of Translation." *Annual Review of Anthropology* 44: 225–40.

Gerlach, Allen. 2003. *Indians, Oil, and Politics: A Recent History of Ecuador*. Wilmington, DE: Scholarly Resources.

Ginsburg, Faye. 1994. "Embedded Aesthetics: Creating a Discursive Space for Indigenous Media." *Cultural Anthropology* 9, no. 3: 365–82.

———. 1998. *Contested Lives: The Abortion Debate in an American Community*. Berkeley: University of California Press.

"'Go Ye and Preach the Gospel': Five Do and Die." 1956. *Life*, January 30: 10–19.

González Gálvez, Marcelo. 2015. "The Truth of Experience and Its Communication: Reflections on Mapuche Epistemology." *Anthropological Theory* 15, no. 2: 141–57.

Gow, Peter. 1991. *Of Mixed Blood: Kinship and History in Peruvian Amazonia*. Oxford: Oxford University Press.

———. 1993. "Gringos and Wild Indians: Images of History in Western Amazonian Cultures." *L'Homme* 126–28: 331–51.

———. 2001. *An Amazonian Myth and Its History*. Oxford: Oxford University Press.

Graeber, David. 2004. *Fragments of an Anarchist Anthropology*. Chicago: Prickly Paradigm Press.

———. 2015. "Radical Alterity Is Just Another Way of Saying 'Reality': A Reply to Eduardo Viveiros de Castro." *HAU: Journal of Ethnographic Theory* 5, no. 2: 1–41.

Graham, Laura. 1995. *Performing Dreams: Discourses of Immortality among the Xavante of Central Brazil*. Austin: University of Texas Press.

———. 2002. "How Should an Indian Speak? Amazonian Indians and the Symbolic Politics of Language in the Global Public Sphere." In *Indigenous Movements, Self-Representation, and the State in Latin America*, edited by Kay Warren and Jean Jackson, 181–228. Austin: University of Texas Press.

———. 2005. "Image and Instrumentality in a Xavante Politics of Existential Recognition: The Public Outreach Work of Eténhiritipa Pimental Barbosa." *American Ethnologist* 32, no. 4: 622–41.

———. 2018. "Transformations of Indigenous Media: The Life and Work of David Hernández Palmar." In *From Filmmaker Warriors to Flash Drive Shamans: Indigenous Media Production and Engagement in Latin America*, edited by Richard Pace, 75–95. Nashville: Vanderbilt University Press.

Greene, Shane. 2009. *Customizing Indigeneity: Paths to a Visionary Politics in Peru*. Stanford, CA: Stanford University Press.

Gudynas, Eduardo. 2011. "Buen Vivir: Germinando Alternativas al Desarrollo." *América Latina en Movimiento* 462: 1–20.

Gutierrez Choquevilca, Andréa-Luz. 2010. "Imaginaire Acoustique et Apprentissage d'une Ontologie Animiste." *Ateliers du LESC* 34: 1–29.

Guyer, Jane. 2016. "'On the Verge': From the Possible to the Emergent." *HAU: Journal of Ethnographic Theory* 6, no. 1: 373–77.

Hage, Ghassan. 2015. *Alter-Politics: Critical Anthropology and the Radical Imagination*. Victoria, Australia: Melbourne University Press.

Haig, Geoffrey, Nicole Nau, Stefan Schnell, and Claudia Wegener, eds. 2011. *Documenting Endangered Languages: Achievements and Perspectives*. Berlin: De Gruyter Mouton.

Halbmayer, Ernst. 2018. "Indigenous Peoples and the Transformations of Modernity: Introductory Thoughts on Contemporary Indigeneities." In *Indigenous Modernities in South America*, edited by Ernst Halbmayer, 1–28. Herefordshire, UK: Sean Kingston Publishing.

Hale, Charles R. 1997. "Cultural Politics of Identity in Latin America." *Annual Review of Anthropology* 26, no. 1: 567–90.

———. 2006 "Activist Research v. Cultural Critique: Indigenous Land Rights and the Contradictions of Politically Engaged Anthropology." *Cultural Anthropology* 21, no. 1: 96–120.

Hanks, William F. 2014. "The Space of Translation." *HAU: Journal of Ethnographic Theory* 4, no. 2: 17–39.

Hanks, William, and Carlo Severi. 2014. "Translating Worlds: The Epistemological Space of Translation." *HAU: Journal of Ethnographic Theory* 4, no. 2: 1–16.

Harrison, Faye V., ed. 1997. *Decolonizing Anthropology: Moving Further Toward an Anthropology for Liberation*. Arlington, VA: American Anthropological Association.

———. 2012. "Dismantling Anthropology's Domestic and International Peripheries." *World Anthropologies Network* 6: 87–110.

Hauck, Jan David, and Guilherme Orlandini Heurich. 2018. "Language in the Amerindian Imagination: An Inquiry into Linguistic Natures." *Language and Communication* 63: 1–8.

Heckenberger, Michael. 2003. "The Enigma of the Great Cities: Body and State in Amazonia." *Tipití: Journal of the Society for the Anthropology of Lowland South America* 1, no. 1: 27–58.

———. 2005. *The Ecology of Power: Culture, Place, and Personhood in the Southern Amazon, A.D. 1000–2000*. New York: Routledge.

Heffernan, Emma, Fiona Murphy, and Jonathan Skinner, eds. 2020. *Collaborations: Anthropology in a Neoliberal Age*. New York: Routledge.

High, Casey. 2006. "From Enemies to Affines: Conflict and Community among the Huaorani of Amazonian Ecuador." PhD diss., London School of Economics, University of London.

———. 2007. "Indigenous Organisations, Oil Development, and the Politics of Egalitarianism." *Cambridge Anthropology* 26, no. 2: 34–46.

———. 2009a. "Victims and Martyrs: Converging Histories of Violence in Amazonian Anthropology and US Cinema." *Anthropology and Humanism* 34, no. 1: 41–50.

———. 2009b. "Remembering the Auca: Violence and Generational Memory in Amazonian Ecuador." *Journal of the Royal Anthropological Institute* 15: 719–36.

———. 2010. "Warriors, Hunters, and Bruce Lee: Gendered Agency and the Transformation of Amazonian Masculinity." *American Ethnologist* 37, no. 4: 753–70.

———. 2012a. "Shamans, Animals, and Enemies: Locating the Human and Non-Human in an Amazonian Cosmos of Alterity." In *Animism in Rainforest and*

Tundra: Personhood, Animals, Plants and Things in Contemporary Amazonia and Siberia, edited by Marc Brightman, Vanessa Grotti, and Olga Ulturgasheva, 130–45. Oxford: Berghahn.

———. 2012b. "Between Knowing and Being: Ignorance in Anthropology and Amazonian Shamanism." In *The Anthropology of Ignorance: An Ethnographic Approach*, edited by Casey High, Ann Kelly, and Jon Mair, 119–36. New York: Palgrave Macmillan.

———. 2013. "Lost and Found: Contesting Isolation and Cultivating Contact in Amazonian Ecuador." *HAU: Journal of Ethnographic Theory* 3, no. 3:196–221.

———. 2014. "'Like the Ancient Ones': The Intercultural Dynamics of Personal Biography in Amazonian Ecuador." In *Fluent Selves: Autobiography and Personhood in Lowland South America*, edited by Suzanne Oakdale and Magnus Course, 35–68. Lincoln: University of Nebraska Press.

———. 2015a. *Victims and Warriors: Violence, History, and Memory in Amazonia.* Urbana: University of Illinois Press.

———. 2015b. "Ignorant Bodies and the Dangers of Knowledge in Amazonia." In *Regimes of Ignorance: Anthropological Perspectives on the Reproduction of Nonknowledge*, edited by Thomas Kirsch and Roy Dilley, 91–114. Oxford: Berghahn.

———. 2015c. "Keep on Changing: Recent Trends in Amazonian Anthropology." *Reviews in Anthropology* 44, no. 2: 93–117.

———. 2016. "'A Little Bit Christian': Memories of Conversion and Community in Post-Christian Amazonia." *American Anthropologist* 118, no. 2: 270–83.

———. 2018. "Bodies That Speak: Languages of Differentiation and Becoming in Amazonia." *Language and Communication* 63, 65–75.

———. 2020. "'Our Land Is Not For Sale!' Contesting Oil and Translating Environmental Politics in Amazonian Ecuador." *Journal of Latin American and Caribbean Anthropology* 25, no. 2: 301–23.

———. 2021. "The Nature of Loss: Ecological Nostalgia and Cultural Politics in Amazonia." In *Ecological Nostalgias: Memory, Affect, and Creativity in Times of Ecological Upheavals*, edited by Olivia Angé and David Berliner, 84–106. New York: Berghahn.

———. 2023. "Civilized Elders and Isolated Ancestors: The Multiple Histories of Contemporary Amazonia." *Tipití: Journal of the Society for the Anthropology of Lowland South America* 19, no. 1: 39–55.

High, Casey, and Roy Elliott Oakley. 2020 "Conserving and Extracting Nature: Environmental Politics and Livelihoods in the New 'Middle Grounds' of Amazonia." *Journal of Latin American and Caribbean Anthropology* 25, no. 2: 236–47.

Hill, Jane. 2002. "'Expert Rhetorics' in Advocacy for Endangered Languages: Who Is Listening, and What Do They Hear?" *Journal of Linguistic Anthropology* 12, no. 2: 119–33.

Holmes, Douglas, and George Marcus. 2008. "Collaboration Today and the Re-Imagination of the Classic Scene of Fieldwork Encounter." *Collaborative Anthropologies* 1, no. 1: 81–101.

Hutchins, Frank. 2007. "Footprints in the Forest: Ecotourism and Altered Meanings in Ecuador's Upper Amazon." *Journal of Latin American and Caribbean Anthropology* 12, no. 1: 75–103.

Hutchins, Frank, and Patrick Wilson, eds. 2010. *Editing Eden: A Reconsideration of Identity, Politics and Place in Amazonia.* Lincoln: University of Nebraska Press.

Ima, Manuela Omari. 2012. *Saberes Waorani y Parque Nacional Yasuní: Plantas, Salud y Bienestar en la Amazonía del Ecuador.* Quito: Iniciativa Yasuní ITT.

Ingold, Tim. 2018. *Anthropology and/as Education.* London: Routledge.

Jackson, Jean. 1995. "Culture, Genuine and Spurious: The Politics of Indianness in the Vaupes, Colombia." *American Ethnologist* 22, no. 1: 3–27.

Janeway, Elizabeth. 1980. *Powers of the Weak.* New York: Alfred Knopf.

Jones, Alison and Kuni Jenkins. 2008. "Rethinking Collaboration: Working the Indigene-Colonizer Hyphen." In *Handbook of Critical and Indigenous Methodologies,* edited by Norman K. Denzin, Yvonna S. Lincoln, and Linda Tuhiwai Smith, 471–86. London: Sage.

Kane, Joe. 1995. *Savages.* New York: Alfred Knopf.

Karl, Terry Lynn. 1997. *The Paradox of Plenty: Oil Booms and Petro-States.* Berkeley: University of California Press.

Kelly, Jose. 2011. *State Healthcare and Yanomami Transformations.* Tucson: University of Arizona Press.

Kenrick, Justin, and Jerome Lewis. 2004. "Indigenous Peoples' Rights and the Politics of the Term 'Indigenous.'" *Anthropology Today* 20, no. 2: 4–9.

Kimerling, Judith. 1993. *Crudo Amazónico.* Quito: Abya-Yala.

Kirsch, Stuart. 2006. *Reverse Anthropology: Indigenous Analysis of Social and Environmental Relations in New Guinea.* Stanford, CA: Stanford University Press.

———. 2018. *Engaged Anthropology: Politics beyond the Text.* Berkeley: University of California Press.

Klein, Harriett, and Louisa Stark, eds. 1985. *South American Indian Languages: Retrospect and Prospect.* Austin: University of Texas Press.

Kohn, Eduardo. 2013. *How Forests Think: Toward an Anthropology Beyond the Human.* Berkeley: University of California Press.

Konrad, Monica, ed. 2012. *Collaborators Collaborating: Counterparts in Anthropological Knowledge and International Research Relations.* New York: Berghahn.

Kopenawa, Davi, and Bruce Albert. 2013. *The Falling Sky: Words of a Yanomami Shaman.* Cambridge, MA: Harvard University Press.

Korak, Christina. 2015. "Indigenous Multilingualism and Translation: The Creation of Intra- and Intersocial Hierarchies in the Communities of the Waorani People of Ecuador." *Tusaaji: A Translation Review* 4, no. 1: 60–81.

Kothari, Uma. 2001. "Power, Knowledge, and Social Control in Participatory Development." In *Participation: The New Tyranny?,* edited by Bill Cooke and Uma Kothari, 139–52. London: Zed Books.

Kroskrity, Paul, ed. 2000. *Regimes of Language: Ideologies, Polities, and Identities.* Santa Fe, NM: SAR Press.

Labaka, Alejandro. 2003. *Crónica Huaorani*. Quito: CICAME.

Larrea, María de Lourdes. 2011. *Del Desarrollo al Buen Vivir: Desafíos para la Construcción de Alternativas Solidarias en Políticas Públicas—Caso Ecuador*. Quito: FLACSO.

Lassiter, Luke Eric. 2005a. "Collaborative Ethnography and Public Anthropology." *Current Anthropology* 46, no. 1: 83–106.

———. 2005b. *The Chicago Guide to Collaborative Ethnography*. Chicago: University of Chicago Press.

Latour, Bruno. 1993. *We Have Never Been Modern*. Cambridge, MA: Harvard University Press.

Lawless, Elaine J. 1993. *Holy Women, Wholly Women: Sharing Ministries of Wholeness through Life Stories and Reciprocal Ethnography*. Philadelphia: University of Pennsylvania Press.

Lévi-Strauss, Claude. 1966. *The Savage Mind*. Chicago: University of Chicago Press.

———. 1976 [1942]. "Guerra e Comércio entre os Índios da América do Sul." In *Leituras de Etnologia Brasileira*, edited by Egon Schaden, 325–39. São Paulo: Nacional.

———. 1995. *The Story of Lynx*. Chicago: University of Chicago Press.

Lima, Tania Stolze. 1999. "The Two and Its Many: Reflections on Perspectivism in Tupi Cosmology." *Ethnos* 64, no. 1: 107–31.

Londoño-Sulkin, Carlos. 2005. "Inhuman Beings: Morality and Perspectivism among Muinane People (Colombian Amazonia)." *Ethnos* 70, no. 1: 7–30.

Low, Setha M., and Sally Engle Merry. 2010. "Engaged Anthropology: Diversity and Dilemmas." *Current Anthropology* 51: 203–26.

Lu, Flora. 2001. "The Common Property Regime of the Huaorani Indians of Ecuador: Implications and Challenges to Conservation." *Human Ecology* 29, no. 4: 425–47.

Lu, Flora, Gabriela Valdivia, and Néstor Silva. 2017. *Oil, Revolution, and Indigenous Citizenship in Ecuadorian Amazonia*. New York: Palgrave Macmillan.

Lu, Flora, and Ciara Wirth. 2013. "Conservation Perceptions, Common Property, and Cultural Polarization among the Waorani of Ecuador's Amazon." *Human Organization* 70, no. 3: 233–43.

Maranhão, Tullio, and Berhard Streck, eds. 2003. *Translation and Ethnography: The Anthropological Challenge of Intercultural Understanding*. Tucson: University of Arizona Press.

Marcus, George. 2001. "From Rapport under Erasure to Theaters of Complex Reflexivity." *Qualitative Inquiry* 7, no. 4: 519–28.

McCallum, Cecilia. 1996. "The Body That Knows: From Cashinahua Epistemology to a Medical Anthropology of Lowland South America." *Medical Anthropology Quarterly* 10, no. 3: 347–72.

———. 2001. *Gender and Sociality in Amazonia: How Real People Are Made*. Oxford: Berg.

McLaren, Peter. 1995. *Critical Pedagogy and Predatory Culture: Oppositional Politics in a Postmodern Era*. London: Routledge.

Mentore, Laura. 2017. "The Virtualism of 'Capacity Building' Workshops in Indigenous Amazonia: Ethnography in the New Middle Grounds." *HAU: Journal of Ethnographic Theory* 7, no. 2: 297–307.

Merlan, Francesca. 2009. "Indigeneity: Global and Local." *Current Anthropology* 50, no. 3: 303–33.

Metcalf, Peter. 2003. *They Lie, We Lie: Getting on with Anthropology.* London: Routledge.

Mignolo, Walter, and Catherine Walsh. 2018. *On Decoloniality: Concepts, Analytics, Praxis.* Durham, NC: Duke University Press.

Mohanty, Chandra Talpade. 1997. "Women Workers and Capitalist Scripts: Ideologies of Domination, Common Interests, and the Politics of Solidarity." In *Feminist Genealogies, Colonial Legacies, Democratic Futures,* edited by M. Jacqui Alexander and Chandra Mohanty, 3–29. New York: Routledge.

Mosse, David. 1994. "Authority, Gender, and Knowledge: Theoretical Reflections on the Practice of Participatory Rural Appraisal." *Development and Change* 25, no. 3: 497–526.

Nadasday, Paul. 2021. "How Many Worlds Are There? Ontology, Practice, and Indeterminacy." *American Ethnologist* 48, no. 4: 357–69.

Narváez, Roberto. 2016. "Intercambio, Guerra y Venganza: El Lanceamiento de Ompore Omehuai y su Esposa Buganei Caiga." *Antropología Cuadernos de Investigación* 16: 99–110.

———. 2018. "La Etnografía: Instrumento de Investigación en Antropología Jurídica; El Caso de un Pueblo Amazónico." *Revista Temas Sociológicos* 23: 307–41.

Narváez, Roberto, and Patricio Trujillo. 2020. "Tiempos de Guerra y Tiempos de Paz, Continuum Simbólico de un Pueblo de Reciente Contacto: El Caso Etnográfico de los Waorani en la Amazonía Ecuatoriana." *Cadernos de Campo* 29, no. 1: 13–37.

Nenquimo, Ima Fabián. 2011. *El Origen de los Waorani: Los Cuatro Dioses de los Waorani y el Hijo del Sol.* Quito: Ministerio del Medio Ambiente del Ecuador.

———. 2014. Tageiri-Taromenani: Guerreros de la Selva. Quito: Fundación Apaika Pee.

Nenquimo, Nemonte, and Mitch Anderson. 2024. We Will Not Be Saved: A Memoir of Hope and Resistance in the Amazon Rainforest. London: Wildfire.

Nuckolls, Janis B. 2010. *Lessons from a Quechua Strongwoman: Ideophony, Dialogue, and Perspective.* Tucson: University of Arizona Press.

Oakdale, Suzanne. 2004. "The Culture-Conscious Brazilian Indian: Representing and Reworking Indianness in Kayabi Political Discourse." *American Ethnologist* 31, no. 1: 60–75.

———. 2005. *I Foresee My Life: The Ritual Performance of Autobiography in an Amazonian Community.* Lincoln: University of Nebraska Press.

———. 2022. *Amazonian Cosmopolitans: Navigating a Shamanic Cosmos, Shifting Indigenous Policies, and Other Modern Projects.* Lincoln: University of Nebraska Press.

Oakley, R. Elliott. 2020. "Demarcated Pens and Dependent Pets: Conservation Livelihoods in an Indigenous Amazonian Protected Area." *Journal of Latin American and Caribbean Anthropology* 25, no. 2: 248–65.

O'Meara, Carolyn, and Jeff Good. 2010. "Ethical Issues in Legacy Language Resources." *Language and Communication* 30, no. 3: 162–70.

Ortner, Sherry B. 1995. "Resistance and the Problem of Ethnographic Refusal." *Comparative Studies in Society and History* 37(1): 173–93.

Osterweil, Michal. 2016. "Collaboration: Translation." Correspondences, *Fieldsights*, October 2. https://culanth.org/fieldsights/collaboration-translation.

Overing, Joanna. 2003. "In Praise of the Everyday: Trust and the Art of Social Living in an Amazonian Community." *Ethnos* 68, no. 3: 293–316.

———. 2012. "The Spectre of the Tyrant: Power, Violence, and the Poetics of an Amazonian Egalitarianism." In *Contesting the State: The Dynamics of Resistance and Control*, edited by Angela Hobart and Bruce Kapferer, 55–85. Herefordshire, UK: Sean Kingston Publishing.

Overing, Joanna, and Alan Passes, eds. 2000. *The Anthropology of Love and Anger: The Aesthetics of Conviviality in Native Amazonia*. London: Routledge.

Pace, Richard. 2018. "Embedded Aesthetics and Envisioning Sovereignty: Some Definitions and Directions in Latin American Indigenous Media Studies." In *From Filmmaker Warriors to Flash Drive Shamans: Indigenous Media Production and Engagement in Latin America*, edited by Richard Pace, 1–28. Nashville: Vanderbilt University Press.

Padoch, Christine, Angela Steward, Miguel Pinedo-Vasquez, and Louis Putzel. 2014. "Urban Residence, Rural Employment, and the Future of Amazonian Forests." In *The Social Life of Forests*, edited by Susanna Hetch, Kathleen Morrison, and Christine Padoch, 322–35. Chicago: University of Chicago Press.

Pandian, Anand. 2019. *A Possible Anthropology: Methods for Uneasy Times*. Durham, NC: Duke University Press.

Peeke, Catherine. 1973. *Preliminary Grammar of Auca*. Norman, OK: Summer Institute of Linguistics.

———. 1979. *El Idioma Huao: Gramatica Pedagogica, Tomo 1*. Cuadernos Etnolinguisticos no. 3. Quito: Instituto Linguistico de Verano.

Pike, Evelyn, and Rachel Saint, eds. 1988. *Working Papers concerning Waorani Discourse Features*. Dallas: Summer Institute of Linguistics.

Postero, Nancy Grey. 2007. *Now We Are Citizens: Indigenous Politics in Postmulticultural Bolivia*. Stanford, CA: Stanford University Press.

Povinelli, Elizabeth A. 2002. *The Cunning of Recognition: Indigenous Alterities and the Making of Australian Multiculturalism*. Durham, NC: Duke University Press.

Praet, Istvan. 2005. "People into Ghosts: Chachi Death Rituals and Shape-Shifting." *Tipití: Journal of the Society for the Anthropology of Lowland South America* 3, no. 2: 131–46.

Quijano, Aníbal. 2007. "Coloniality and Modernity/Rationality." *Cultural Studies* 21, no. 2: 168–78.

Rabinow, Paul. 2007. *Marking Time: On the Anthropology of the Contemporary*. Princeton, NJ: Princeton University Press.

Ramos, Alicida Rita. 1998. *Indigenism: Ethnic Politics in Brazil*. Madison: University of Wisconsin Press.

———. 2012. "The Politics of Perspectivism." *Annual Review of Anthropology* 41: 481–94.

Rappaport, Joanne. 2008. "Beyond Participant Observation: Collaborative Ethnography as Theoretical Innovation." *Collaborative Anthropologies* 1, no. 1: 1–31.

Redford, Kent. 1991. "The Ecologically Noble Savage." *Orion Nature Quarterly* 9, no. 3.

Reeve, Mary Elizabeth, and Casey High. 2012. "Between Friends and Enemies: The Dynamics of Inter-Ethnic Relations in Amazonian Ecuador." *Ethnohistory* 59, no. 1: 141–62.

Riederer, Rachel. 2019. "An Uncommon Victory for an Indigenous Tribe in the Amazon." *New Yorker*, May 15.

Riles, Annelise. 2015. "From Comparison to Collaboration: Experiments with a New Scholarly and Political Form." *Law and Contemporary Problems* 78, no. 1/2: 147–83.

Rival, Laura. 1993. "The Growth of Family Trees: Understanding Huaorani Perceptions of the Forest." *Journal of the Royal Anthropological Institute* 28, no. 4: 635–52.

———. 1996a. *Hijos del sol, padres del jaguar: Los Huaorani de Ayer y Hoy.* Quito: Abya-Yala.

———. 1996b. "Blowpipes and Spears: The Social Significance of Huaorani Technological Choices." In *Nature and Society: Anthropological Perspectives*, edited by Philippe Descola and Gisli Palsson, 145–64. London: Routledge.

———. 1998. "Prey at the Center: Resistance and Marginality in Amazonia." In *Lilies of the Field: Marginal People Who Live for the Moment*, edited by Sophie Day, Evthymios Papataxiarchis, and Michael Stewart, 61–79. Boulder, CO: Westview.

———. 2000. "Marginality with a Difference, or How the Huaorani Preserve Their Sharing Relations and Naturalize Outside Powers." In *Hunters and Gatherers in the Modern World*, edited by Peter Schweitzer, Megan Biesele, and Robert Hitchcock, 244–62. New York: Berghahn.

———. 2002. *Trekking through History.* New York: Columbia University Press.

———. 2007. Commentary on Carlos Fausto's "Feasting on People: Eating Humans and Animals in Amazonia." *Current Anthropology* 48, no. 4: 519.

———. 2016. *Huaorani Transformations in Twenty-First-Century Ecuador.* Tucson: University of Arizona Press.

———. 2022. *Caso Pueblos Indígenas Tagaeri y Taromenani vs Ecuador.* Public hearing.

Rivas Toledo, Alexis. 2003. "Sistema Mundial y Pueblos Indígenas en la Amazonía: A Propósito del Ataque a los Tagaeri." *Íconos* 17: 21–31.

———. 2020. *Antropología, Ecología y Derechos Humanos: Los Pueblos Indígenas Aislados del Amazonas; Los Últimos Grupos de Yasuní.* Almería, Spain: Círculo Rojo.

Robarchek, Clayton, and Carole Robarckeck. 1998. *Waorani: The Contexts of Violence and War.* Fort Worth, TX: Harcourt Brace.

Robbins, Joel, and Alan Rumsey. 2008. "Introduction: Cultural and Linguistic Anthropology and the Opacity of Other Minds." *Anthropological Quarterly* 81, no. 2: 407–20.

Rosaldo, Renato. 1989. *Culture and Truth: The Remaking of Social Analysis.* Boston: Beacon.

Rubel, Paula, and Abraham Rosman. 2003. Introduction to *Translating Cultures: Per-*

spectives on Translation and Anthropology, edited by Paula Rubel and Abraham Rosman, 1–22. Oxford: Berg.

Rumsey, Alan. 2013. "Intersubjectivity, Deception and the 'Opacity of Other Minds': Perspectives from Highland New Guinea and Beyond." *Language and Communication* 33, no. 3: 326–43.

Sahlins, Marshall. 1999. "What Is Anthropological Enlightenment? Some Lessons of the Twentieth Century." *Annual Review of Anthropology* 28, no. 1: i–xxiii.

Said, Edward W. 1978. *Orientalism*. New York: Pantheon Books.

Santos, Boaventura de Sousa, and Agustín Grijalva Jiménez, eds. 2012. *Justicia Indígena, Plurinacionalidad e Interculturalidad en Ecuador*. Quito: Abya Yala.

Sawyer, Suzanne. 2004. *Crude Chronicles: Indigenous Politics, Multinational Oil, and Neoliberalism in Ecuador*. Durham, NC: Duke University Press.

———. 2022. *The Small Matter of Suing Chevron*. Durham, NC: Duke University Press.

Scazza, Margherita. 2022. "Resistencia Waorani: A Study of Anti-Extractivist Resistance, Territorial Defence, and Indigenous Autonomy in Ecuadorian Amazonia." PhD diss., University of Edinburgh.

Scazza, Margherita, and Opi Nenquimo. 2021. "From Spears to Maps: The Case of Waorani Resistance in Ecuador for Their Defense of Their Right to Prior Consultation." *International Institute for Environment and Development*, London.

Scott, James C. 1985. *Weapons of the Weak: Everyday Forms of Peasant Resistance*. New Haven, CT: Yale University Press.

Seeger, Anthony. 1987 *Why Suyá Sing: A Musical Anthropology of an Amazonian People*. Cambridge: Cambridge University Press.

Seifart, Frank, Sebastian Drude, Bruna Franchetto, Jurg Gasche, Lucia Golluscio, and Elizabeth Manrique. 2008. "Language Documentation and Archives in South America." *Language Documentation and Conservation* 2: 130–40.

Sempértegui, Andrea. 2019. "Indigenous Women's Activism, Ecofeminism, and Extractivism: Partial Connections in the Ecuadorian Amazon." *Politics and Gender* 17, no. 1: 197–224.

Sherzer, Joel, and Greg Urban. 1986. Introduction to *Native South American Discourse*, edited by Joel Sherzer and Greg Urban, 1–14. Berlin: De Gruyter Mouton.

Shore, Cris. 2020. "Symbiotic or Parasitic? Universities, Academic Capitalism, and the Global Knowledge Economy." In *Collaborations: Anthropology in a Neoliberal Age*, edited by Emma Heffernan, Fiona Murphy, and Jonathan Skinner, 23–44. New York: Routledge.

Shulist, Sarah. 2013. "Collaborating on Language: Contrasting the Theory and Practice of Collaboration in Linguistics and Anthropology." *Collaborative Anthropologies* 6, no. 1: 1–29.

———. 2018. *Transforming Indigeneity: Urbanization and Language Revitalization in the Brazilian Amazon*. Toronto: University of Toronto Press.

Sillitoe, Paul, ed. 2015. *Indigenous Studies and Engaged Anthropology: The Collaborative Moment*. New York: Routledge.

Simpson, Audra. 2014. *Mohawk Interruptus: Political Life across the Borders of Settler States*. Durham, NC: Duke University Press.

Smith, David M. 1985. "Big Stone Foundations: Manifest Meaning in Chipewyan Myths." *Journal of American Culture* 8: 73–77.

———. 1998. "An Athapaskan Way of Knowing: Chipewyan Ontology." *American Ethnologist* 25, no. 3: 412–32.

Smith, Linda Tuhiwai. 1999. *Decolonizing Methodologies: Research and Indigenous Peoples*. London: Zed Books.

Sneath, David, Martin Holbraad, and Morten Axel Pedersen. 2009. "Technologies of the Imagination: An Introduction." *Ethnos* 74, no. 1: 5–30.

Stasch, Rupert. 2009. *Society of Others: Kinship and Mourning in a West Papuan Place*. Berkeley: University of California Press.

Strathern, Marylin. 1987. "An Awkward Relationship: The Case of Feminism and Anthropology." *Signs* 12, no. 2: 76–92.

———. 1988. *The Gender of the Gift: Problems with Women and Problems with Society in Melanesia*. Berkeley: University of California Press.

———. 1991. *Partial Connections*. New York: Rowman and Littlefield.

———. 2006. "A Community of Critics? Thoughts on New Knowledge." *Journal of the Royal Anthropological Institute* 12, no. 1: 191–209.

———. 2012. "Currencies of Collaboration." In *Collaborators Collaborating: Counterparts in Anthropological Knowledge and International Research Relations*, edited by Monica Konrad, 109–25. New York: Berghahn.

Tassi, Giovanna, ed. 1992. *Náufragos del Mar Verde: La Resistencia de Los Huaorani a Una Integración Impuesta*. Quito: Abya-Yala.

Taussig, Michael. 1987. *Shamanism, Colonialism, and the Wild Man: A Study in Terror and Healing*. Chicago: University of Chicago Press.

Taylor, Ann Christine. 1983. "The Marriage Alliance and Its Structural Variations among Jivaroan Societies." *Social Science Information* 22, no. 3: 331–53.

———. 1993. "Remembering to Forget: Identity, Mourning, and Memory among the Jívaro." *Journal of the Royal Anthropological Institute* 28: 653–78.

———. 2007. "Sick of History: Contrasting Regimes of Historicity in the Upper Amazon." In *Time and Memory in Indigenous Amazonia: Anthropological Perspectives*, edited by Carlos Fausto and Michael Heckenberger, 133–68. Tallahassee: University Press of Florida.

Taylor, Charles. 1992. "The Politics of Recognition." In *Multiculturalism and the Politics of Recognition*, edited by Amy Gutmann, 25–74. Princeton, NJ: Princeton University Press.

Tedlock, Barbara. 1991. "From Participant Observation to the Observation of Participation: The Emergence of Narrative Ethnography." *Journal of Anthropological Research* 47, no. 1: 69–94.

Thomason, Sarah. 2015. *Endangered Languages*. Cambridge: Cambridge University Press.

Todd, Zoe. 2016. "An Indigenous Feminist's Take on the Ontological Turn: 'Ontology' Is Just Another Word for Colonialism." *Journal of Historical Sociology* 29, no. 1: 4–22.

Townsley, Graham. 1993. "Song Paths: The Ways and Means of Yaminahua Shamanic Knowledge." *L'Homme* 33, no. 126/128: 449–68.

Trujillo, Patricio. 2011. *Boto Waorani, Bito Cowuri: La Fascinante Historia de los Hombres Verdaderos*. Quito: Fundación FIAAM.

Tsing, Anna. 2005. *Friction: An Ethnography of Global Connection*. Princeton, NJ: Princeton University Press.

Turner, Terence. 1991. "Representing, Resisting, Rethinking: Historical Transformations of Kayapo Culture and Anthropological Consciousness." In *Colonial Situations: Essays on the Contextualization of Ethnographic Knowledge*, edited by George Stocking, 285–313. Madison: University of Wisconsin Press.

———. 2009. "The Crisis of Late Structuralism. Perspectivism and Animism: Rethinking Culture, Nature, Spirit, and Bodiliness." *Tipití: Journal of the Society for the Anthropology of Lowland South America* 7, no. 1: 3–42.

Urban, Greg. 2001. *Metaculture: How Culture Moves through the World*. Minneapolis: University of Minnesota Press.

Uzendoski, Michael. 2012. "Beyond Orality: Textuality, Territory, and Ontology among Amazonian Peoples." *HAU: Journal of Ethnographic Theory* 2, no. 1: 55–80.

Uzendoski, Michael, Mark Hertica, and Edith Calapucha Tapuy. 2005. "The Phenomenology of Perspectivism: Aesthetics, Sound, and Power in Women's Songs from Amazonian Ecuador." *Current Anthropology* 46, no. 4: 656–62.

Uzendoski, Michael, and Edith Calapucha Tapuy. 2012. *The Ecology of the Spoken Word: Amazonian Storytelling and Shamanism among the Napo Runa*. Urbana: University of Illinois Press.

Vargas-Cetina, Gabriela, ed. 2013. *Anthropology and the Politics of Representation*. Tuscaloosa: University of Alabama Press.

Veber, Hanne, and Pirjo Virtanen, eds. 2017. *Creating Dialogues: Indigenous Perceptions and Changing Forms of Leadership in Amazonia*. Boulder: University of Colorado Press.

Venuti, Lawrence, ed. 2000. *The Translation Studies Reader*. London: Routledge.

Vigh, Henrik, and David Sausdal. 2014. "From Essence Back to Existence: Anthropology beyond the Ontological Turn." *Anthropological Theory* 14, no. 1: 49–73.

Vilaça, Aparecida. 2002. "Making Kin out of Others in Amazonia." *Journal of the Royal Anthropological Institute* 8, no. 2: 347–64.

———. 2016. *Praying and Preying: Christianity in Indigenous Amazonia*. Berkeley: University of California Press.

Viveiros de Castro, Eduardo. 1992. *From the Enemy's Point of View: Humanity and Divinity in an Amazonian Society*. Chicago: University of Chicago Press.

———. 1996. "Images of Nature and Society in Amazonian Ethnology." *Annual Review of Anthropology* 25: 179–200.

———. 1998. "Cosmological Deixis and Amerindian Perspectivism." *Journal of the Royal Anthropological Institute* 4, no. 3: 469–88.

———. 2002. "O Nativo Relativo." *Mana* 8, no. 1: 113–48.

———. 2003. "Anthropology and Science." Manchester Papers in Social Anthropology 7. Manchester: University of Manchester Press.

———. 2004. "Perspectival Anthropology and the Method of Controlled Equivocation." *Tipití: Journal of the Society for the Anthropology of Lowland South America* 2, no. 1: 3–22.

———. 2011. *The Inconstancy of the Indian Soul: The Encounter of Catholics and Cannibals in 16th-Century Brazil.* Chicago: Prickly Paradigm.

———. 2019. "Aucun Peuple n'est une Île." In *Au Seuil de la Forêt: Hommage à Philippe Descola: L'antropologie de la Nature,* edited by Geremia Cometti, Pierre Le Roux, Tiziana Manicone, and Nastassja Martin, 1063–80. Mirebeau-sur-Bèze, France: Tautem.

Voeltz, F. K. Erhard, and Christa Kilian-Hatz. 2001. *Ideophones.* Typological Studies in Language 44. Amsterdam: John Benjamins.

Wagner. Roy. 1981. *The Invention of Culture.* Chicago: University of Chicago Press.

Walker, Christopher, dir. 1996. *Trinkets and Beads.* New York: Icarus Films.

Walker, Harry. 2010. "Soulful Voices: Birds, Language, and Prophecy in Amazonia." *Tipití: Journal of the Society for the Anthropology of Lowland South America* 8, no. 1: 1–21.

———. 2012. *Under a Watchful Eye: Self, Power, and Intimacy in Amazonia.* Berkeley: University of California Press.

———. 2015. "Justice and the Dark Arts: Law and Shamanism in Amazonia." *American Anthropologist* 117, no. 1: 47–58.

Wallis, Ethel. 1960. *The Dayuma Story: Life under Auca Spears.* New York: Harper and Brothers.

———. 1973. *Aucas Downriver.* New York: Harper and Row.

Walsh, Catherine. 2010. "Development as Buen Vivir: Institutional Arrangements and (De)colonial Entanglements." *Development* 53, no. 1: 15–21.

Warren, Kay, and Jean Jackson, eds. 2002. *Indigenous Movements, Self-Representation, and the State in Latin America.* Austin: University of Texas Press.

Wasserstrom, Robert. 2016. "Waorani Warfare on the Ecuadorian Frontier, 1885–2013." *Journal of Latin American and Caribbean Anthropology* 21, no. 3: 497–516.

West, Paige. 2006. *Conservation Is Our Government Now: The Politics of Ecology in Papua New Guinea.* Durham, NC: Duke University Press.

———. 2016. *Dispossession and the Environment: Rhetoric and Inequality in Papua New Guinea.* New York: Columbia University Press.

Whiteley, Peter. 2003. "Do 'Language Rights' Serve Indigenous Interests? Some Hopi and Other Queries." *American Anthropologist* 105, no. 4: 712–22.

Whitten, Norman. 1996. "The Ecuadorian Levantamiento of 1990 and the Epitomizing Symbol of 1992: Reflections on Nationalism, Ethnic-Bloc Formation, and Racialist Ideologies." In *History, Power, and Identity: Ethnogenesis in the Americas, 1492–1992,* edited by Jonathan Hill, 193–218. Iowa City: University of Iowa Press.

———. 2008. "Interculturality and the Indigenization of Modernity: A View from Amazonian Ecuador." *Tipití: Journal of the Society for the Anthropology of Lowland South America* 6, no. 1–2: 3–36.

Whitten, Norman, and Dorothea Whitten. 2011. *Histories of the Present: People and Power in Ecuador.* Urbana: University of Illinois Press.

Wierucka, Aleksandra. 2016. *Huaorani of the Western Snippet*. New York: Palgrave Macmillan.

Witherspoon, Gary. 1977. *Language and Art in the Navajo Universe*. Ann Arbor: University of Michigan Press.

Woolard, Kathryn, and Bambi Schieffelin. 1994. "Language Ideology." *Annual Review of Anthropology* 23, no. 1: 55–82.

Wroblewski, Michael. 2021. *Remaking Kichwa: Language and Indigenous Pluralism in Amazonian Ecuador*. London: Bloomsbury.

Yeti Caiga, Cawetipe. 2012. *Gramática Waodani Tededo para Nivel Básico*. Cuenca, Ecuador: Universidad de Cuenca.

Yost, James. 1981. "Twenty Years of Contact: The Mechanisms of Change in Wao (Auca) Culture." In *Cultural Transformations and Ethnicity in Modern Ecuador*, edited by Norman Whitten, 677–704. Urbana: University of Illinois Press.

Zanotti, Laura. 2016. *Radical Territories in the Brazilian Amazon: The Kayapó's Fight for Just Livelihoods*. Tucson: University of Arizona Press.

Ziegler-Otero, Lawrence. 2004. *Resistance in an Amazonian Community: Huaorani Organizing against the Global Economy*. New York: Berghahn.

INDEX

Page numbers in italics denote figures, and endnotes are indicated by "n" followed by the endnote number.

The authorized representative in the EU for product safety and compliance is:
Mare Nostrum Group B.V.
Mauritskade 21D
1091 GC Amsterdam
The Netherlands
Email address: gpsr@mare-nostrum.co.uk

KVK chamber of commerce number: 96249943

The authorized representative in the EU for product safety and compliance is:
Mare Nostrum Group
B.V Doelen 72
4831 GR Breda
The Netherlands

www.ingramcontent.com/pod-product-compliance
Lightning Source LLC
Chambersburg PA
CBHW030818270326
41928CB00007B/792